PRINCIPLES OF BITCOIN

PRINCIPLES OF
Bitcoin

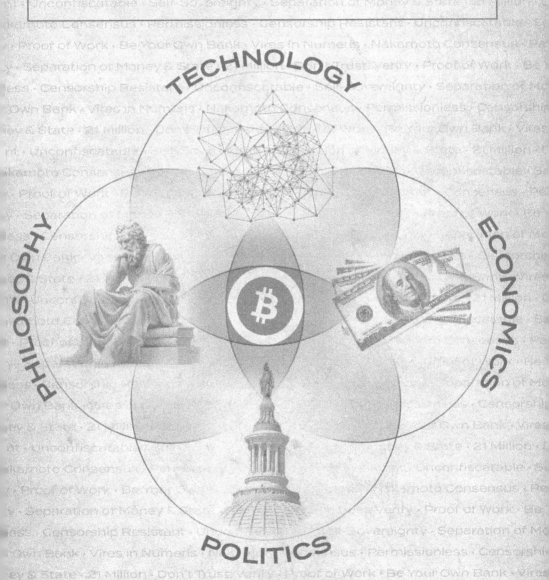

TECHNOLOGY

PHILOSOPHY

ECONOMICS

POLITICS

VIJAY SELVAM

FOREWORD BY ALEX GLADSTEIN

Columbia Business School Publishing

Columbia University Press
Publishers Since 1893
New York   Chichester, West Sussex

Library of Congress Cataloging-in-Publication Data
Names: Selvam, Vijay, author.
Title: Principles of Bitcoin : technology, economics, politics, and philosophy / Vijay Selvam.
Description: New York : Columbia University Press, [2025] | Includes index.
Identifiers: LCCN 2024051611 | ISBN 9780231220125 (hardback) |
    ISBN 9780231563079 (ebook)
Subjects: LCSH: Bitcoin. | Economics—Political aspects.
Classification: LCC HG1710 .S47 2025 | DDC 332.4/048—dc23/eng/20250218

Cover design: Jason Enterline

GPSR Authorized Representative: Easy Access System Europe,
Mustamäe tee 50, 10621 Tallinn, Estonia, gpsr.requests@easproject.com

We shall not cease from exploration

And the end of all our exploring

Will be to arrive where we started

And know the place for the first time.

—T. S. Eliot, "Little Gidding"

Contents

PART IV: THE POLITICS

PART V: THE PHILOSOPHY

Foreword

We sit on the brink of a historic shift in money, markets, finance, and global trade. A new digital currency, created fifteen years ago by an unknown civil liberties activist, is now worth more than $1 trillion; is being mined by nation states; has become the national currency of a country; is being traded via ETFs by the world's largest firms on Wall Street; and is being adopted as a tool of savings and commerce by tens of millions of people worldwide, from individuals stuck in collapsing economies to visionary investors.

And yet this is just the beginning of the Bitcoin story.

Deplatforming and currency devaluation are on the rise around the world. Governments are trying to restrict who can spend and on what, and are eroding the purchasing power of currencies through inflation. Central bank digital currencies (CBDCs)—which shift monetary power from private banks and tech companies to the state—are coming. More than 130 central banks are researching CBDCs, while more than sixty countries are building pilots, and more than twenty have launched some form of this new digital cash. The goal is micro control over your wallets, payments, and savings.

Meanwhile, billions face hyperinflation, financial exclusion, and a lack of access to banks or even personal identification. Interest rate decisions made by an unelected group of financial elites in Washington, DC, have a staggering impact on the developing world. And stranded energy exists all around us (e.g. enormous solar, wind, geothermal, biomass, and hydro energy sits untapped in rural areas of the planet), while people starve and suffer in energy poverty without a way to monetize these abundant resources.

In this world, Bitcoin is destined to become a bigger and bigger part of our lives. The only way it won't is if governments stop disenfranchising people and devaluing their savings, people from Argentina to Turkey to Zimbabwe are somehow magically bestowed with reliable money, totalitarian regimes build private digital cash, and people find other ways to bootstrap renewable energy resources in remote places. But none of this is currently foreseeable. This is why Bitcoin will grow.

People, companies, and governments worldwide, whether they know it yet or not, yearn for an open, neutral, scarce digital currency: something that preserves purchasing power over time, that can teleport peer to peer anywhere in the world in seconds, that no dictator can stop or censor, and that can transform energy into capital anywhere.

This is Bitcoin, and it has the potential to change the world forever.

In 2024, it might seem like you've missed the boat. But the reality is that we are just on the brink. Investing your time and energy in learning about Bitcoin today is one of the smartest decisions you can make. Whether you are investing for your family or professionally; you operate an international business or like to travel frequently; you have family abroad where it's hard to send money; or you are trying to figure out how to keep your corporate, state, or retirement assets from melting away, learning about Bitcoin is one of the most important things you can do for your future and the people and communities you care about.

And in your hands is a perfect guide for that critical mission. Vijay Selvam has written a brilliant and beautiful book that very simply, but very thoroughly, covers all aspects of Bitcoin. In these pages, Selvam takes you from someone with zero knowledge about the subject to a budding expert.

Unlike other books on the topic, this is not an ideological book. It is reasonable and even-handed. It is accessible and fun to read. It includes diverse global perspectives, covers the basics, and dives deep into what makes Bitcoin tick and what kind of impact it will have on the world around us.

In short, it will help you begin a journey that will never end: your trip down the Bitcoin rabbit hole. See you on the other side.

Alex Gladstein

Chief Strategy Officer, Human Rights Foundation

Preface

I do not recall when I first heard the word "bitcoin," but the first time I read about it in any detail was in 2013. An article in the *Financial Times* (*FT*) titled "The Bitcoin Believers" caricatured a band of young evangelists who believed bitcoin was the economic future. "To be a Bitcoin user is to be a Bitcoin evangelist," the article declared. It went on to quote one of the said evangelists' description of bitcoin:

> It's a hot tech start-up, mixed with emerging markets, mixed with gold, mixed with forex. It's a gold rush. It's a land-grab. It's the Wild West. There's going to be a Goldman Sachs in this economy. If you build a better mousetrap, you could be a millionaire.[1]

As an employee of Goldman Sachs myself at the time, this statement was incomprehensible gibberish to me.

Prior to Goldman Sachs, I had practiced as a lawyer at law firms in New York and London. My first legal job involved complex real estate mortgage-backed securities and their subsequent repackaging into collateralized debt obligations (CDOs), and related financial derivatives, including credit default swaps (CDSs): precisely the products that caused the 2007–2008 global financial crisis. In 2008, as a New York attorney at a white-shoe Wall Street law firm, I was involved in putting together the bailout package for one of the largest Wall Street banks in the immediate aftermath of the Lehman Brothers bankruptcy. The financial system was under siege, and it seemed almost inevitable that other major banks, including Morgan Stanley and Goldman Sachs, might collapse as well. In the eye of this storm, the atmosphere was charged with extreme uncertainty and fear.

Amid these historic events, I was struck by a cold, hard truth: my colleagues, despite their esteemed educational backgrounds, illustrious careers, impressive credentials, and renowned expertise, had not the faintest clue about what would happen next. This experience left me deeply cynical.

But then lawyers are anyway possibly the most cynical members of society. It is a function of our training and, I will concede, the personalities of those of us drawn to the profession. The adversarial nature of legal practice, the focus on conservative risk mitigation, and dealing with uncertain outcomes make us, by nature, cynical and skeptical beings. Anyone trying to convince us of anything is generally assumed to be lying or misleading until proven otherwise. It would be many years before I learned that one of bitcoin's core philosophies, "Don't trust, verify" is in fact a fundamental tenet of legal practice.

My innate cynicism presented a virtually insurmountable hurdle for me to understand something as avant-garde as bitcoin in 2013. And my educational background did not help either. While at Harvard Law School, I had cross-registered for the acclaimed investment management course at Harvard Business School, which had been taught by financial luminaries like Mohamed El'Erian, along with guest lecturers like Jeremy Grantham. As a result, the concept of *intrinsic value* and the different valuation models based on cash flow, revenue multiples, etc. had been etched in my brain as the only methods of evaluating an asset. Naturally, that was the mental model that I instinctively brought to bitcoin before dismissing it as obviously valueless based on those methodologies.

Shortly after I read the *FT* article in 2013, I was invited as a guest speaker to a university in Hong Kong to talk about CDOs, CDSs, MBSs and my experiences during the Global Financial Crisis. During the Q&A session, a student at the back of the classroom (who had not seemed interested in any of the proceedings) stuck his hand up and asked a question that seemed to come out of the blue: "What do you think about Bitcoin?" As if on cue, I instantly launched into a ten-minute monologue—a dismissive and intellectually snobbish discourse about intrinsic value; expected future cash flows; EBITDA multiples; and how bitcoin was essentially no more than online gambling. Jeremy Grantham would have been proud. Bitcoin was trading at a little over $100 at the time. The student said nothing in response. I do not know where he is today, but I often imagine that he immediately added to his bitcoin investment after listening to me. Perhaps he took it as a sign of how early he was to the investment opportunity based on how little was broadly understood about it.

The reality is that I did not really have much of a shot at bitcoin back in 2013. The cognitive hurdle that I had to overcome in order to take it seriously was simply too high. On the one hand, there was my mindset, a product of my education and training, which got in the way, and on the other hand, there was simply no accessible and credible resource to study the subject. I had no recourse except for the *FT*'s supercilious assessment, which only reinforced my instinctively negative intellectual response (or, rather, nonintellectual response).

The first time I heard bitcoin described as "digital gold" was in 2016.[2] A friend at lunch said that bitcoin was about to make gold redundant. As a gold bug myself (who had been languishing in my underwater gold investments for several years at that time), I distinctly remember how absurdly outrageous it was to hear this "magic-internet-money-Ponzi-scheme" being uttered in the same breath as an investment in gold, the revered and historic store of value.

But the sheer absurdity of that statement piqued my interest and made me dig deeper. It had already been a few years since I called it a scam in 2013. Yet it was still around, with people continuing to make increasingly outlandish claims about it. Some of those people, like my friend, were even rather intelligent! I therefore started to take baby steps down the "rabbit hole." Even at the time, however, there were precious little resources available on the topic.[3] On the internet, I mostly ran into ideological rants on obscure blogs by anarchists and anti-state libertarians. None of it really "spoke my language" back then.

Nevertheless, I did commence a multiyear journey in studying it—a journey that I am still on. Technology entrepreneur and investor Naval Ravikant describes bitcoin as a "mind virus."[4] Once you are first exposed to it, you often find yourself totally captivated by its intricacies and possibilities, unable to shake off its influence. Like a virus, it spreads through the mind, prompting continuous contemplation and reflection about its technological innovation; economic, political, and social implications; and philosophical meaning. Its decentralized nature and promise of financial sovereignty become recurring themes in one's worldview, leading further and further down the rabbit hole of exploration and discovery that seemingly has no bottom. Speaking for myself, I can attest to the accuracy of Ravikant's "mind virus" analogy. Several years after contracting a rather virulent strain, I am yet to shake the infection.

As my understanding of bitcoin grew, so did my regret over my dismissiveness in years gone by. In 2021, when the bitcoin price skyrocketed to over $50,000, I ran into my friend from that lunch in 2016 when we discussed digital gold.

By 2021, I imagined that he would have been well into his retirement, having identified bitcoin's potential so early, when it was trading at a few hundred dollars. To my utter astonishment, he said he had zero bitcoin. "It's too volatile," he said, true to form, as someone also with a traditional Wall Street banking background. It seemed like he, too, had never really understood it after all. Apparently he was exposed to the virus but not infected.

The goal in writing this book was to create the type of resource that I wish I had in those early days when I struggled to understand bitcoin. In recent years, particularly since 2020, there has been an explosion of learning materials on the subject, and it is not difficult to find several excellent resources (some of these resources even have the names of Fidelity and Blackrock put to them). The field has many incredibly deep-thinking investors, political theorists, and philosophers (not to mention meme artists) who have produced some exceptional works on bitcoin. In writing this book, I am undeniably standing on the shoulders of giants.

As a popular meme goes, bitcoin is for *anyone* but not necessarily *everyone*. Countless individuals have casually explored it, only to dismiss it for various reasons, and many more will continue to do so in the future. The elusiveness of bitcoin, I believe, stems from its intersection with numerous fields and disciplines. Viewing it solely through a technological lens, such as its function as a payment service, might render it seemingly worthless and antiquated without acknowledging its profound implications in the realms of macro and monetary economics. Contemplating its geopolitical potential without understanding its technological robustness and game theoretic incentive structures could make it appear a fool's errand that will be crushed by governments. And focusing exclusively on its price movements or its role as a store of value without delving into its philosophical foundations might lead one to overlook its societal significance and enduring cultural narrative.

This book endeavors to weave together these multifaceted themes into a cohesive fabric anchored in first principles thinking. Understanding bitcoin is just as much an *unlearning* process as it is a *learning* process. Thinking in first principles is an effective method of accelerating the former process. First principles thinking lies at the heart of bitcoin, and the more one delves into its fundamental aspects, the deeper their comprehension becomes. While concepts like decentralized consensus, stateless money, and self-sovereignty may seem distant and abstract to most, the notion of first principles thinking permeates all walks of life. It serves as a cornerstone for almost all professions and vocations and is indispensable for navigating society and life generally.

This book is intended to be a simplified, accessible, and comprehensive resource for those seeking an introduction to bitcoin. It may appeal to those who find it natural to think in first principles. This is a demographic that includes individuals across various sectors including, but not limited to, my own—investment banking and law. It may include students seeking a mental model to understand this subject amid the cacophony of social media clutter about NFTs and meme tokens. And it may be appealing to members of an older generation, like my own parents—medical doctors far removed from finance or technology but whose worldview is firmly grounded in first principles thinking.

The impetus behind a person's drive to write a book can be complex. At its core, the act of writing might indeed resonate with Aristotle's concept of eudaimonic self-actualization, where the pursuit of writing serves as a pathway to realizing one's highest potential and virtues.[5] On the other hand, the drive to write may also stem from a deep-seated urge to rectify the misrepresentations of truth that pervade society. This is particularly strong in the case of bitcoin, where narratives are distorted by the news media and members of the political and financial establishment. Misinformation is rife. Writing, in this sense, becomes an act of philosophical defiance—a way to challenge and remediate misunderstandings and misrepresentations. One might say that the pursuit and presentation of factual accuracy is not merely an intellectual exercise but a moral imperative.

Distilling such a vast spectrum of information and literature into a cohesive whole was always going to be an ambitious and formidable undertaking. Ernest Hemingway had some words of inspiration: "All you have to do is write one true sentence. Write the truest sentence that you know."[6]

The essence of writing is in the clarity of communicating one's truth with honesty and simplicity. This book is an endeavor to cut through the noise and reveal the authentic core of a multifaceted, multidisciplinary, and revolutionary innovation. Eleven years after it was first posed to me by that student in Hong Kong, this is a revised response to that enduring question: "What do you think about bitcoin?"

Acknowledgments

I extend my deepest gratitude to Alex Gladstein, Richard Byworth, Lyn Alden, Jameson Lopp, Jeff Booth, Tyler Meade, Oliver Pearson, Andrew Bailey, Alexander Benard, and Shubhi Goyal for their invaluable contributions to this book. Their guidance and expertise were instrumental in shaping its final form.

I am thankful to Columbia University Press for publishing this book, and to Brian Smith, Marielle Poss, Ben Kolstad, and Marianne L'Abbate for their help with the editorial process. I acknowledge Lee McGorie for his work on the images, and Jason Enterline for his help with the cover art. Most importantly, my sincere gratitude goes to Myles Thompson, who saw the potential in this manuscript from the beginning and provided me great encouragement.

To my family and friends: thank you for your boundless love, support, and kindness.

Finally, I am grateful to Satoshi for the inspiration and for giving me something to write about.

PART I

The Framework

CHAPTER 1

Why Are We Talking About This?

The average person's engagement with bitcoin is reminiscent of the ancient Indian parable about the blind men and the elephant. In the parable, a group of blind men encounter an elephant for the first time, and each touches a different part of the animal to learn what it is like. One man feels the elephant's side and declares the elephant is like a wall. Another feels the elephant's tusk and says the elephant is like a spear. A third touches the elephant's trunk and insists that the elephant is like a snake. The one who feels the elephant's leg argues that the elephant is like a tree. Another who feels the elephant's ear claims the elephant is like a fan. Finally, the last man holding the elephant's tail asserts that the elephant is like a rope.[1]

The creator of bitcoin himself, Satoshi Nakamoto, expressed his frustration about trying to describe it: "Writing a description for this thing for general audiences is bloody hard. There's nothing to relate it to."[2] Thinking in first principles, a fundamental question to ask on the subject of bitcoin should be: why are we talking about it? Or, more specifically, what is bitcoin's core innovation that makes it worthy of discussion?

The answer to this question is that, in 2008, a monumental and pathbreaking invention occurred: a whitepaper was published that resulted in the creation, for the first time in history, of a commodity on the internet, that is, a "digital commodity."

DIGITAL COMMODITY

The words "digital commodity" have become so trite, commonplace, and abused that they are virtually meaningless today. The unfortunate truth is that most people who utter them, including many purported crypto experts, do not truly understand their meaning and significance. The words have been tortured to such a degree that they now confess to a meaning far removed from reality.

For just a moment, let us imagine we have never heard the words "bitcoin," "crypto," "blockchain, "NFT," or "web3" before. Let us cleanse our minds of everything we have seen and heard about them in the media and from the Silicon Valley venture capital industry. Now analyze the words:

> "Digital" refers to the encoding and transmission of information in a binary format, represented by the numerals "1" and "0." Anything that is digital is purely informational.
>
> "Commodity" typically describes a tangible physical good, for example, agricultural produce like rice, raw materials like crude oil, or precious metals like gold bars. Commodities are made of physical matter, subject to the laws of physics.

A digital commodity, therefore, implies a magical combination of the properties of the digital with that of the physical.[3] But the challenge here is that what is digital, being informational, is infinitely replicable at no cost.

> If you have an apple and I have an apple, and we swap apples—we each end up with only one apple. But if you and I have an idea and we swap ideas—we each end up with two ideas.[4]
>
> —George Bernard Shaw

If I send you a digital photo via email, I could subsequently send the exact same photo to a million other people via email, and they would all have exact replicas of the photo. That is because the digital photo is purely informational, composed of 1's and 0's, which can be copied at no cost. You, as the recipient of that photo from me, can have no absolute assurance that you are the only recipient of the photo.[5] You might have to take my word for it, or you would need some third party (a trusted intermediary) to monitor or gatekeep my emails to ensure that I do not send the photo elsewhere. In short, the transfer of value digitally has historically been possible only with the involvement of a trusted intermediary or recordkeeper.

On the other hand, if I hand you a gold bar, you now possess that gold bar and I do not. The laws of physics prevent me from handing you the gold bar and then, a few minutes later, handing the same gold bar to someone else. If you walk away from me holding the bar in your hands, you have absolute assurance that you, and only you, possess it, to the exclusion of all others at that moment in time. You do not need me to promise you not to give it to anyone else. Nor do you need someone else to monitor me to ensure that I do not give it (i.e., what is in your hands) to someone else. Physical custody of the commodity is final and does not rely on any form of trust. It relies on physics.

The innovation at the heart of bitcoin was to bridge the digital and physical, and create an instrument that has properties of physical matter and that can be transmitted around the world at speeds only conceivable in the digital space. In other words, bitcoin somehow enabled the laws of physics to apply to 1's and 0's in the digital world. It effectively gave digital information a certain type of physicality: physical-digital-information. This is such a mind-bending and pathbreaking concept that it takes an immense amount of reflection and introspection to appreciate.

When you do understand this *physical* nature of bitcoin, it becomes apparent that the invention is so much more than merely a new payment technology. Its multiple dimensions and implications in the fields of economics, politics, philosophy, and beyond begin to open up. And once you finally see it holistically from all these perspectives, it is hard to unsee. It is as if the blind men in the Indian parable suddenly regained their vision and could see the elephant in its true and holistic form.

THE ROCK OF CENTAURUS (A THOUGHT EXPERIMENT)

In the ancient mythical land of Atlantis, around 7,000 BCE, a rock was discovered that was composed of a material from a galaxy in the Centaurus constellation, over five light-years away. It was deposited on Earth through a celestial phenomenon millions of years prior. The said Centaurus constellation was devoured by a black hole subsequently and, as a result, this solitary rock was the last remaining one of its unique material in the universe. In other words, the Rock was absolutely scarce—there could never be more of the Rock of Centaurus.

Being from a far-off galaxy, the Rock was observed to exhibit certain mysterious and otherworldly properties. For one, it was perfectly divisible into one quadrillion particles. Even more incredibly, if you held a particle in your hand

and whispered a secret word to it, it turned invisible. You could make the particle reappear on any part of the planet at will, by uttering the same secret word. You could pick up a particle and throw it to another person, and regardless of where that person was in the world, even thousands of miles away, they could reach out and catch it with their hands.

Throwing the particles around was as simple as playing catch with a tennis ball. You did not need any special skill nor any sort of approval. All you needed to do was to pick it up and throw it, and the particle would physically move at the speed of light to the desired recipient. No need for the involvement of any other third party in the process. After all, it was a *physical* rock that you could *physically* give anyone or receive from anyone. Because the particles could be turned invisible, you could throw a particle to any recipient without anyone else knowing

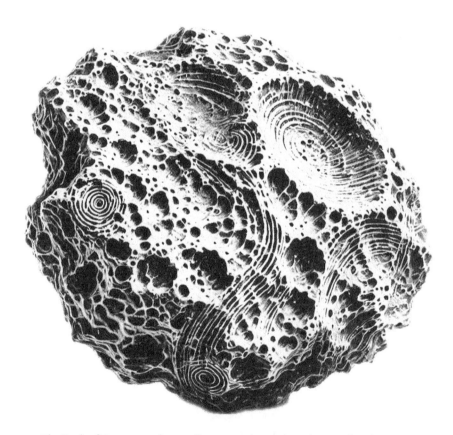

1.1 The Rock of Centaurus: the metallic gray rock was the only one of its distinctive material in the universe, making it the scarcest material known to humankind. Image source: by author.

about it or having any ability to stop it or interfere (just like two people tossing a tennis ball back and forth in the privacy of their backyard).

Over several years, the Rock was split into its quadrillion particles and was distributed organically among the Atlanteans. Several marketplaces popped up where people bought and sold the particles. Many Atlanteans bought and held some particles as a store of wealth—they were accustomed to holding gold as a store of value, and, therefore, recognized the importance of storing their wealth in a scarce asset. They could see that the Rock was far scarcer than even gold because it was made of a material that was entirely lost to a black hole, except for this single remaining fragment. They understood that its unique and magical properties would increase demand for it over time. Unlike gold, the supply of the Rock could not increase with rising demand, which implied that its price would appreciate substantially over time as demand grew.

Atlanteans were also weary of how heavy and difficult gold was to transport and how easily it could be confiscated by the Atlantean authorities or stolen by robbers. But the Rock particles that could be turned invisible and were almost weightless were impossible to confiscate and could be securely transported. Owners did not need to trust any third party to store the particles (as they did with other physical commodities like gold). Also, given its unique and self-evident properties, there was no possibility of counterfeit Rock particles, which was a significant problem with gold and fool's gold.

If you were an Atlantean, would you have considered the Rock of Centaurus to be of any value or utility?

While this story is obviously, and lamentably, pure fiction and no more than a thought experiment, what if you learned that today, in the twenty-first century, there exists a commodity that has near-identical properties to the mythical Rock of Centaurus? It just goes by a different name.

As a thought experiment, imagine there was a base metal as scarce as gold but with the following properties: boring grey in colour, not a good conductor of electricity, not particularly strong, but not ductile or easily malleable either, not useful for any practical or ornamental purpose, and with one special, magical property: can be transported over a communications channel.

If it somehow acquired any value at all for whatever reason, then anyone wanting to transfer wealth over a long distance could buy some, transmit it, and have the recipient sell it.[6]

—Satoshi Nakamoto, August 27, 2010

FIRST PRINCIPLES THINKING

Grasping the complexities of bitcoin is a challenging endeavor. Comedian John Oliver once noted: "Bitcoin is everything you don't understand about money combined with everything you don't understand about computers."[7]

The concern stems primarily from the absence of a relatable mental model to understand bitcoin. It does not help that a lot of noise surrounds the subject in the crypto industry. And in that noise, the original signal is most often lost or garbled at best. This book is not about NFTs or web3 or about the crypto industry, which, at its peak, ex-bitcoin, reached $2 trillion in market capitalization in 2022 and witnessed some of the largest financial fraud schemes in history. Rather, the goal of this book is to encourage readers to engage in some first principles thinking.

Aristotle, often considered the father of first principles thinking, articulated the importance of identifying the first cause or the "principle" of everything. In his work, *Metaphysics*,[8] he describes the process as the "first basis from which a thing is known":

> In every systematic inquiry (methodos) where there are first principles, or causes, or elements, knowledge and science result from acquiring knowledge of these; for we think we know something just in case we acquire knowledge of the primary causes, the primary first principles, all the way to the elements.[9]
>
> —Aristotle, 335-323 BCE

He posited that, by understanding the essential elements of a thing, you could deduce its true underlying properties. This understanding will afford an appreciation of the thing's fundamental laws and principles.[10] This method of analytical thinking calls for breaking down complex problems into their most basic, foundational elements and then moving up in one's understanding from there.

Embracing first principles thinking could help society confront and correct many normalized distortions. For example, people today seemingly accept a multitude of economic and political missteps by governments and central banks without question. People have acquiesced to endless currency debasement and debt accumulation globally. They often fail to ask basic, first principles questions with regard to such matters that are of paramount importance to our society and future generations. Asking these questions may prompt a reevaluation of established norms with respect to many things, including, for the purposes of our discussion in this book, money and its relationship with the state. As John Kenneth Galbraith observed:

> The study of money, above all other fields in economics, is the one in which complexity is used to disguise the truth, not to reveal it. Most things in life—automobiles, mistresses, cancer—are important principally to those who have them. Money, in contrast, is equally important to those who have it and those who don't. Both, accordingly, have a concern for understanding it. Both should proceed in the full confidence that they can.[11]

Henry Ford had a more cynical view: "It is well enough that people of the nation do not understand our banking and monetary system, for if they did, I believe there would be a revolution before tomorrow morning."[12]

Within the realm of cryptocurrencies, the dazzling prospects of NFTs and web3 often distract from the core innovation and promise of bitcoin. In the frenzy to capitalize on the latest trend, the central question is often lost: what was bitcoin's original innovation and purpose? A return to first principles thinking here may reveal the true potential of bitcoin as not just another cryptocurrency but a foundational shift in the way we view monetary policy, central banks, and the state. First principles thinking urges us to peel back the layers of complexity that cloud our judgment and to construct knowledge from the ground up.

It seems clear that a first principles approach to understanding bitcoin should involve analyzing why it exists and where it derives its purported value from. The hardest part is developing the correct mental model to think about it. Is it like a tech stock or a meme stock? Is it a currency, or is it just another payments service like Visa or PayPal? Is it a commodity like gold? Is it a bubble, like tulip bulbs during the Dutch tulip mania in the 1600s?[13]

What mental model do we use to study the subject? This book takes the approach that the best mental model for understanding bitcoin, or the best thing to "relate it to" per Satoshi, is a physical commodity with certain magical properties, that is, the hypothetical Rock of Centaurus, or, in Satoshi's words, a boring gray metal with nothing special about it other than its ability to be transported over a communications channel. This is why the "digital gold"[14] analogy works well—bitcoin is gold 2.0. As we shall discuss in this book, bitcoin retains or improves upon most of gold's most valued properties and eliminates many of its weakest ones.

FOUNDATIONAL INVENTIONS

Consider the invention of the wheel 5,500 years ago, and the invention of the automobile 140 years ago. Both rank among humanity's greatest inventions. But are they the same "category" of inventions?

There are some inventions where the innovation is so fundamental and revolutionary that it essentially becomes timeless. It requires little or no modification. We may refer to such inventions as "foundational inventions." The wheel falls into this class. The original invention is said to have occurred in Mesopotamia, where the Sumerians inserted rotating axles into solid discs of wood. Only minor adjustments to the wheel have occurred over the ensuing 5,500 years. For example, subsequent civilizations hollowed out the discs to make them lighter weight, and the wood was replaced by other materials in subsequent millennia. But the core principle—that rotational movement via an axle reduces friction between surfaces, enabling smooth motion by rolling rather than dragging—has remained constant. The invention was timeless and needed no improvement in its operating principle.

In a similar category as the wheel is the lever. It is a simple machine invented over seven thousand years ago, possibly in ancient Egypt. Its principle of leverage to lift heavy objects is timeless and complete. The innovative concept required no further development in and of itself. The basic form of a nail, used in woodwork to join two objects, has also been largely unchanged since at least 3,500 BCE in Egypt. The magnetic compass, invented in ancient China, has remained unchanged in terms of its basic principle for over two thousand years. These are all examples of foundational inventions. The innovations were of an elemental nature and were complete since inception.

By contrast, consider the invention of the automobile. German engineer Karl Benz invented the first gasoline-powered car in 1886. This laid the foundation for the automobile industry. Around the same time, innovators like Gottlieb Daimler and Wilhelm Maybach also contributed to the development of early automobiles. Then, in the early twentieth century, Henry Ford revolutionized car production with the introduction of the assembly line. Throughout the twentieth century, the automobile evolved with innovations such as automatic transmissions and fuel-efficient engines. The past two decades have seen the rise of electric and hybrid vehicles. Today, we see further transformation of the industry with the development of autonomous driving technology. Unlike the wheel, Karl Benz's invention, although pathbreaking, was not the final product—it was merely the starting point for subsequent development and innovation. Like the automobile, the telephone has changed drastically from rotary phones to touch-tone phones, to mobile phones, and to smartphones. Computers have changed fundamentally from the ENIAC in 1945 to desktops, laptops, and tablets, with significant improvements in processing power, size, and functionality. Light bulbs have changed from Thomas Edison's invention of the incandescent light bulb in 1879, to fluorescent bulbs, halogen bulbs, LED lights, and newer versions that are brighter and more energy efficient. And cameras today have virtually nothing in common with the original invention by Nicéphore Niépce in 1826. These inventions, in their original forms, were *not* foundational inventions.

Which category of invention does bitcoin fall into? Bitcoin should be considered a foundational invention. It is the wheel, not the automobile. While minor incremental developments may take place (e.g., related to the protocol's programmability), and layered technologies may be built "on top" of it (not affecting the protocol itself), the core invention remains unchanged. Similar to the wheel, bitcoin is the finished product. Thousands of other cryptocurrencies have been developed, each claiming to use and improve upon bitcoin's underlying blockchain technology. While they may well serve other important purposes (the discussion of which is beyond the scope of this book), the concept of digital scarcity, which makes bitcoin digital gold, was a foundational invention that is irreplicable, final, and complete.

Bitcoin is analogous to a new "substance" that was created—only once—with absolutely limited supply: the Rock of Centaurus. And needless to say, the Rock of Centaurus would not be absolutely scarce if there also existed a Rock of Andromeda from another galaxy with interchangeable magical properties. Another analogy that has been used to make this point is that of a new element in the periodic table whose molecular structure cannot be re-created. This may be the hardest concept to grasp in one's study of bitcoin (and perhaps the most controversial, too) because it has little to do with bitcoin' code but rather arises from game theory, human psychology, network effects, and path dependency. Part 2, in particular, chapters 3, 4, and 7, lay out the rational basis for this thesis.

THE HOLISTIC METHOD

In Plato's *Charmides*, Socrates refers appreciatively to physicians who cure the "whole body" of their patients:

> You have probably heard this about good doctors, that if you go to them with a pain in the eyes, they are likely to say that they cannot undertake to cure the eyes by themselves, but that it will be necessary to treat the head at the same time if things are also to go well with the eyes. And again, it would be very foolish to suppose that one could ever treat the head by itself without treating the whole body. In keeping with this principle, they plan a regime for the whole body with the idea of treating and curing the part along with the whole.[15]

The "holistic approach" to medical diagnosis traces its origins to Hippocrates, a contemporary of Plato. Two thousand five hundred years ago, he wrote the first ever textbook of Western medicine, *Corpus Hippocraticum*, which includes the collective medical knowledge of the era. Hippocrates is considered the father of Western medicine—medical students around the world today take the Hippocratic oath upon graduation from medical school.

The word "holistic" originates from the Greek word "holos" meaning "whole" or "complete." The holistic approach involves addressing the entirety of an entity rather than analyzing its individual parts in isolation. In medicine, it acknowledges the interconnectedness of various components of the body and the importance of a comprehensive view to gain a full appreciation of a subject. "Holism" is a philosophy based on the idea that all dimensions of life are interconnected. Rather than just thinking "outside the box," the approach would be to remove the "box" altogether.[16]

Gestalt psychology is a field of psychology that focuses on how people perceive and organize sensory information as whole patterns or configurations rather than just a collection of individual components. This contrasts with the traditional scientific method, which divides the object into a set of elements that are analyzed separately, with a view to reducing complexity. Gestalt psychology is based on the idea that when individual elements are combined, they can produce perceptions that are not apparent when considering each part separately. Human nature is inclined to understand objects as entire structures. By extension, the understanding of a part depends on the entire structure in which it is embedded. The whole is greater than the sum of its parts.

In seeking to understand bitcoin's meaning and significance, a holistic approach makes all the difference. When people perform an isolated analysis, they view the subject through a unitary lens, forming a negative impression because of a lack of appreciation of the other dimensions, and passing judgment too soon. Bitcoin cannot be viewed in a silo. It can only be appreciated holistically. The holistic philosophy is the basis for the multidisciplinary approach that this book takes to study bitcoin. It is suggested that the key faculties in this regard are technology, economics, politics, and philosophy. Why are each of these fields relevant?

Let us start with economics. Bitcoin represents a direct challenge to the centralized monetary systems that have dominated for centuries. Satoshi's idea was to create an uninflatable reserve asset immune to the discretionary monetary policies of central banks and governments. An appreciation of bitcoin's role in this regard can only be possible, however, with a clear grasp of the problem, namely, currency debasement, inflation, and moral hazard. To understand why bitcoin matters, one must appreciate that fiat money governed by central banks is a relatively new concept in monetary history and that alternative systems have existed in the past. Only by studying economics can we better appreciate the malignancies of the current system, as well as bitcoin's disruptive potential.

An awareness of politics and political history is necessary to appreciate bitcoin's role as a censorship-resistant asset that cannot be confiscated. Throughout history, governments have overstepped their authority, using financial control as a means of oppression. Understanding cases of government overreach—from asset seizures to financial censorship—reveals the importance of bitcoin's properties. Contemporary politics shows that authoritarian regimes continue to suppress dissent and impose financial restrictions on people. In the geopolitical context, the U.S. dollar faces increasing scrutiny as the global reserve currency, and the world's political landscape grows ever more unstable. An understanding of these tensions illuminates the value of a politically neutral currency and the unique solution that it offers.

A study of bitcoin's philosophy is crucial to comprehend the deeper narratives that underpin it. It prompts questions about values, morality, and the kind of world we wish to live in. Bitcoin embodies a libertarian philosophy, advocating for individual sovereignty and financial privacy. Understanding where one aligns on the political spectrum—whether with libertarian ideals of personal freedom or authoritarian views that prioritize state control—requires philosophical reflection. For instance, it raises questions about how important privacy and autonomy are in one's life and how much control we would be willing to surrender. As a scarce uninflatable asset, bitcoin challenges modern debt- and inflation-driven consumerism. It raises questions about whether instant gratification through spending, or saving for the future, leads to a more meaningful existence.

Economics, politics and philosophy answer the "why" of bitcoin. To understand the "how," we need to study the technology, which lends credence to the ambitious claims put forward on the other fronts. Only by studying the underlying technology can we appreciate the monumental breakthrough that made decentralized, peer-to-peer digital transactions possible. To truly believe in bitcoin's absolute scarcity of 21 million coins, it is necessary to analyze how this is actually achieved through economic incentive structures masterfully and ingeniously engineered through code. The words "censorship resistant" and "unconfiscatable" are no more than just that—mere words—without an understanding of how they might hold true in the face of a nation-state attack on bitcoin. Technological insight is also key to recognizing the potential risks and vulnerabilities of the network, such as how hard and soft *forks* operate and how power is distributed across the decentralized system.

Many, particularly in the financial news media, analyze bitcoin purely from an economic standpoint. Focused entirely on price, they dismiss bitcoin as no more than a speculative investment akin to a small-cap stock. While obsessing over the volatility of bitcoin's price, they often remain blind to the political implications of censorship resistance and unconfiscatability—properties that offer a lifeline to billions living under authoritarian regimes. Some may explore the political promise of bitcoin without understanding the technological basis from which its unstoppable potential arises. This may lead them to dismiss the purported political benefits altogether. "It is just a matter of time before governments shut it down," they may scoff.

Others steeped in bitcoin's technology may believe that the software is all there is to bitcoin. They may miss the fact that the code is only a small component of what makes bitcoin *bitcoin*. Economic incentive structures based in game theory, as well as the philosophical and cultural narratives that underpin it, are arguably of far greater importance to bitcoin's ultimate success. Bitcoin's legacy lies in its uncodified social contract rather than lines of C++ code. Technologists who do not appreciate this fact often move on to the latest trend in cryptocurrency, thinking that bitcoin's software is outdated and irrelevant.

The only way to overcome these blind spots in one's study of bitcoin is to approach it holistically. While this book has selected the domains of technology, economics, politics, and philosophy to focus on, these are by no means the only fields that bitcoin touches on. One might take the view that mathematics, physics, statistics, psychology, history, anthropology, and quantitative financial analysis, among many others, are equally important. However, for the moment, we shall focus our lens on the four key enumerated domains, establishing a preliminary foundation from which more expansive studies may evolve in the future.

THIS BOOK

Part I will set the framework for the ensuing discussion. In the next chapter, we will explore the practical implications of bitcoin as a digital commodity and how this reshapes our understanding of money. Through a comparative analysis of bitcoin against historical competitors like fiat currency and gold, we evaluate time-tested attributes of money to understand bitcoin's place in the arc of monetary history.

In part II, we will perform a thorough examination of the claim that bitcoin is akin to a physical commodity on the internet. It is important to appreciate what a lofty claim this is in the first place. A digital asset with physical properties seems absurd and fantastical if you think about it. We will analyze the heart of the technological breakthrough that achieved this incredible feat through a discussion of the decades-old computer science problem that was solved using an intricate design of incentive structures rooted in game theory. In the context of bitcoin's technological underpinnings, we will address a central debate in the crypto industry around decentralized consensus mechanisms: Proof-of-Work versus Proof-of-Stake. We will discuss the long-term "security budget" concerns relating to bitcoin's diminishing block rewards and its impact on incentives to mine bitcoin and secure the network. We will analyze bitcoin's resilience by examining potential attack vectors, and we will address a question that frequently arises in the context of the more than twenty thousand cryptocurrencies that have been launched and continue to be launched each day: what makes bitcoin unique as a monetary asset in a landscape of purportedly faster, cheaper, and more programmable cryptocurrencies? We will seek to answer this question in part II by demonstrating, objectively, why bitcoin is a path-dependent, irreplicable, once-in-history invention.

In part III, we will consider bitcoin through the lens of macro and monetary economics. We will look at the state's control of money and how this came to be from a historical perspective. This is particularly relevant in the context of the role of central banks in controlling monetary policy. The perils of inflation and monetary debasement will be considered against a deflationary hard asset like bitcoin. And with this backdrop, we will assess the rate of adoption of bitcoin, its price appreciation, and its potential to emerge as the fastest horse in the race against inflation by soaking up profligate money printing by central banks. In this respect, we will consider bitcoin's infamous volatility to help frame it in a more rational light, with a better appreciation of investment horizons in order to dispel a myopic viewpoint.

In part IV, we will evaluate the political case for bitcoin. The dark shadow of the surveillance state will be considered both from historical and contemporary perspectives. We will embark on a thought-provoking journey to imagine the impact that a hypothetical asset like bitcoin could have wielded during pivotal moments of sovereign and political crises and wars throughout history. We will evaluate what a government ban on bitcoin might involve and its feasibility from a practical, legal, and game theoretical perspective. We will also delve into the geopolitical implications for bitcoin vis-à-vis the U.S. dollar and the SWIFT payment systems. And we will postulate how the current geopolitical landscape might present a role for an apolitical asset like bitcoin. In the context of the politics that surrounds the topic, we will address one of the primary subjects of media hysteria over bitcoin: its energy usage. Through a quantitative and qualitative analysis, we see that reality is far removed from media perceptions.

In part V, we will explore the philosophical underpinnings of bitcoin, focusing on the concept of the sovereign prerogative in contrast with the notion of the self-sovereign individual. Bitcoin emerges as an unprecedented tool in the pursuit of self-sovereignty, offering a new level of autonomy and empowerment. We will discuss the influence of "A Cypherpunk's Manifesto" on bitcoin's inception, offering insight into the cultural and ideological framework that shaped bitcoin's ideals. The evils of consumerism spurred by inflationary monetary policies will be considered from a philosophical angle, as well as the role that a deflationary hard money like bitcoin could play in this context. We will explore the critical role of philosophical narratives in the endurance of an idea, particularly in the age of social media where narratives can shape and shift public opinion. This discussion will include an examination of memes, highlighting their potency in disseminating complex ideas and fostering community around bitcoin. The difficulty in understanding what bitcoin really is, which this book aims to address, has led to a long list of misconceptions. In this part, we will discuss some of the most notorious misconceptions about great inventions throughout history, which bear a striking resemblance to the narratives propagated by bitcoin skeptics.

CHAPTER 2

Bitcoin and Money

Man-made rules can be bent and broken, physical laws not so much. For example, you can't simply "make up" a physical gold coin. You have to dig it out of the ground. You can, however, absolutely make up a gold coin on paper.

—Gigi

THE PHYSICAL AND THE DIGITAL

A peer-to-peer transaction is one where two parties transact directly with one another without the involvement of any third-party recordkeeper. Historically, such transactions have been exclusively confined to physical assets, wherein the act of handing over an item tracks the transfer of value with finality and certainty via possession (referred to as *final settlement*). Shells, beads, teeth, coins, and cash are examples of physical objects that have been used to transfer value in this manner throughout human history. Such peer-to-peer exchanges do not require a third-party recordkeeper because the laws of physics guarantee that the item cannot appear in more than one place at the same time.

The alternative to using physical items is to use a ledger to track transfers of value. Ledgers are purely informational and require trusted intermediaries to maintain.

The distinction between the two systems for keeping track of things is illustrated by the following example.[1] Imagine you are a shepherd with a hundred sheep. At the end of each day, you want to ensure that all one hundred sheep have returned home, safe and sound. There are two ways you could go about this. You could buy a hundred collars and put one on each sheep. As soon as a sheep returns home, you could remove the collar and hang it up on a hanger in your shed. At the end of each day, if you look at the wall and see the hundred hangers with a collar on each one, you know, beyond a shadow of a doubt, that all your sheep are home. The laws of physics guarantee that a collar cannot simultaneously appear on a hanger and also in a wolf's den that evening.

The second method would be to maintain a list and count the sheep as they walk through the gate. You would need to be careful not to make an error while counting. If you count a hundred sheep, would you know with absolute certainty that all sheep are in fact home? What if you double-counted a sheep?

A collar on a hanger *directly* represents its location in your shed as opposed to anywhere else. It is self-evident. The list produced by counting the sheep is purely informational—it *indirectly* represents the sheep's location. You would have to trust that you did a good job counting.[2]

The digital world has traditionally relied exclusively on the second method for tracking and transferring value. The first option was not available because we could not use physical items in the digital space. Everything that is digital is no more than information comprising 1's and 0's. Unlike physical matter, information can be perfectly copied at virtually no cost. The problem described in chapter 1 whereby a single photo can be sent online to any number of recipients in a costless manner is referred to as the double-spending problem. To solve this, we use digital ledgers that record who owns what in the real world. This way, even though we cannot hold a digital item in our hands, we can still *trust* to whom it belongs because the ledger, maintained by a trusted third party, keeps track of everything.

Today's global banking and financial system runs almost entirely on ledgers. Ledger entries have become the money of humanity. "Wealth" takes the form of ledger entries on electronic databases. These electronic databases reside at one's bank (at a subledger level) and ultimately at the relevant central bank (at the general ledger level). Around 90 percent of money in the United States and 97 percent in the United Kingdom has no physical existence at all.[3] What we take for granted as our store of value is essentially a digital entry residing on the server or cloud of a centralized trusted entity.

The Map Is the Territory

As discussed, ledgers may be used as informational representations of real-world assets. Consider gold-backed certificates. You could transfer a certificate representing a gold bar from Tokyo to New York digitally in a second. However, the actual gold bar sitting in a vault in London would not move an inch. The transfer at the certificate level is purely informational. The transaction and ownership are tracked on a ledger through several layers of trust. You trust the custodian in London to safeguard the gold. You trust the recordkeeper—a broker based in the Cayman Islands perhaps—to maintain accurate books and records. And you trust the legal system and the rule of law to enforce your rights against the aforementioned parties.

If you think of the real-world asset as the *territory*, then the information pertaining to the territory would be the *map*.[4] With a gold bar, the map and the territory are the same—when you hold the piece of gold in your hand, all information pertaining to its nature and location is in your hand. With a gold certificate, the map and the territory are *not* the same. The gap between the two is where trust resides. And where trust resides, so does the abuse of trust, as history bears witness. The unavoidable need for a real-world recordkeeper to track a real-world asset in the digital space is referred to as the oracle problem. The custodian or recordkeeper (the oracle) has to be trusted to secure the asset and also to update the ledger on an ongoing basis with information regarding transfers of ownership and so on. Without the actual gold, the informational ledger is of zero value.

Now imagine that we had a means in the digital world to unify the map and the territory. To illustrate the idea, consider that when you look at the map of a town on Google Maps, you trust Google to ensure that the map is an accurate representation of the physical town. But imagine if the map in your hand and the actual town, with roads and buildings, were magically the same. It is a rather mind-bending notion (and, of course, impossible in the case of maps of a town). In such a scenario, where the map is the territory, there would be no need for trust.

This is the crux of bitcoin's technological achievement. With bitcoin, as we know, there is no real-world asset sitting in a vault somewhere that imparts value to it. The ledger and the asset are the same. This raises the question, What exactly is the asset that gives bitcoin its value? Where does this value reside? The answer to this question, in the simplest of terms, is that *the record of ownership of the asset is, itself, the asset.* The process by which ownership information is produced and memorialized imparts value to the record in and of itself. In other words, *the map is the territory.*[5]

What makes this method of producing and recording information so special that it imparts monetary value to the record? First, the record is kept on ledgers maintained independently and voluntarily by tens of thousands of computers dispersed around the world. Second, the sanctity of the record is ensured by hundreds of thousands of specialized computers that expend tens of millions of dollars a day to keep the records secure from manipulation. Third, cryptographic techniques are used by which users control their ownership record on the distributed ledger and securely enter into transactions. These factors together attribute monetary value to these digital ownership records. This attribution, of course, is ultimately based on the belief system and narratives that surround bitcoin (this is explored in part V), similar to the process by which gold acquired and has retained monetary value.

The second point above, which is referred to as mining (discussed in detail in part II), is crucial in this regard. As we shall see, this involves brute-force computation to produce information memorializing bitcoin transactions and ownership. These computations incur substantial electricity cost. The energy expended gives the information an "unforgeable costliness"[6] that ensures bitcoin's scarcity, contributing to its value (see chapter 4 for a detailed discussion on this point). The information produced through the real-world energy expenditure may be described as a *digital manifestation of a real-world phenomenon*. The digital product of the energy, which cost real-world dollars to produce, is the bitcoin. Bitcoin thus flips the oracle problem on its head.

> Bitcoin fixes [the oracle problem] by going in the *opposite* direction. It starts with information and makes its own reality via its continued operation. It defines the map and implies the territory. All participants voluntarily "act out" Bitcoin and a shared reality emerges because of it . . . Ergo: in Bitcoin, the map is the territory.[7]
>
> —Gigi

Bitcoin overcomes the need for a centralized trusted intermediary by establishing an autonomous and self-regulating network of participants through an intricate balance of economic incentive structures. The technological architecture that makes this possible is discussed in part II, but at a high level, transactions are created, validated, and included in an immutable record through a self-sustaining ecosystem with different participants performing different functions in an open and trustless manner. The result of this complex yet harmonious process is that digital information is turned into a scarce and valuable commodity. It is achieved through the actions of individuals acting voluntarily in their own economic interests.

To summarize, prior to bitcoin, peer-to-peer transactions were only possible in the physical world because "value" could not reside independently in the digital world—it was exclusively a conception of the real world. The only way to transfer value digitally was by using a centralized recordkeeper who maintained a ledger and tracked the movement of value in the real world. Bitcoin creates a paradigm shift, imbuing the informational landscape with the unequivocal assurance of physical exchange. Bitcoin is thus a *digital incarnation of physical certainty.*

Why does this matter? And what does a digital commodity achieve? These are first principles questions that should be addressed. In short, the ability to transact peer to peer in the digital realm using an asset that mimics the properties of a physical commodity has profound economic and political implications. As we shall see, this is especially the case with respect to money itself. But before we evaluate these monetary implications, we need to lay the groundwork for the discussion by asking another first principles question.

WHAT IS MONEY?

Money does not make the world go round, but it certainly is the lifeblood of almost all economic activity on the planet. It also underpins social structures and plays a central role, if not *the* central role, in the development and sustenance of human civilizations. It affects international relations, serving as a tool of stability and power. It provides a means for individuals to store the fruits of their labor and plan for the future. It fuels the engine of capitalism. Without money, the complexity and scale of human society would be inconceivable.

But what makes money *money*? This is a question we will return to at several junctures and in different contexts throughout this book. But let us analyze this question here in first principles.

When you hand over a dollar bill in exchange for a candy bar, the transaction, on the face of it, is not too different from a barter exchange that may have taken place in ancient civilizations prior to the advent of money. In both transactions, the parties exchange items that they perceive as valuable. But there is a key difference.

Consider a barter exchange, where you have mangoes and I have strawberries. You might set the price of your mangoes at ten strawberries per mango. I might argue that eight of my strawberries should be worth one mango on the basis that my strawberries are particularly fresh and juicy. You may disagree. However, if you price your mangoes at $10 each, and I only have $8 on me, it would be nonsensical for me to argue that my dollars should be *worth more in mango terms*. Instead, I would argue that your mangoes should be *worth less in dollar terms*. Dollars take centerstage. I might negotiate an $8 price on the basis that the mangoes are small and not as sweet as those at the grocery store down the street. The value of the dollars in my pocket is beyond reproach—a debate over the Federal Reserve's forward guidance affecting inflation rates is unlikely (though not impossible) at the checkout counter. Money is special. There is something about its standardized acceptance that fundamentally changes how the average person thinks about commercial exchanges.

Carl Menger, economist and founder of the Austrian School of Economics, sought to address this issue in 1892 in his paper, "On the Origin of Money."[8] He observed that it is nothing short of "mysterious" and "enigmatic" that people accept "little metal disks apparently useless as such" or "documents representing them" as money:

> What is the nature of those little disks or documents, which in themselves seem to serve no useful purpose, and which nevertheless, in contradiction to the rest of experience, pass from one hand to another in exchange for the most useful commodities, nay, for which every one is so eagerly bent on surrendering his wares? Is money an organic member in the world of commodities, or is it an economic anomaly? Are we to refer its commercial currency and its value in trade to the same causes conditioning those of other goods, or are they the distinct product of convention and authority?

In seeking to solve this mystery, Menger introduced the concept of salability of money, which essentially refers to the marketability of the asset that society accepts as money. The relative ease with which an item retains its marketability with regard to transactions over long distances (spatial salability) and over time by retaining or increasing its purchasing power into the future (temporal salability), the more likely it is that society would converge on it as their money, according to Menger. In chapter 8, we will discuss the history and evolution of money in this context, but for now, let us consider two broad categories of money: commodity money and fiat money.

Commodity money has its origins in ancient civilizations. People used physical items of intrinsic value as mediums of exchange with the primary purpose of facilitating trade and overcoming the limitations of barter. Cattle and grain were used early on. For example, Mesopotamians used barley, and various societies across Asia and Africa used cowrie shells. These gave way to precious metals like gold and silver because of their durability, divisibility, portability, and inherent value. Then came coinage, where governments minted coins from precious metals. Because of limitations around portability, divisibility, and so on, people moved to paper currency backed by commodities—in the case of gold, the gold standard (this is sometimes referred to as representative money). Under this system, paper currency could be exchanged, by legal mandate, for a specified quantity of the precious metal.

Fiat money, in contrast to commodity money, is not tied to any physical commodity but instead is simply created by government decree ("fiat" in Latin means, "let it be done"). Its value is derived from the trust and confidence in the issuing government, and its acceptance in a nation is *mandated* by the law of the land. Given that it is not subject to physical limitations of scarcity imposed by commodity money, fiat can be produced in unlimited quantities by the issuing government. At the heart of the fiat system is trust in the central banking institution of a nation to act responsibly in exercising its immense powers over money creation. Fiat money offers governments unprecedented flexibility and control over economic affairs and policymaking.

The transition from commodity money to fiat money was gradual, and the factors influencing this transition will be discussed in chapter 8. In summary, the constraints and limitations of the gold standard, particularly during times of economic stress like World War I, the Great Depression, and World War II, prompted governments to seek more flexible monetary systems; the death knell for the gold standard came in 1971, when President Richard Nixon ended the convertibility of the U.S. dollar into gold. This move effectively marked the beginning of the modern era of fiat money.

As a digital *commodity*, bitcoin is a potential avenue and opportunity for the world to return to principles of commodity money. Unlike fiat money, bitcoin has a finite supply capped at 21 million coins. This scarcity is reminiscent of gold. Unlike fiat, bitcoin's transparent issuance process, governed by a decentralized network, ensures that its creation and distribution are predictable and immune to human discretion.

A COMPARATIVE ANALYSIS

How do the three monetary systems—gold, fiat and bitcoin—compare in terms of Menger's notion of salability? To perform such an evaluation, we must first determine the key properties under which they are to be compared. The monetary properties analyzed hereunder are derived from economic principles and theories that are widely discussed and debated (and usually disagreed upon) in the field of economics. Foremost among them are scarcity, portability, verifiability, divisibility, durability, fungibility and history. Some of these properties, like portability, divisibility, verifiability, and fungibility, contribute to *spatial* salability, while the others, like scarcity, durability and history, arguably contribute towards *temporal* salability. In the digital era, and in the context of the unprecedented power wielded by the surveillance state (a discussion reserved for parts IV and V of this book), there are two additional properties that are highly relevant: censorship resistance and unconfiscatability.

Let us evaluate gold, fiat and bitcoin on the basis of each of these properties:

1. Scarcity

The extent to which fiat money is inflated over time is entirely subject to the absolute discretion of the government or central bank that issues the currency. Supply can literally be inflated to infinity at no cost by the click of a button. As Ben Bernanke, former chair of the Federal Reserve, famously observed in 2009 about the money creation process via commercial bank intermediation: "we simply use the computer to mark up the size of the account they have with the Fed." Suffice to say here that countries like Weimar Germany, Zimbabwe, Argentina, and Venezuela, as well as almost all developed country central banks today including the Federal Reserve and the European Central Bank have invariably fallen victim to inflationary policies and currency debasement in varying degrees.

Scarcity is certainly one of gold's defining characteristics, contributing to its value and appeal as a store of wealth for millennia. Its scarcity arises from

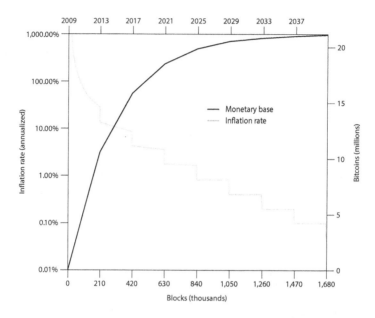

2.1 Bitcoin inflation rate. *Source*: Kevin Schellinger

geology—it is limited by the amount present in the Earth's crust[9] and the feasibility of extracting it. However, this scarcity is not fixed. When the price of gold rises, it becomes economically viable to mine gold from more difficult and less accessible sources. Higher prices can justify the increased costs of extraction, leading to an increase in supply. This feedback mechanism means that the supply of gold is elastic; its scarcity can decrease as prices increase, at least in the short to medium term. This elasticity is a result of the economics of gold mining. New technologies can also make previously uneconomical deposits viable, further adjusting the scarcity dynamically in response to market conditions.[10]

Unlike gold and fiat, bitcoin operates under a predetermined supply model. The total supply of bitcoin is capped at 21 million coins, with new bitcoins introduced to the market at a predictable rate. Unlike gold, no matter how much the price of bitcoin increases, the rate of new bitcoin creation does not accelerate. *Bitcoin is the first asset in history, whose supply is entirely unaffected by increased demand for it.*[11] The algorithmic nature of bitcoin's supply ensures that its scarcity is absolute and predictable, unaffected by price increases or advances in mining technology.

Figure 2.1 shows that new bitcoin is created in every block, and the number of such new bitcoin created per block is halved every four years. Thus, bitcoin's maximum total supply is 21 million. By ensuring that its supply is capped, rule-based, and predetermined, bitcoin offers a level of predictability and security that is unmatched by any physical commodity or fiat currency.

2. *Portability*

Transporting gold requires security measures to prevent theft, loss, or interception. Moving gold between countries or even within a country necessitates armed escorts, secure vaults, and ships or planes equipped to handle valuable cargo. For instance, the transfer of gold reserves during World War II demonstrated these challenges vividly. Various nations moved their gold reserves to prevent them from falling into enemy hands, and such movements involved complex logistics and significant risks. The United Kingdom, for example, shipped much of its gold to Canada for safekeeping, a perilous journey across U-boat-infested waters.[12]

The cost of transporting gold includes the physical logistics, such as secure packaging and the means of transport, and also insurance to cover the immense value being moved. These costs can be prohibitive, especially for large quantities, and they directly affect the efficiency of gold as a medium for international trade or as a means of storing wealth.

Physical cash, or fiat, suffers similar shortcomings as gold. Carrying physical currency for large transactions can be impractical because of weight and volume, and it poses significant security risks, including theft and loss. Physical fiat currency is not easily portable across borders because of different currencies in different countries, exchange rate issues, and legal restrictions on the amount of cash that can be carried across borders. Digital fiat currency solves many of these portability issues because it can be transferred instantaneously around the world without needing to stuff a suitcase with cash and get on a plane. But such transactions may be subject to compliance, red tape, regulatory hurdles, and intermediary fees. Digital fiat is not in bearer form and thus relies on trusted intermediaries, which comes with associated risks such as confiscation and censorship, as we shall discuss later in this chapter.

Bitcoin can be transported around the globe instantly via layered protocols,[13] with final settlement occurring in ten minutes on average via the internet, regardless of the amount being transferred.[14] In terms of security, the bitcoin protocol has never been hacked. The task of breaking bitcoin's cryptography is estimated to be orders of magnitude more difficult than finding a single grain of sand in the entire universe. Of course, services built on top of bitcoin, such as exchanges, individual computers, and so on, have been hacked, thus compromising people's bitcoin (i.e., bitcoin that is not held by individuals in self-custody). The different types of bitcoin storage infrastructure and their relative levels of security and convenience will be discussed in chapter 3.

3. Verifiability

The physical nature of fiat currency makes it susceptible to counterfeiting. Despite advanced security features, counterfeit notes circulate widely around the world. The U.S. Treasury Department estimated in 2021 that there were between $70 and $150 million worth of counterfeit U.S. dollar bills in circulation at any given time in the United States alone.[15] This is an even bigger problem in developing countries.

The verification process for gold is critical because the value of gold is tied directly to its purity, measured in karats or fineness. The accurate assessment of gold requires specialized equipment and expertise.[16] Common methods include X-ray fluorescence (XRF) analyzers, which can measure the purity of gold and other precious metals without destroying them.[17] However, such equipment is expensive and requires trained personnel to operate. Other methods, like acid tests, can determine the gold content, but they may cause slight damage to the item being tested.[18]

Counterfeit gold products have become increasingly sophisticated. Forgeries include gold-plated tungsten, which has a density similar to that of gold, making it difficult to detect through traditional means like weight and size measurements.[19] Counterfeiters also produce fake gold coins and bars that mimic the appearance and markings of genuine products, requiring experts to identify the subtle differences.

The history of gold is rife with examples of counterfeiting and fraud. As far back as the Lydians, who are credited with creating the first gold coins in the seventh century BCE, there were attempts to counterfeit gold.[20] Recent decades have seen several high-profile cases of gold-bar counterfeiting, including bars filled with tungsten.[21] These incidents have occurred in the vaults of major banks, highlighting the ongoing challenge of verification.

Bitcoin's consensus mechanism allows immediate and transparent verification of transactions and ownership without the need for third-party intermediaries.

The integrity of each unit can be verified easily and transparently at almost no cost through its digital ledger.

4. Divisibility

Gold's divisibility, or the ability to break it down into smaller units without losing value, presents practical challenges that affect its usability as a currency for everyday transactions. Gold's physical nature means that dividing it into smaller pieces requires melting and refining, processes that are costly and require technical expertise and equipment.[22] This makes dividing physical gold into smaller, transaction-friendly amounts impractical.

When gold is divided into very small pieces, the value of these pieces can become less clear, especially if they are not standard weights or if the division process incurs costs. For small transactions, the cost of verifying the weight and purity of each piece could outweigh the value of the transaction itself.

Gold coins were minted in various sizes historically to facilitate transactions of different values.[23] However, the smallest denominations were often limited by the practicality of minting and handling very small coins. Dividing gold into smaller parts also raises issues with storage and handling. Small pieces of gold are easier to lose and more difficult to store securely than larger bars or coins.

Fiat, or cash, suffers divisibility constraints based on its denomination. Divisibility is limited to the smallest denomination issued by the relevant central bank. Digital fiat, of course, overcomes this constraint to an extent, although fees and charges limit micro transactions. As with portability, digital fiat (unlike cash) comes with additional risks, as we shall discuss later in this chapter.

Bitcoin can be divided into very small units (100 million "satoshis" per bitcoin), facilitating transactions of any size—including micro transactions at a fraction of a cent—with precision.

5. Durability

Gold's durability is one of its most defining and valued characteristics, and contributes to its status as a store of wealth for thousands of years. Unlike many other metals, it does not react with oxygen, making it resistant to rusting, tarnishing, and corrosion.[24] Gold's chemical inertness is why it retains its luster and beauty even after being buried for millennia. It does not dissolve in most acids (with the exception of a mixture known as aqua regia). It remains solid at a wide range of temperatures found on the Earth's surface. Gold coins can remain in circulation for centuries without significant wear. Similarly, gold jewelry can be passed down through generations and still retain its beauty and increase in value.

Bitcoin enjoys a comparable (and, in many respects, superior) level of durability that may be much harder to comprehend at first. It exists on a decentralized network that is maintained across tens of thousands of nodes, ensuring its longevity and resilience against disasters that could affect physical or centralized assets. This aspect will be explored further in chapter 6.

Physical fiat currencies score the lowest here because they are subject to wear and tear. Notes can become damaged or deteriorate, which affects their usability and acceptance. This necessitates periodic replacement and incurs additional costs for governments. Digital fiat, of course, enjoys comparatively better durability than the physical form, but it ultimately depends on the integrity of the centralized financial institution maintaining the ledger entries as well as the legal and government systems that legitimize and enforce the societal belief system in fiat.

6. Fungibility

Fungibility is a crucial monetary property that denotes the interchangeability of individual units of a currency or commodity with another of the same type, ensuring that each unit's value is identical and indistinguishable from another. Gold may be said to exhibit a high degree of fungibility. A gram of pure gold is functionally and economically identical to any other gram of pure gold, regardless of its origin or form (coin, bar, or ingot).[25]

Every bitcoin is technically equal to another, ensuring no distinction in value between units. However, bitcoin's public ledger, the blockchain, records every transaction, potentially affecting fungibility. If certain bitcoins were flagged as tainted because of past illegal transactions, they might be refused by parties fearing legal repercussions.

Fiat currencies issued by governments as legal tender are designed to be perfectly fungible within their respective systems. One hundred dollars in one denomination is worth the same as one hundred dollars in another, and it makes no difference to the transaction's parties which specific notes or coins are used (though it often happens that, for smaller transactions, large denominations may be refused by merchants for want of change). Fiat's fungibility, while comprehensive within its national borders, encounters limitations when assessed in the context of international transactions and exchanges because of its nationality. Each country issues its own fiat currency, which is legally recognized and mandated for use within its jurisdiction. This increases transaction costs, regulatory complexities, and other points of friction given the global nature of trade and commerce. Fiat is not and never can be a borderless apolitical money like gold and bitcoin.

7. Censorship Resistance

Fiat currency is issued and regulated by governments, and thus inherently operates within a permissioned framework, subject to state oversight and control. This centralized nature allows governments to exercise significant authority over transactions, including the ability to freeze bank accounts, restrict international transfers, and impose capital controls. Physical currency can be demonetized by governments.[26] Such measures can be enacted for various reasons that may be entirely arbitrary at times. The state holds the power to censor or limit transactions at will, leveraging the financial system to enforce legal and policy objectives. While this may not seem too concerning for those lucky to be living in developed nations, billions live in oppressive, authoritarian regions where financial freedom is limited.

A transaction in gold (i.e., you physically give me a gold bar) cannot be censored as such, but the aspect of physical possession can be compromised. Despite its physical and decentralized nature, gold can also be subject to state control and censorship. Several countries, such as India and China, have historically limited the importation of gold and curbed its use in domestic transactions because of concerns around managing their trade deficits[27] and protecting local industries.

Anyone with internet access can use bitcoin without needing approval from a central authority. When bitcoin is transmitted on the bitcoin network, there is no authority deciding whether the transaction should be allowed. Bitcoin levels the financial playing field and thus offers inclusive access to global financial systems. Transactions in bitcoin can be executed without interference from governments or financial institutions.

8. Unconfiscatability

Fiat currency can be confiscated through various means, often as part of legal or government actions. Governments have the power to seize assets, including fiat currency, under certain circumstances. Confiscation can occur directly through law enforcement actions, where cash is physically taken, or by freezing bank accounts. This process is facilitated by the centralized control inherent in fiat currency, which allows governments to enforce their will through the banking and financial system.

In the exchange of physical assets like gold or a swath of land, ownership is transferred and solidified through the act of possession.[28] This is a concept deeply rooted in natural law and physical reality. "Possession is said to be nine-tenths of the law," where the tangible transfer of property signifies ownership.[29] Gold's physical nature makes it more resistant to confiscation than fiat currency, which, by its nature, operates within the state's framework. At least you could dig a hole in your backyard and bury your gold. With digital fiat, no such possibility exists—your money is just a ledger entry that can vanish in a second if the state wills it. While it is true that physical fiat may also be buried in a treasure chest like gold, it is nevertheless a creation of the state and is therefore susceptible to demonetization (speak to any Indian who experienced the government's sudden invalidation of 500 and 1,000 rupee notes in 2016).

Although better than fiat, gold still suffers portability constraints because of its weight and size, as discussed earlier. History has shown that physical assets can be seized or confiscated, often leaving individuals without recourse. One of the most notable examples in modern history is Executive Order 6102, issued in the United States in 1933, which required citizens to relinquish their gold holdings to the government. Other instances abound globally, from the seizure of property during the Russian Revolution to the expropriation of land during the Zimbabwean land reforms in the early 2000s.[30] Such actions, often perpetrated by authoritarian regimes, left citizens powerless and often impoverished.

In contrast to the vulnerability of tangible assets, bitcoin offers a revolutionary solution by transforming physical value into information. By encoding value as data, bitcoin can be stored on a device or remarkably, memorized as a sequence of words or characters, thus becoming impervious to traditional methods of confiscation. Imagine transporting or holding one's life savings, family wealth, or ancestral treasure troves within the confines of one's memory, not in a bank vault or under one's mattress. Reflect on the historical implications of this capability, especially during times of crisis and migration. One could envisage its dramatic impact during events like the Jewish diaspora, the partitions of India and Pakistan,[31] or the mass migrations during the world wars, where displaced populations might have preserved and transported their wealth securely and discretely. We shall revisit this discussion in chapter 12.

9. History

Most do not appreciate that the modern fiat money system is actually an experiment a little over fifty years old. The world's transition to a full fiat money system took place as recently as 1971 when President Nixon announced the suspension of the dollar's convertibility into gold (i.e., the gold standard), effectively ending the Bretton Woods system. Our current monetary era, characterized by floating exchange rates and central banks' discretionary control over the money supply, thus commenced.

Gold has been used as money for thousands of years, making it one of the oldest forms of currency in human history. It was used by ancient Egyptians in 3,000 BCE, by the Lydians in 700 BCE, and several other civilizations through time. Over the centuries, gold played a central role in the economies of empires and nations, underpinning currencies, backing paper money, and serving as a store of value and a hedge against inflation. Even after the abandonment of the gold standard in the twentieth century, gold continues to be an important financial asset, symbolizing wealth and financial security across cultures and economies worldwide.

Bitcoin's fifteen-year history is the shortest of the three. But it cannot really be faulted for that: a disruptive technology, by definition, has a shorter history than that which it disrupts. And in the technology space, where innovation moves at lightning pace, a fifteen-plus-year history is actually comparable to eons. Bitcoin has established a perfect track record over this period with a 99.99 percent uptime.[32] It has never been hacked or compromised in any way. And with each passing day, it gets stronger and more resilient.

Final Scorecard

The comparative performances of the three monetary systems—fiat currency, gold, and bitcoin—may be tallied up using the proposed grades in table 2.1.[33]

The results of this comparative analysis of the three competing forms of money are quite stark. Bitcoin's superiority over fiat and gold based on key monetary attributes is hard to ignore. The reason for this is bitcoin's monumental achievement in fusing a tangible asset's finality with the ethereal nature of digital information. It inherits the definitive qualities of traditional commodities while also offering the advantages of digital information. This convergence represents a significant stride in the economic empowerment of humanity. The imbuing of physical attributes in cyberspace is not an incremental leap. It is an exponential leap. It represents a new watermark in what money can be for humankind.

If bitcoin is such a perfect form of money, then why is it not more widely used? The answer to this question is simply that tectonic shifts do not occur overnight. Consider the enormity of the stated objective here—the disruption of global central banking and money itself. Consider the distance that bitcoin has covered in just fifteen years. From a price of less than $0.01 in 2011, it currently trades at over $60,000 in 2024, commanding a market capitalization greater than the precious metal silver (which itself, alongside gold, has been a store of value for thousands of years). Consider the journey it has traveled from skepticism

TABLE 2.1 Comparative performance

Attribute	Fiat	Gold	Bitcoin
Scarcity	D	A	A+
Portability	B	D	A+
Divisibility	B	C	A+
Verifiability	B	C	A+
Durability	C	A+	A+
Fungibility	B	A+	B
Censorship Resistance	D	C	A+
Unconfiscatability	D	C	A+
History	B	A+	C

about it being no more than a tulip mania to its embrace by multi-trillion-dollar asset managers like Blackrock and Fidelity. Consider that it has been adopted as legal tender by a nation-state, El Salvador, and that other regions, such as Lugano in Switzerland and Madeira in Portugal, are actively promoting its mass adoption. While the number of people who hold any bitcoin may run into over a hundred million, those who truly understand it are arguably still only in the tens of thousands. Consider the implications of a steady increase of that number to cover a significant portion of the world.

The expression "gradually, then suddenly" illustrates how incremental changes accumulate until reaching a tipping point,[34] leading to rapid and transformative outcomes. This pattern is observable in various phenomena: technological adoption, cultural shifts, and even in nature. For instance, the internet, once a novelty, gradually integrated into daily life until its use became suddenly ubiquitous. A dam under pressure may hold for a while, but it can fail suddenly if erosion continues. Paradigm shifting changes often build over time unnoticed until a critical threshold is breached, leading to swift, sweeping transformations. Truth has a persistent nature, breaking through barriers of concealment and eventually emerging clearly in the light of day.

THE ENDGAME

> Using Bitcoin for consumer purchases is akin to driving a Concorde jet down the street to pick up groceries. . . . Consumer payments are a relatively trivial engineering problem which the modern banking system has largely solved with various forms of credit and debit arrangements.[35]
>
> —Saifedean Ammous

A popular and stubborn misconception in the news media and the economic and financial establishment is that bitcoin represents a payment technology for everyday use. The bitcoin network's "slow" ten-minute settlement time is often pointed to as being vastly inferior to Visa, Mastercard, and Venmo, all three of which allow you to complete your coffee purchase transaction within seconds. This leads to quibbles around bitcoin having no real use on the transactional front. Leaving aside the fact that such claims are now entirely invalid given layered technologies like the Lightning Network that allow for instantaneous bitcoin transactions (discussed in chapter 3), such perceptions entirely miss the point.

Bitcoin's goal has always been to serve as a decentralized asset with a fixed, transparent, and immutable monetary policy, with the potential to emerge as an alternative to central banking monetary policy.[36] This intention is clear from Satoshi's own statements regarding the problem that bitcoin was intended to address:

> The root problem with conventional currency is all the trust that's required to make it work. The central bank must be trusted not to debase the currency, but the history of fiat currencies is full of breaches of that trust.[37]
>
> —Satoshi Nakamoto, February 11, 2009

While gold has historically served the role of an immutable asset, we have seen its shortcomings earlier in this chapter. Satoshi's intention was to create digital gold rather than a mere transactional payment system. This is evident in his hidden clues embedded in the protocol, which reference Executive Order 6102, dated April 5, 1933, whereby President Franklin D. Roosevelt forbade ownership of gold coins, bullion, and gold certificates: (1) Satoshi states his birthday as April 5, the same month and day as the Executive Order, and (2) the "difficulty adjustment" in the bitcoin protocol (see chapter 3) adjusts every 2016 blocks (Order 6102 in reverse). Gold, or rather, digital gold, was unquestionably on Satoshi's mind. The intention was to create an asset that is immune to debasement or corruption by any governmental or other authority and that does not suffer the shortcomings of physical gold.

It is quite clear that payment technologies like VISA and PayPal were never the target of Satoshi's intended disruption. Thousands of cryptocurrencies have been spawned based on the single purported "improvement" over bitcoin that they settle faster than bitcoin's ten-minute transaction time. They are entirely irrelevant, however, to bitcoin's intended purpose of challenging central banking monetary policy.

Hal Finney, cryptographer, inventor, and early bitcoin developer, made this observation as early as 2010, yet there are many, even within the bitcoin community today, who appear surprised by this notion, or simply choose to ignore it. He noted that bitcoin's ultimate fate would be its use as a base layer reserve currency, with bitcoin-backed banks issuing bitcoin-backed digital cash currency for everyday transactions:

> Actually, there is a very good reason for Bitcoin-backed banks to exist, issuing their own digital cash currency, redeemable for bitcoins. **Bitcoin itself cannot scale to have every single financial transaction in the world be broadcast to everyone and included in the block chain.** There needs to be a secondary level of payment systems which is lighter weight and more efficient. Likewise, the time needed for Bitcoin transactions to finalize will be impractical for medium to large value purchases.
>
> Bitcoin-backed banks will solve these problems. **They can work like banks did before nationalization of currency.** Different banks can have different policies, some more aggressive, some more conservative. Some would be fractional reserve while others may be 100 percent Bitcoin-backed. Interest rates may vary. Cash from some banks may trade at a discount to that from others . . .
>
> **I** believe this will be the ultimate fate of Bitcoin, to be the "high-powered money" that serves as a reserve currency for banks that issue their own digital cash.** Most Bitcoin transactions will occur between banks, to settle net transfers. **Bitcoin transactions by private individuals will be as rare as . . . well, as Bitcoin based purchases are today.**[38]

Bitcoin banks holding your bitcoin may seem antithetical to one of bitcoin's greatest strengths—self-custody and thus the ability to resist confiscation, as discussed earlier. Bitcoins held in such banks are susceptible to state capture (just like gold was confiscated under Order 6102 in the United States). However, a distinction should be drawn between bitcoin used as one's savings and bitcoin used for daily transactions. In that sense, perhaps the majority of an individual's bitcoin could be under self-custody on-chain (i.e., akin to a savings account), which rarely moves, and a small portion for daily transactions could be held through third-party-custodied solutions (i.e., akin to a checking account).

The main point is that there are always trade-offs. Self-custody of a digital commodity comes with the trade-off that *final* settlement may not be instantaneous and will likely incur non-negligible fees. In contrast to bitcoin's ten-minute settlement, fiat money requires several days to achieve final settlement, first at the commercial bank level and then ultimately at the central bank level. The global banking system, costing tens of trillions of dollars, exists primarily to manage the counterparty risks associated with these multiple layers of settlement, which bitcoin eliminates entirely. The final settlement of a gold transaction (i.e., transfer of possession) can also take weeks because it involves the physical shipment and delivery of gold from one location to another, costing enormous amounts of money and resources.

Furthermore, here is a revelation that may be surprising to some: contrary to what many bitcoin influencers may tell you, bitcoin is *not* for everyone! Or, more specifically, the use of bitcoin's base layer (making on-chain transactions) will inevitably become too costly for the vast majority of the world. As Hal Finney observed, the bitcoin protocol will ultimately be reserved for very large (likely batched) transactions. This is by design. As we shall discuss in chapter 5, the long-term security of the bitcoin network (which directly relates to the compensation that bitcoin miners receive for directing computational power to the network) depends on transaction fees getting a lot higher than they are today to compensate the miners. Thus, fees becoming too high for on-chain coffee purchases was always a necessary feature of bitcoin's design.

The debate over bitcoin's intended target disruption (central banking versus payment services) was borne out in a series of events, referred to as the Blocksize Wars, that took place between 2015 and 2017.[39] At the heart of the conflict were two very different visions for bitcoin's future. On one side were those who viewed bitcoin mainly as a payment service and who planned to make changes to the protocol to improve transaction settlement time. And on the other side of the debate were those who saw bitcoin as a revolutionary disruption of traditional monetary policy and central banking and who were thus opposed to any changes that might compromise this core value (which the proposed changes risked doing).

The latter ideology prevailed ultimately. In August 2017, a chain split (known as a hard fork) created Bitcoin Cash, representing the payment service vision as distinct from the original bitcoin blockchain. In subsequent years, bitcoin has achieved a vastly higher market capitalization than Bitcoin Cash, which has gradually trended to zero versus bitcoin. This resolution underscored the community's emphasis on bitcoin's security, scarcity, and decentralization over the convenience of everyday transactions.

In chapter 3, we will explore bitcoin's layer 2 technologies, such as the Lightning Network, which allow instantaneous and virtually free transactions, operating on a layer that sits on top of bitcoin. As these technologies gain further traction globally, they could render this entire debate moot. Nevertheless, the core point is this: in the almanac of historic disruptions, we should not confuse bitcoin's position with that of a payment services disrupter. Technological solutions built on bitcoin may well ultimately disrupt payment systems like VISA, PayPal, and Venmo; however, that was never the primary objective of bitcoin. Bitcoin's purpose is, and has always been, to disrupt fiat money and the institution of central banking.

PART II

The Technology

CHAPTER 3

Bitcoin's Architecture

I n part I, we conceptualized bitcoin as a digital commodity wherein digital information is made to exhibit properties of physical matter. While a helpful mental model, it would be useless if the claim does not hold water in practical terms. In part II, we will analyze the technological basis for this lofty claim. Let us begin by analyzing the underlying computer science problem that Satoshi set out to solve in order to create a digital commodity.

THE BYZANTINE GENERALS' PROBLEM

Before 2008, the digital world faced a significant challenge in designing and implementing a system for achieving trustless consensus, known as the Byzantine Generals' Problem. This problem, a cornerstone issue in computer science, is particularly relevant to systems that need consensus despite the presence of unreliable or malicious entities. It was first articulated in 1982 by Leslie Lamport, Robert Shostak, and Marshall Pease.[1] They highlighted the difficulties of achieving reliable agreement among parties that do not necessarily trust one another.

To understand the problem, envision a group of Byzantine generals planning to attack a fortified city. Stationed around the city, they must agree on a unified strategy, but their only means of communication is through messengers. The problem is that there may well be traitors present who might send false messages or contradict orders. This would obviously cause chaos, undermine the attack strategy, and cause the attack to fail.[2] A solution to this problem would require a consensus mechanism to ensure that: (1) all loyal generals decide on the same plan of action, and (2) a few traitors cannot lead the loyal generals to adopt a flawed plan.

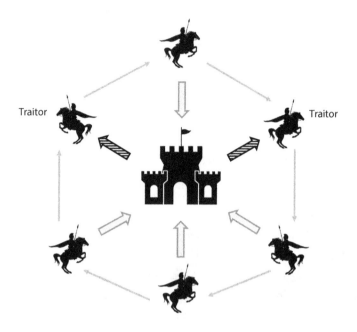

3.1 The Byzantine Generals' Problem. *Source*: Author.

Solving the Byzantine Generals' Problem, therefore, involves creating a system that guarantees agreement among the loyal parties despite the presence of traitors. In distributed computing systems and in the absence of a central trusted party, this problem features where communication might be unreliable, and participants could act maliciously. The term *Byzantine Fault Tolerance (BFT)* refers to a system's ability to continue operating correctly even if some participants act maliciously. Traditional BFT solutions were not easily scalable and necessitated a centralized group of participants. The historical need for such a centralized authority made this an elusive and insurmountable problem.

THE BITCOIN WHITEPAPER

On October 31, 2008, an individual or group under the pseudonym Satoshi Nakamoto introduced a seminal paper titled "Bitcoin: A Peer-to-Peer Electronic Cash System."[3] This paper effectively proposed a solution to the Byzantine

Generals' Problem. The innovation was a combination of several key technological advancements in cryptography, distributed systems, and economic incentives that enabled the creation of an asset on the internet that was immune to double spending. This was accomplished without requiring a centralized authority by implementing a solution to the Byzantine Generals' Problem.

The solution is an ingenious system by which participants achieve consensus in a decentralized manner. A public ledger is distributed across tens of thousands of network participants—each voluntarily maintaining a copy. This ledger records all transactions in the network's native asset, that is, bitcoin, in a secure, transparent, and immutable manner, using cryptography and a system known as Proof-of-Work, which secures the network. This achieves what is termed *distributed consensus* or *decentralized consensus* (as opposed to centralized consensus) that is inherently resistant to malicious actors despite not having a recordkeeping supervisory authority.

Noted mathematician and bitcoin developer Andrew Poelstra has described the mechanism as follows:

> A distributed consensus, as the term is used in Bitcoin, is a consensus (i.e., global agreement) between many mutually distrusting parties who lack identities and were not necessarily present at the time of system setup . . . The reason that this consensus is needed is called the double-spending problem. That is, in any decentralized digital currency scheme there is the possibility that a spender might send the same money to two different people, and both spends would appear to be valid. Recipients therefore need a way to be assured that there are no conflicts, or that if there are conflicts, that the network will recognize their version as the correct one. A distributed consensus on transaction ordering achieves this: in the case of conflict, everyone agrees that the transaction which came first is valid while all others are not. (The other problems with digital currency, e.g., authentication and prevention of forgery, are comparatively easy and can be handled with traditional cryptography.)[4]

This solution to the double-spending problem enabled digital currency for the first time. Prior attempts, such as David Chaum's DigiCash, Wei Dai's b-money, and Nick Szabo's Bit Gold, either relied on a central authority or did not fully address the double-spending problem in a decentralized context.[5]

Satoshi's solution to the Byzantine Generals' Problem (which, in turn, solved the double-spending problem), is referred to as Nakamoto Consensus. It utilizes the Proof-of-Work system to create a cost in sending a message. More specifically, Proof-of-Work requires computational effort and thus the incurring of real-world expense. The cost acts as a deterrent against malicious behavior. A traitorous Byzantine general proposing to send a malicious message would have to incur a significant cost in doing so. Such cost, if instead incurred honestly, would be profitable to the general. Therefore, game theoretically, a rational actor would act honestly rather than maliciously.

The Participants

Bitcoin's decentralized network ecosystem consists of different participants playing different roles. They participate voluntarily and are driven by economic incentives. Collectively, they maintain and secure the network and enable transactions in its native asset, bitcoin.

Nodes are computers that connect to the bitcoin network and enforce a set of rules based on software that they run. They store, spread, and preserve the history of bitcoin transactions (the bitcoin blockchain), acting as the network's distributed ledger. They validate transactions and blocks of transactions, ensuring that they meet the consensus rules encoded in their software. By doing so, nodes take the place of a centralized recordkeeper, thus making the network decentralized. The number of reachable nodes spread around the world is currently around 20,000, though the total number is estimated to be well over 100,000.[6]

Miners are entities with specialized hardware that perform the computational work required to secure the network from potential attackers and bad actors (i.e., traitorous Byzantine generals) through a process known as mining. A miner bundles transactions (i.e., transactions submitted by bitcoin users to the network for processing) into a *block* and then competes against thousands of other miners around the world for the privilege of adding that block to the bitcoin blockchain. The competition involves finding a solution to a cryptographic puzzle requiring brute-force computation, which expends electrical energy. When a miner creates a new block successfully, it is rewarded with newly minted bitcoins (the block subsidy) and transaction fees from the transactions included in that block. There are estimated to be hundreds of thousands of individual bitcoin miners dispersed around the world.

Users are individuals or entities that own and transact in bitcoin (directly or through intermediaries). They use bitcoin for a variety of purposes, including investment, remittance, and purchasing goods and services. Users may interact with the bitcoin network through software applications called wallets (explained below), which enable them to send, receive, and store bitcoin. By buying, holding, and transacting in it, users collectively impart economic value to bitcoin. There are estimated to be over 200 million bitcoin users around the world.[7]

Transaction Life Cycle

The bitcoin consensus mechanism, from the moment a transaction is initiated to its final addition to the blockchain, involves several steps:

Step 1. Transaction creation: A user initiates a bitcoin transaction by creating and signing a transaction with their *private key*. The transaction includes the amount of bitcoin to be transferred, the recipient's *address* (a unique identifier used to send and receive bitcoin), and a transaction fee. The cryptographic process involved in this step is discussed later in this chapter.

Step 2. Transaction broadcast: The transaction is broadcast via the internet to the bitcoin network, where it is picked up by tens of thousands of nodes around the world and added to the memory pool (*mempool*), a holding area for transactions waiting to be included in a block.[8]

Step 3. Block creation: Each miner selects transactions from the mempool to create a block. Transactions with higher fees are typically prioritized because miners receive these fees in addition to the block subsidy if the block is added successfully to the blockchain.

Step 4. Mining (Proof-of-Work): To win the right to add a block to the blockchain, miners compete against each other to solve a cryptographic puzzle. This involves guessing a value through trial and error to find a number (known as a nonce) that, when combined with the block's data and put through a cryptographic algorithm, produces a result that meets a target set by the protocol. This target is periodically adjusted automatically by the algorithm—a process known as the *difficulty adjustment*—to ensure that it takes miners ten minutes, on average, to find the nonce (in other words, as more miners enter the network and competition increases, the difficulty of the puzzle correspondingly increases, and vice versa).

Step 5. Block broadcast: When a miner successfully finds a nonce, they broadcast the new block to the network for verification. The block includes the nonce, the transactions in the block, and a reference to the previous block in the chain (which creates a link in the blockchain).

Step 6. Block verification: The nodes in the network validate the new block. They check the nonce and ensure that all transactions within the block are valid.

Step 7. Block addition to the blockchain: Once validated, the new block is added to the blockchain maintained by the nodes. The successful miner is rewarded with newly minted bitcoins and the transaction fees from the transactions included in the relevant block.

Step 8. Transaction completion: The addition to the nodes' ledger is considered confirmation of the relevant transactions included in the block. The process continues with miners moving on to create the next block. If two miners solve the puzzle simultaneously, the network may temporarily *fork*. Nodes choose which chain to continue based on the chain that has the most computational energy expended on it. The network returns to consensus eventually, and the transactions in the forked (shorter) chain are returned to the mempool to be included in future blocks.

This sequence ensures a decentralized, secure, and verifiable ledger of transactions, which is the essence of bitcoin's Nakamoto Consensus mechanism.

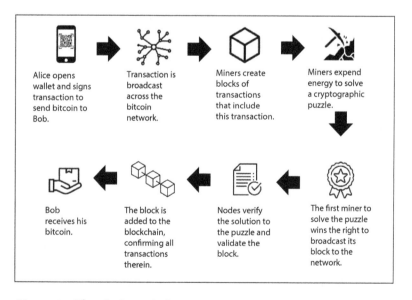

Alice opens wallet and signs transaction to send bitcoin to Bob.

Transaction is broadcast across the bitcoin network.

Miners create blocks of transactions that include this transaction.

Miners expend energy to solve a cryptographic puzzle.

The first miner to solve the puzzle wins the right to broadcast its block to the network.

Nodes verify the solution to the puzzle and validate the block.

The block is added to the blockchain, confirming all transactions therein.

Bob receives his bitcoin.

3.2 Transaction life cycle. *Source:* Author.

Cryptography

In step 1 above, the creation of a bitcoin transaction involves use of public key cryptography—a technology with origins deeply rooted in espionage, military strategy, and the clandestine communication needs of governments. Cryptography's evolution began in ancient civilizations using simple substitution ciphers and continues today in complex algorithms designed to secure digital communications in the modern era.[9]

In bitcoin, public key cryptography enables users to generate a cryptographic pair of keys: a *public key*, which can be shared with others, and a *private key*, which is kept secret (a *key* is a unique cryptographic code, represented as a long string of alphanumeric characters). The public key can be derived from the private key, but not vice versa.[10] The public key is used to create a bitcoin address to which others can send bitcoin, while the private key is used to *sign* transactions digitally, proving ownership of the bitcoin being sent. When a transaction is made, the transaction is signed with the sender's private key in a way that can be verified by others using the corresponding public key. This process ensures that bitcoin can be spent only by its rightful owner—the holder of the related private key.

Public-private key pairs are created using a cryptographic algorithm known as the Elliptic Curve Digital Signature Algorithm (ECDSA). This mathematical operation generates a public key from a private key. It is used to create and verify *digital signatures* in transactions, ensuring that they are authentic and unaltered. Secure Hash Algorithm 256-bit (SHA-256) is a cryptographic operation used to create a bitcoin address (used to send and receive bitcoin) from a public key. SHA-256 is also used in the bitcoin mining process (i.e., the mathematical puzzle that miners have to solve). It is a cryptographic function that takes an input string of numbers and produces an output known as a *hash*. Each output hash is unique to the corresponding input. It is like a digital fingerprint for data. Changing even a small part of the input produces a completely different output hash. The process works by taking the input and running it through a series of mathematical operations that scramble and mix the data to produce the hash.

These cryptographic processes are deterministic, meaning that the same input will always result in the same output, but it is designed to be one-way: while it is easy to generate an output from an input, it is practically impossible to reconstruct the original input from the output. In other words, it is practically impossible to identify one's private keys by reverse-engineering the corresponding bitcoin address generated using the keys. This makes cryptography a powerful tool for verifying peer-to-peer transactions in the absence of a gatekeeper who would traditionally perform such verifications in a centralized manner.

The probability of successfully hacking SHA-256 or ECDSA is extremely low from a thermodynamic standpoint. It would be significantly easier to find a single solitary grain of sand in the entire universe than it would be to hack SHA-256 through brute force.[11] Needless to say, bitcoin has never been hacked. While quantum computing has been described as a potential future threat, discussions on this subject remain highly theoretical at this stage (see chapter 6 regarding the risks quantum computing poses to bitcoin).

The applications that allow users to store their private keys securely, manage their bitcoin holdings, and conduct transactions are referred to as digital wallets. These wallets allow bitcoin users to interact with the bitcoin network, offering a user-friendly interface for storing and transacting in bitcoin. There are broadly three types of wallets providing different levels of security and convenience:

Software wallets: These applications can be installed on a computer or mobile device. The wallet stores the user's private keys and enables them to be used on the go to sign transactions. Software wallets connected to the internet are referred to as hot wallets. These wallets offer the greatest degree of convenience, but they are also relatively less secure because the device on which the private keys are stored is connected to the internet and thus could potentially be hacked. Note that this has nothing to do with the bitcoin protocol itself being hacked.

Hardware wallets: These physical devices are designed to store private keys securely offline, away from potential online threats. They can connect to a computer to sign transactions, then be stored away again safely. This form of offline storage is referred to as cold storage, and the wallet is called a cold wallet.

Paper wallets: These are physical pieces of paper on which the private keys may be written down and stored in a secure location. The private keys take the form of a series of words—mnemonic phrases—that back up the keys in a human-readable format. Paper wallets are the ultimate form of cold storage because they are incapable of being directly connected to the internet. As long as they are physically secured, there is no means by which they may be hacked.

The ultimate result of these cryptographic techniques used in bitcoin is that users can exercise self-sovereignty over their financial assets. Users control their private keys and, by extension, their bitcoin holdings without the need for intermediaries like banks. This self-sovereignty extends to privacy and security because transactions can be made pseudonymously. While bitcoin addresses are recorded on the blockchain, the identities of the users behind these addresses are not inherently tied to them unless they are revealed through other means. Former President Barack Obama has referred to such a capability as "everybody walking around with a Swiss bank account in their pocket."[12]

Network Security

As discussed earlier, Proof-of-Work represents the key solution to the Byzantine Generals' Problem. It is the process by which bitcoin ensures the security of the network and the prevention of double spending of bitcoin. The solution is achieved by (1) offering a reward (the block reward) to participants as an incentive to propose transactions for inclusion in the blockchain, and (2) adding a cost (electrical energy expense) to each such proposal to disincentivize malicious behavior.

The addition of a block to the blockchain (akin to a Byzantine general sending a message that proposes a battle plan) requires miners to compete at solving a complex mathematical puzzle.[13] This puzzle involves finding a numeric solution (i.e., the nonce) using the SHA-256 hashing algorithm. The solution can be found only through brute force trial and error (the number of guesses per second is known as the *hash rate*). This exercise requires significant computational power, which in turn demands financial investment in electricity and hardware. The requirement to solve this mathematical puzzle before being able to propose a block ensures that attempting to act maliciously incurs significant costs. For a dishonest miner to alter the blockchain or double-spend transactions, they would need to outcompete honest miners consistently over time, requiring an unsustainable amount of computational power and energy.

Miners are rewarded with new bitcoin and transaction fees for solving the puzzle and adding a block to the blockchain. Therefore, the benefits of cooperating with the system outweigh the costs of attempting to undermine it.

The high cost of "sending a message" (solving the puzzle and proposing a block) serves as a natural barrier against dishonesty. It ensures that the effort and resources required to act maliciously are so significant that supporting the integrity of the system becomes more advantageous. Miners are incentivized to create and maintain this energy threshold barricade, a protective force field, that secures the network against bad actors. The greater the competition among miners, the higher the energy threshold and corresponding cost that a bad actor would need to incur to attack the network.

This force field, that is, the total hash rate, currently stands at over six hundred exahashes per second. This represents the total computational power being used to mine and secure the bitcoin network. This is an unfathomable amount of power. Bitcoin expert Yassine Elmandjra describes the enormity of this computational power through different analogies:

- For every star in our galaxy, the bitcoin network is calculating 5 billion computations per second.
- It would take about two thousand years for the entire global population, each performing one computation per second, to match the bitcoin network's hash rate.
- The bitcoin network performs about sixty-seven times more computations per second than there are grains of sand on Earth.

The network hash rate continues its steady upward trend over time, having peaked at just under nine hundred exahashes per second in July 2024.

Each block created through the above mining process contains a list of transactions (selected by the miner from the mempool) and a block header. The block header includes the hash of the previous block. As a result of this architecture, altering any block's content would invalidate the hash of all subsequent blocks. Changing any block postconfirmation would necessitate redoing the Proof-of-Work for that block and all following blocks, an effort so costly and time consuming that it is practically impossible. These mechanisms ensure the blockchain's integrity, making it extremely difficult, if not impossible, to alter past transactions. The bitcoin blockchain achieves immutability as a result.

The bitcoin protocol targets a ten-minute interval for block creation. This duration has been criticized as being too long, resulting in "slow" bitcoin transaction confirmations. However, bitcoin's core commitment to decentralization, yet again, was Satoshi's rationale: ten-minute intervals ensure sufficient time for blocks to propagate across the global network of tens of thousands of nodes, minimizing the risk of chain splits or forks and ensuring ledger consistency.[14] Every 2,016 blocks, the protocol adjusts the difficulty of the mathematical problem—the process known as the *difficulty adjustment*—to ensure that the time to find a block remains approximately ten minutes, regardless of the network's total hash rate.

Through the above processes, Nakamoto Consensus uses Proof-of-Work to achieve consensus (solving the Byzantine Generals' Problem) without needing a trusted third party. The relevant miner publishes its successfully hashed block to the network of nodes around the world. The block is then validated by the nodes' software and, if deemed valid, recorded on their ledgers. The process operates under a trustless model—each node validates every transaction independently, from the very first block from 2009 (known as the Genesis Block) to the latest. If a miner presents a block that violates consensus rules, it is rejected by the nodes. When blocks are simultaneously propagated by miners and result in competing chains (i.e., a fork), the nodes adopt the chain with the most accumulated Proof-of-Work (usually the longest chain) as the valid ledger. Through this process of independent verification and distributed consensus, the protocol enables secure and trustless peer-to-peer transactions.

ABSOLUTE SCARCITY

The 21-million bitcoin cap is hardcoded into the protocol, representing a foundational rule that all participating nodes and miners agree to enforce. This scarcity is maintained through *halving* events that occur approximately every four years, where the block subsidy for miners is cut in half.[15] These halving events, which are programmed into the bitcoin protocol, ensure that the creation of new bitcoins slows over time until the cap is reached, which is projected to occur around the year 2140. As of 2024, almost 20 million bitcoins have already been mined out of the maximum 21 million, representing over 94 percent of the total.

The concept of immutability in bitcoin's protocol parallels the constancy of physical commodities like gold. Just as gold's value and recognition are contingent on its unchanging molecular composition, the essence of a digital commodity lies in its steadfast characteristics. How can we be sure that this supply cap is true and immutable? After all, the supply cap is just open-source software and can be changed. The crucial question we need to ask is, What would it take to change bitcoin's 21-million-coin supply cap?

Technically, it would require a coordinated update to the protocol, known as a *hard fork*. A hard fork represents a significant change or divergence in the blockchain protocol that is not backward compatible, which means that the changes introduced by the fork are not compatible with the previous version of the protocol. Transactions or blocks created under the new rules cannot be validated by nodes that have not been upgraded to the new version of the software. This lack of backward compatibility is what distinguishes a hard fork from a *soft fork*, where the changes are made so that they remain compatible with older versions, allowing nonupgraded nodes to participate still in validating transactions, albeit without recognizing or enforcing the new rules. In simple terms, a loosening of consensus rules (making the rules less strict) typically requires a hard fork, while a tightening of consensus rules (making the rules stricter) may be achieved by a soft fork.

A change to bitcoin's 21-million supply cap would involve a loosening of the rules and thus would necessitate a hard fork. The hard fork is effectively a chain split. It creates a new divergent chain from the original blockchain wherein blocks comply with the new loosened set of rules. There will, therefore, exist two parallel blockchains that share a common history up to the point of divergence. A key question arises at this stage: how is the dominant chain determined following such a hard fork?

Game Theory

Game theory explores strategic interactions among rational decision-makers. In the case of a bitcoin hard fork, economic incentives ultimately dictate whether the old or the new chain emerges as the dominant one: the potential increase in the value of the chosen chain drives users to purchase and hold it, anticipating a price appreciation of the asset on that chain. The higher prices result in higher-value block rewards, which drive miners to expend money to mine on that chain. This correspondingly increases the security of that chain, attracting more users and investors to it. A virtuous cycle thus arises on the chosen chain.

The decision-making process is influenced by several factors, including the perceived future value of each chain, and the actions of other network participants. Users, including holders and traders, evaluate which chain to support based on potential future value, security, utility, history, and narratives. The decision-making process for users involves predicting network effects and the actions of other users and miners, creating a complex game-theoretical scenario where the choices of others significantly affect individual outcomes.

For miners, the decision to support a chain is often a calculation of potential rewards versus costs. Miners must consider the immediate block rewards and transaction fees in comparison to their operational costs, primarily electricity and hardware depreciation. Game theory suggests that miners will migrate to the chain that maximizes their net profits. However, this decision is complicated by uncertainty about the future value of rewards from each chain, which depends on user adoption and market acceptance.

Network effects play a crucial role. As mentioned, the chain that attracts more users and miners becomes more secure and valuable, creating a positive feedback loop that further attracts participation. This effect is critical in the early stages following a fork because it can quickly tip the balance in favor of one chain over another. Users tend to gravitate toward the chain that maintains compatibility with existing services, infrastructure, and standards within the bitcoin ecosystem. The chain that is perceived as the legitimate continuation of the bitcoin protocol is more likely to benefit from existing network effects, including user trust and developer support.

In summary, the interplay of game theory and network effects following a bitcoin hard fork creates a complex decision-making environment for miners and users.

How have bitcoin hard forks played out historically? Several hard forks have occurred in bitcoin's history. Bitcoin Cash (BCH) forked in August 2017 because of disagreements over block size (as discussed in chapter 2). BCH proponents advocated for larger blocks to facilitate more transactions and improve scalability. The original bitcoin chain (BTC) remained dominant, largely because of its established network effect, higher security through a greater hash rate, and the broader community's preference for a more conservative approach to scalability enhancements. Bitcoin SV (BSV) forked from BCH in November 2018, further implementing block size increases with the objective of increasing scalability.

The continued dominance of BTC over its forks illustrates the community's preference for the original chain's security, stability, and development environment.

Changing the Rules of Chess

As we have seen, users tend to prefer the dominant bitcoin blockchain over competing forks. In response to such user preferences, miners driven by profit motives tend to follow suit, contributing hash rate to the dominant chain. This dynamic, as discussed, establishes a feedback loop where increased mining support enhances the chain's security, further attracting user and developer activity, which in turn increases the chain's value and appeal.

The historical responses of the bitcoin community to forks highlight a central aspect of bitcoin: the unchangeable nature of its core protocol features. Proposals to alter the fixed supply cap of 21 million bitcoins fundamentally challenge its narrative and are likely to be rejected overwhelmingly. As history has shown, the original bitcoin chain has remained dominant because of its foundational principles, network security, and the economic incentives that align miners and users with the original protocol. The network effects and the Lindy effect discussed in chapter 7 have only become exponentially stronger since the last hard fork.[16]

Regardless of which chain wins as the dominant chain, it is important to appreciate that as long as there is someone, somewhere in the world, interested in running a node with the original bitcoin software, and there is someone, somewhere in the world, interested in expending electricity to mine new blocks in return for the original bitcoin, there is no way to change bitcoin. This is the primary feature: bitcoin is voluntary.

Bitcoin is no more than an opt-in social contract. Nobody forces you to adopt it or use it or even to stick to its 21-million cap. The source code is open source. You may copy the code and change the supply schedule to 100 million coins if you so please. But your software will no longer be compatible with all the other 100,000-plus nodes enforcing the original 21-million cap. By analogy, if you desired to change the rules of chess, you are free to do so. But no one will play with you.[17]

CENSORSHIP RESISTANCE

Users benefit from permissionless access by engaging with the bitcoin network without requiring approval from any central authority. This means anyone can send and receive bitcoin transactions, regardless of their geographical location, socioeconomic status, or identity. The only requirement is access to the internet and a bitcoin wallet, which can be created freely in a few minutes. This democratizes access to financial services, particularly for those underserved by traditional banking systems.

For anyone who voluntarily desires to participate in the bitcoin consensus system as a node, they may do so at a cost less than $100 and thereby contribute to the network's security and governance. This is critical for the network's health and resilience because a higher number of nodes increases decentralization, making the network more robust against attacks and censorship. The mining process is also open to anyone with the necessary computational resources. The specialized equipment, known as ASIC mining machines, can cost anywhere between $300 and $3,000 as of this writing.

From a technical standpoint, the notion that bitcoin is censorship resistant derives ultimately from economic incentive structures relating to the participants. As long as you are willing to pay a high enough transaction fee, there is always likely to be a miner somewhere in the world willing to process your transaction.

This is why bitcoin is often described as censorship resistant rather than censorship proof.[18] The distinction is crucial: while individual miners have the freedom to choose *not* to include certain transactions in the blocks they mine (effectively censoring them), this does not stop other miners from including those transactions in their blocks. This ensures that the system maintains a level of censorship resistance overall.

The key ingredient here is the system's decentralization—no single entity controls all the hash rate. If a miner decides to censor certain transactions, they are losing fees related to those transactions. For the censorship to have a significant impact, miners with a majority of the mining power would need to censor the relevant transaction collaboratively. This action is not economically rational because it would lead to a loss of revenue for the miners involved in such an effort, especially if the censored transaction offers higher fees. There may, of course, be noneconomic reasons for censoring transactions for a period, but economic incentives ultimately make such an attack unsustainable.

Noncensoring miners can earn higher fees by not discriminating between transactions because they will have more transactions competing for their block space. This will increase their revenue compared to censoring miners, who have less competition for block space and therefore potentially lower fees. Over time, the higher revenue earned by noncensoring miners could incentivize the censoring miners to stop censoring. Alternatively, the noncensoring miners may use their extra revenue to acquire more mining hash rate by expanding their mining operations, further increasing their share of the network's hash rate. As a result of this process, the system trends toward an equilibrium over time.[19]

Market forces and economic incentives encourage miners to process all transactions and thus ensure that the network remains open and accessible. Bitcoin's technical design inherently discourages censorship through a combination of decentralized control and economic incentives. While individual miners can choose to censor transactions, the majority's pursuit of profit ultimately supports the system's resilience against censorship. Nakamoto Consensus ingeniously aligns the interests of users, nodes, and miners, ensuring that each group contributes to and benefits from the network. By allowing anyone to participate in these roles without permission, bitcoin maintains its decentralized environment, promoting a transparent, secure, and inclusive financial ecosystem.

POWER OF INCENTIVES

> It is not from the benevolence of the butcher, the brewer, or the baker that we expect our dinner, but from their regard to their own interest.[20]
>
> —Adam Smith, 1776

Bitcoin's architecture represents a shift from centuries-old centralized systems that have long governed financial transactions. Centralized systems utilized concentrated control to streamline decision-making in the name of efficient governance. As we have seen, the genius of bitcoin lies in its sophisticated coordination of incentive mechanisms, ensuring trustless interactions between parties without the need for a central authority.

Bitcoin employs a decentralized framework where trust is not assumed but engineered. This is achieved through a complex interplay of incentives between the different participants. These incentive structures are meticulously crafted to ensure the functional integrity of the system. They balance the competing interests of the participants (namely, the nodes, miners, and users) and thus ensure the equilibrium necessary for a self-sustaining and autonomous trustless system.

The economic theory behind these incentives resonates with the principles articulated by Adam Smith, the father of modern economics. Smith's assertion that individual self-interest inadvertently supports the broader good is exemplified in bitcoin's design. The idea is that the harmonious interplay of actions driven by the self-interest of individual participants achieves systemwide goals. Participants in the bitcoin network are motivated by their gains, yet their actions collectively underpin the security and functionality of the entire system. It is a perfect example of Smith's invisible hand at work in the digital age.[21]

Bitcoin leverages this idea to construct a system where incentives are the foundational pillars. The cryptographic rules and consensus mechanisms that govern bitcoin are game-theoretic principles in digital form. The idea is that the actions beneficial to the individual align with what is beneficial for the network, thus creating a trustless yet reliable system for financial exchange. Bitcoin's architecture is a testament to the power of incentives, proving that, with thoughtful design, it is possible to orchestrate a symphony of self-interested actions that result in a game theoretic harmony of collective trust.

TIMECHAIN, NOT BLOCKCHAIN

Many bitcoin experts prefer the term "timechain" to "blockchain." This reflects the critical role of time in bitcoin's solution to the double-spend problem.

> Viewing Bitcoin through the lens of time should make clear that the "block chain"—the data structure that causally links multiple events together—is not the main innovation. It is not even a new idea, as is evident by studying the timestamp literature of the past. What is a new idea—what Satoshi figured out—is how to independently agree upon a history of events without central coordination.[22]
>
> —Gigi

Mathematician and software developer Andrew Poelstra also observes:

> For the purposes of cryptocurrency, it is sufficient to achieve distributed consensus on the time-ordering of transactions (and nothing else). This implies consensus on the "first transaction which moves these particular funds," which assures the funds' new owner that the network recognizes them as such.[23]

As discussed in chapter 2, in the realm of physical transactions, the transfer of physical matter, for example, a gold coin, is self-verifying. The physical transfer of the coin inherently prevents double spending because a coin cannot exist in two places simultaneously. This physical constraint ensures that transactions are trustless and also timeless. The question as to whether the coin had in fact been transferred to someone else a few minutes prior, resulting in a double spend, does not arise.

To use money in the digital realm, we have to rely on ledgers because we cannot use physical objects. A ledger works only if we have a definitive order of transactions to be reflected that prevents double spending. In other words, the time of a transaction is crucial in order to reflect its accurate place on the ledger. And to establish order, timestamps are necessary. Trustless money in the digital realm thus requires the elimination of any centralized entity that creates and manages timestamps and any single entity that is in charge of time itself.

It is clear that creating a decentralized timestamping system was the root of the problem that Satoshi set out to solve. He did so by creating an entirely new conception of time itself that is unique to bitcoin. As Gigi notes, "The fact that bitcoin is a clock is hiding in plain sight."[24] Satoshi himself alludes to the fact that the bitcoin network as a whole acts as a clock:

> [W]e propose a solution to the double-spending problem using a peer-to-peer distributed timestamp server to generate computational proof of the chronological order of transactions.[25]
>
> —Satoshi Nakamoto

Rather than relying on a centralized external source of time, Satoshi's innovation was to create an internal source of time that operates independently. Bitcoin's Proof-of-Work system and the difficulty adjustment (discussed earlier) are designed to maintain a constant average block time of ten minutes, regardless of the total computational power on the network or advances in mining technology. The aim is not to keep energy expenditure or difficulty constant but rather to keep the timing of block creation constant. This stabilizes the rate at which new bitcoins are created and transactions are confirmed.

The idea is that a truly scarce asset should be costly in terms of time, not just energy. As Gigi has observed, energy costs can fluctuate, and technological advancements can make energy generation more efficient, but time is finite.

We cannot create more time. This finite nature of time contributes to the absolute scarcity of bitcoin. Without the difficulty adjustment, the time it takes to create a block could decrease as more miners join the network or as mining technology improves.

If block times became too fast (e.g., a few milliseconds), it would be impossible to order transactions reliably and prevent double spending. Even the speed of light, which takes 66 milliseconds to travel around the planet, imposes a physical limit on the speed at which transactions can be received and ordered. In addition, with sufficient power, it would be possible to mine all bitcoins at once rather than stick to the predefined schedule that has played a crucial role in achieving a broad dispersion of bitcoin over the years.

From the perspective of the bitcoin network, Proof-of-Work and the associated difficulty adjustment create a steady pace of block creation, effectively creating an alternate reality of time altogether that is inherent to the network. They ensure that the cadence of block creation allows for the delays inherent in global communication, thus maintaining network synchronization and reliability. By adjusting difficulty every 2,016 blocks, bitcoin ensures that the average time to find each block remains around ten minutes. This internal rhythm allows for the reliable propagation of blocks across the network, considering the asynchronous nature of global communications.

Transactions in the bitcoin network's mempool are considered "timeless" until they are included in a validated block. The inclusion of a transaction in a block assigns it a specific time based on the block's position in the blockchain. This simplifies the process of determining the sequence of events without having to deduce the timing of a transaction based on the multitude of clocks and timepieces that different network participants may refer to around the world. By redefining time within its system, bitcoin allows for a clear and straightforward understanding of transaction sequences.

> The difficulty adjustment makes sure that the ticks of Bitcoin's internal metronome are somewhat constant. It is the conductor of the Bitcoin orchestra. It is what keeps the music alive.[26]
>
> —Gigi

While Satoshi drew on several existing technologies to create bitcoin (e.g., Adam Back's Hashcash for Proof-of-Work, and Whitfield Diffie and Martin

Hellman's public key cryptography), it can be argued that his most original contribution was the difficulty adjustment. It was the secret ingredient that crystallized decades of computer science research and development in this space.

The time-based nature of block production, coupled with the decentralized verification of each block by nodes, means that bitcoin effectively functions as a distributed timestamp server. Each block represents a consensus of the verified transactions up to that point, with a reliable timestamp that is agreed upon by the network.

By decentralizing control over the ledger's timing, bitcoin prevents the double-spending problem and establishes a form of digital money that does not rely on trust in a centralized timestamper. Where the laws of physics address timestamping in the physical world, in bitcoin's world Proof-of-Work, orchestrated through the difficulty adjustment, creates its own conception of time: hence, timechain, not blockchain.

MEDIUM OF EXCHANGE

As discussed in chapter 2, Satoshi wanted to solve the problem of centralized monetary control (i.e., central banking). Creating a medium of exchange that disrupts Visa, Mastercard, and PayPal was not his objective. This nevertheless remains a topic of heated debate within the bitcoin community. In any event, several technological innovations may make the debate moot by permanently solving the medium of exchange constraints of bitcoin. These technologies are referred to as layer 2 solutions (on the basis that bitcoin's protocol is layer 1 and these technologies sit on top of it as layer 2 protocols).

The primary complaint about bitcoin's layer 1 serving as a medium of exchange is its ten-minute settlement time. This interval makes bitcoin impractical for everyday transactions such as purchasing coffee or groceries. When the bitcoin network experiences high demand, the limited block space leads to increased transaction fees as users compete to have their transactions included in the next block.

Layer 2 solutions alleviate this issue by enabling a vast number of transactions to occur outside layer 1, instantaneously and at close to no cost. This makes bitcoin usable as a medium of exchange for smaller, daily transactions. By conducting transactions off the main blockchain, layer 2 solutions offer enhanced privacy. Layer 2 transactions are not recorded on the public blockchain and thus provide users with greater privacy for their financial activities. Layer 2 protocols also allow for the development of new applications and use cases, from micropayments to complex financial contracts.

There are numerous layer 2 solutions but let us focus on the most well known and widely adopted one, the Lightning Network.[27] This layer 2 technology facilitates instant, low-cost transactions that are achieved through a network of payment channels that operate off the main bitcoin blockchain. Here is a summary of its operating process:

Opening channels: Imagine Alice wants to send frequent, small payments to Bob without enduring the usual delays and fees associated with the bitcoin network. To do this, Alice and Bob open a payment channel on the Lightning Network. They each commit a certain amount of bitcoin into a multisignature wallet—a digital wallet that requires more than one signature to authorize a transaction. This initial deposit is akin to opening a tab at a bar: it represents the maximum amount that can be transacted within their channel. This transaction is recorded on the bitcoin blockchain, establishing their payment channel.

Conducting transactions: With the channel open, Alice can send multiple payments to Bob instantly and without the need for each transaction to be recorded on the bitcoin blockchain. Instead of broadcasting their transactions to the entire network, they simply adjust the balance of their deposits in the multisignature wallet. For example, if Alice wants to send one bitcoin to Bob, she adjusts the balance sheet within their channel to reflect this. These transactions are secured through the use of cryptographic proofs, ensuring that either party can claim their rightful share at any time.

Closing the channel: When Alice and Bob decide to close their channel, the final balance is settled on the bitcoin blockchain. If Alice initially deposited three bitcoins and Bob deposited two, and Alice sent one bitcoin to Bob through their Lightning transactions, the channel would close by distributing two bitcoins to Alice and three to Bob. This final settlement is the only other transaction (after the opening one) that is recorded on the bitcoin blockchain.

Network of channels: The true power of the Lightning Network lies in its vast network of channels. If Alice has a channel open with Bob, and Bob has another channel open with Charlie, Alice can pay Charlie through Bob without needing to open a direct channel with Charlie. This capability is facilitated through a mechanism called routing, where transactions can hop across multiple channels until they reach their destination. Thus, a user may transact with anyone else on the network regardless of whether they have a direct channel open with them, significantly increasing the scalability and speed of transactions.

Through the above mechanism, the Lightning Network can process almost instantaneously millions of transactions per second (vastly more than any traditional payment system like Visa or Mastercard or any other cryptocurrency like Ethereum or Solana). Lightning transactions work both online and with a customer physically coming into a store. The customer simply opens a Lightning app on their phone (provided by any one of numerous software service providers) and scans the quick-response (QR) code on the merchant's screen. The transactions settle instantly and are final. The fees are miniscule: a fraction of a penny compared to fees of around 1.5 percent to 3.5 percent for the traditional card payment networks.

Such layer 2 solutions drastically reduce the burden on the bitcoin blockchain, avoiding congestion, high fees, and slow confirmation times. They enable the kind of rapid, microtransaction capability that is necessary for everyday purchases. Bitcoin is thus transformed into a genuinely usable currency for daily transactions. By operating outside the main Bitcoin blockchain (except for settling accounts when channels are opened or closed), the Lightning Network offers a scalable, efficient, and more private way of conducting bitcoin transactions.

Bitcoin as Payment Rails

It is important to appreciate the dual roles of bitcoin. On the one hand, bitcoin is an asset like gold (digital gold); on the other hand, the bitcoin network may be utilized as payment rails not restricted to the bitcoin asset.[28] Numerous service providers have created platforms and applications that manage the conversion from bitcoin to different currencies instantaneously for a nominal fee. This service allows merchants to invoice and receive payments in their local currency while utilizing the bitcoin network for transactions.

The key point here is that merchants do not have to take ownership of bitcoin at any point. Their interaction with bitcoin is purely in its capacity as payment rails. This is especially useful to those who wish to avoid the price volatility risks associated with holding bitcoin. The conversion from bitcoin to the local currency is instant, ensuring that merchants receive the exact invoiced amount in their currency of choice, regardless of any fluctuations in the price of bitcoin. The transaction fees, as mentioned earlier, are a fraction of any traditional payment network. Final settlement may be achieved immediately and without any counterparty risk, unlike with traditional money transmitters.

This demonstrates a broader trend toward the integration of bitcoin into everyday commerce. Developers continue to build software applications connecting to bitcoin's payment rails, thereby bridging the gap between traditional financial systems and bitcoin.

Before the Senate Banking Committee in 2018, Peter Van Valkenburgh of Coin Center delivered the below insightful description of bitcoin as public payments infrastructure, drawing an analogy with the internet being public information infrastructure:

> The lack of any corporation in-between means that bitcoin is the world's first public digital payments infrastructure. And by "public" I simply mean open to all and not owned by any single entity. We have public information infrastructure for websites and email, it's called the Internet, but the only public payments infrastructure that we have is cash, as in paper money, and it only works for face-to-face transactions.
>
> Before bitcoin, if you wanted to pay someone remotely—over the phone, wire, or internet—then you could not use public infrastructure. You would rely on a private bank to open their books and add a ledger entry that debits you and credits the person you are paying. And if you both don't use the same bank, then there will be multiple banks and multiple ledger entries in between.
>
> With bitcoin, the ledger is the public blockchain and anyone can add an entry to that ledger transferring their bitcoins to someone else. And anyone, regardless of their nationality, race, religion, sex, or creditworthiness can (for absolutely no cost) create a bitcoin address in order to receive payments digitally . . .
>
> Before the Internet, if you wanted to deliver a message you'd have to go through one of three TV broadcasters or a handful of newspapers . . . No critical infrastructure

should be wholly dependent on one or two. The Internet removed single points of failure in communications infrastructure and ushered in a wave of competition among new media corporations building on top of its public rails.

This comparison of bitcoin to the internet is a helpful mental model because what the internet is to information, bitcoin is to money. The description also eloquently encapsulates bitcoin's unique and unprecedented technological achievement in creating public infrastructure for digital payments.

This public nature of the bitcoin protocol is critical to permissionless financial transactions. You do not need the permission of any gatekeeping corporation or government to use its service. In developing countries, for example, many smartphone users do not have bank accounts. Bitcoin opens the possibility of financial inclusion for many such people for the first time. All you need is a smartphone and a connection to the internet to use it. To fund a wallet, an unbanked individual could either pay someone in physical cash or be paid for work directly in bitcoin. Self-contained and independent economies such as this continue to grow organically outside the traditional financial system in various parts of the developing world.

CHAPTER 4

Proof-of-Work Versus Proof-of-Stake

Unfortunately, Proof-of-Work is the only solution I've found to make p2p e-cash work without a trusted third party. Even if I wasn't using it secondarily as a way to allocate the initial distribution of currency, PoW is fundamental to coordinating the network and preventing double-spending.

— Satoshi Nakamoto, May 3, 2009

The most contentious topic within the cryptocurrency industry arguably centers around the comparison of consensus protocols, particularly Proof-of-Stake (PoS) and Proof-of-Work (PoW). Bitcoin's PoW is often criticized as being antiquated and inefficient, especially in terms of energy consumption. Advocates for change argue that PoS, hailed for its energy efficiency, represents a more sustainable future for cryptocurrencies.[1] This call for transition underscores a broader concern over the environmental impact of bitcoin's energy-intensive PoW algorithm.

Before delving into the environmental considerations of bitcoin's energy use—a topic reserved for chapter 16—let us again return to the primary feature that qualifies something as a digital commodity. As discussed in chapter 1, bitcoin's technological breakthrough was in the invention of digital property that mirrors the unalterable constancy of physical matter. The very prospect of changing something as fundamental as bitcoin's consensus protocol from PoW to PoS would be antithetical to this idea. Gold has never changed its molecular constitution; bitcoin mirrors this constancy in the digital world. Satoshi's core innovation—digital absolute scarcity—is entirely undercut by even the *ability* to change the protocol in any such manner.

Ethereum, the second largest cryptocurrency, transitioned from PoW to PoS in 2023. This transition followed a history of over a dozen changes to its protocol and supply schedule that establish that it is not, and never was, an unalterable protocol. Bitcoin, by contrast, has maintained a consistent protocol and supply schedule since its inception (despite numerous failed attempts by powerful and well-funded parties to change it), establishing its status as an unchangeable digital commodity.[2] The question of *whether* we should change the protocol is itself moot if bitcoin's protocol were in fact unchangeable in the first place! If bitcoin's claim to absolute scarcity (discussed in chapter 3) holds true (meaning that its protocol cannot be changed in any such fundamental manner), the debate over shifting from PoW to PoS is redundant and circular.

For the purposes of illustrating this point and the key differentiation between PoW and PoS, we shall look at two hypothetical scenarios, one where a group of powerful miners attempt to alter bitcoin's supply schedule and another where a group of powerful validators attempt to alter Ethereum's supply schedule (again). The contention here is that there is no substitute for PoW, and any suggestion otherwise about "improvements" is entirely naïve, misinformed, and/or outright malicious.

We have already discussed the mechanics of PoW in detail in chapter 3. Let us examine some of the core features of Ethereum's PoS protocol. Unlike bitcoin's PoW system, which requires miners to solve complex mathematical problems to validate transactions and create new blocks, PoS relies on validators who stake their Ether or ETH, (Ethereum's native token) as a form of security deposit. To become a validator, a participant must stake a minimum of thirty-two ETH.[3] This stake acts as collateral to incentivize validators to act in the network's best interest (their staked ETH may be seized by the network—*slashed*—if they act in a manner that the network deems to be against its interests). Validators are responsible for proposing new blocks and voting on block validity. Their chances of being chosen to propose a block or vote are proportional to the amount of ETH they have staked.

The act of staking involves an ETH holder sending their ETH to a staking address. The process of validating this staking transaction and accepting the person submitting it as a validator within the PoS validator set can take several days or even weeks. This is a design choice that introduces a latency into the onboarding and offboarding of validators via throughput limitations. This is intended to discourage rapid withdrawals by malicious validators who launch an attack and seek to exit quickly to escape the network's punitive action.

Consensus in PoS is achieved differently than in PoW. Validators are "randomly"[4] selected to bundle transactions into blocks. Other validators then attest to the validity of these blocks. A block is considered finalized when enough attestations have been gathered. This process eliminates the computational race and related costs (i.e., energy use) that are characteristic of PoW mining. Validators receive rewards for proposing and attesting to blocks accurately. Conversely, their staked ETH can be slashed for behaviors that threaten the network's integrity, such as voting on the "wrong" chain during a chain split or being offline and not participating in the consensus process when chosen.[5] These incentives and penalties are aimed at maintaining network security and integrity.

A COMPARATIVE ANALYSIS

The problem with a PoS system when compared with PoW is that it leads to a degree of centralization and thus diminished immutability, permissionless access, and censorship resistance. A core feature of PoS is the requirement for validators to stake thirty-two ETH, an investment that, at current valuations, amounts to approximately $100,000. This entry barrier naturally privileges those with substantial financial resources, potentially skewing network control toward wealthier participants. A significant portion of the network's validation power is concentrated within a handful of entities; currently, five corporate entities jointly control about two-thirds of all validators in their staking pools. This concentration of power diverges from bitcoin's distributed consensus.

The most common counterargument here in support of PoS is that bitcoin mining is also centralized given that a handful of mining pools (which individual miners can voluntarily join, pool their hash rate, and earn a share of the block rewards) control the majority of the total network hash rate, thereby causing centralization. This narrative is flawed for several reasons:

1. PoW mining pools have far less power over individual participants in the mining pool compared to the power wielded by PoS staking pools over individual participants in the staking pool. Participants in a PoW mining pool can switch pools instantly with the click of a

button if, for example, they disagree with the political stance adopted by a given mining pool, whereas it can take several days (by design) to unstake your ETH and exit a staking pool if you disagree with the pool's behavior for any reason. A blockchain coming under attack by a large staking pool (or mining pool) requires a reaction in a matter of minutes. The latency in the ability to withdraw staked ETH effectively annuls any checks and balances that the individual stakers have over PoS staking pools. This problem is not present in PoW mining pools, as discussed.

2. The small group of ETH staking pools who control almost two-thirds of staked ETH can technically censor every single new staking transaction and prevent any new validators from entering the validator set. This means that they can consolidate all staking rewards and decision-making power among themselves, thwarting any threatened dissent. This is a result of the inherent nature of PoS, wherein power (the amount of ETH you have staked) is derived from *inside* the system itself. This scenario does not arise in the case of PoW. Miners acquire power to add blocks from *outside* the system—they need to go out in the real world and acquire application-specific integrated circuit (ASIC) machines and expend real electricity. This is beyond the purview of incumbent dominant players, who have no power over anyone's ability to acquire machines and spend cheap energy they have access to.[6]

3. PoW is inherently distributive of bitcoin because miners, to cover costs like electricity, equipment, labor, and other operating expenses, must sell the bitcoins they earn, thus distributing it more widely. Conversely, PoS inherently concentrates wealth because ETH holders earn more coins simply by holding and staking their existing coins, with no need for any resource expenditure whatsoever. Validators thus compound their stake indefinitely and exponentially over time with no need to sell any ETH to cover expenses incurred in earning the ETH. This difference means that, while PoW encourages the natural dispersion of bitcoin through its operational model, PoS tends to concentrate wealth because holders who can stake more earn more without a natural mechanism for dispersion.

4. PoS incumbent validators also have the power to raise the entry threshold gradually for new validators. It currently sits at thirty-two ETH, which itself is exorbitantly high. The fact is that given staking

rewards are finite, the more the number of validators, the less share of the staking rewards each validator receives. This would make a rational, self-interested validator contrive to restrict new validators from entering. When all incumbent validators are aligned on the incentive to consolidate the economics and power in their hands, it is hard to see how this will not result in steps being taken over time to make entry as validators harder and harder. Beyond the cost of physical mining equipment and electricity, which no bitcoin incumbent player can influence directly, there is no entry threshold in bitcoin's permissionless PoW consensus system.

Another crucial aspect of PoS is that, unlike bitcoin's PoW, its blockchain and transaction history are inherently not trustless. As we have discussed, Satoshi used the PoW transaction ordering system in his design due to its trustless nature:

> Proof-of-Work has the nice property that it can be relayed through untrusted middlemen. We don't have to worry about a chain of custody of communication. It doesn't matter who tells you a longest chain, the Proof-of-Work speaks for itself.[7]

The primary advantage of PoW is that the history of the ledger is unforgeable unless someone is willing and able to commit more processing power than the total of the entire history of the bitcoin network to undo it.[8] As Hugo Nguyen observes, each new block effectively "buries" all prior transaction history under its weight, thus making it nearly impossible to forge.[9]

Nick Szabo, computer scientist, cryptographer, and legal scholar, in his highly acclaimed paper "Shelling Out" notes that a store of value requires an "unforgeable costliness."[10] This concept underlies the fact that assets derive their value from the difficulty and cost of their production, thus ensuring their scarcity and value. Szabo's idea is central to bitcoin, which requires computational work, making it costly and unforgeable. As Lyn Alden observes:

> We can imagine Bitcoin's blockchain ledger as a giant decentralized digital monument dedicated to preserving the objectivity of the past, built out of processing power, and growing larger each day. To rearrange the past according to Bitcoin's consensus mechanism, an entity would need to wield an unfathomable amount of energy and processing power in the present.[11]

Turning to PoS, validators temporarily stake their ETH as collateral rather than commit electricity to create new blocks. Given this detachment from the physical realm, the history of transactions in a PoS ledger has *no* unforgeable costliness. Anyone can re-create an infinite number of alternative histories of transactions.[12] It is therefore impossible for someone to look at them and independently determine which is the "real" history.

The only way that a PoS system may solve this is for a node to never go offline. New entrants could trust this specific designated node to point out the "correct" PoS blockchain. However, this is, by definition, trust-based.[13] The ability for a node to leave and rejoin the network without relying on trust is crucial to a truly decentralized digital commodity. This is evident in Satoshi's design as mentioned in the Bitcoin whitepaper:

> Messages are broadcast on a best efforts basis, and nodes can leave and rejoin the network at will, accepting the longest proof-of-work chain as proof of what happened while they were gone.[14]

If a validator leaves and then rejoins the PoS network, they have no way to prove what the true history of the ledger is and what occurred when they were offline. If there are competing versions of the history, they have no ability to determine which one is valid. They would have to look to some authority and trust that authority.

> Proof-of-Work is not only useful but absolutely essential. Trustless digital money can't work without it. You always need an anchor to the physical realm. Without this anchor, a truthful history that is self-evident is impossible. Energy is the only anchor we have.
> Proof-of-Work = trust physics to determine what happened.
> Proof-of-Stake = trust humans to determine what happened.[15]

> —Gigi

When a PoS network goes down (a weekly or daily occurrence in most PoS protocols, compared to bitcoin's 99.99 percent uptime over fifteen years), Lyn Alden observes that major validator operators of PoS systems literally get into a chatroom and manually figure out where to restart the blockchain based on their own records. This manual governing process is the alternative if one wishes to avoid the real-world energy expenditure of PoW.[16]

HYPOTHETICAL SCENARIO 1: MINER ATTACK ON BITCOIN

In this hypothetical scenario, a group of bitcoin miners who control the majority of hash rate (the miner majority) propose to increase the block reward from 3.125 to 10 bitcoins, indefinitely—that is, putting an end to the quadrennial halving of bitcoin's supply, and the 21 million supply cap. They argue that bitcoin's "security budget" needs an increase in the block subsidy to incentivize miners sufficiently to secure the network over the long term.[17] Under the influence of the miner majority, numerous bitcoin thought leaders support the change, claiming it is crucial for bitcoin's ongoing viability, relevance, and survival.

This change of code (a loosening of bitcoin's consensus) requires a hard fork, leading to the creation of two separate chains: the original BTC chain and the forked chain, BTC-X. The ultimate winner in this split, that is, the dominant chain, as discussed earlier,[18] is determined by the market response to the forked chains. Users, who will end up holding both chains after the split, will decide to hold one chain and sell the other. This in turn will result in price appreciation of one chain versus the other. The higher-priced chain will attract more miner hash rate because the block rewards will be more profitable on that chain compared to the chain whose coins are falling in price. More hash rate in turn will make the network more secure, which in turn attracts more capital, leading to a virtuous cycle (contrasting with a vicious downward spiral that will likely grip the competing chain).

If the market prefers BTC-X, then BTC will gradually descend into oblivion (similar to other chains that have hard-forked away from bitcoin in the past).[19] What is of interest here, however, is the scenario where most bitcoin users actually prefer BTC and want to fight back against the miner majority. How does that play out, and does the PoW system keep the dominant group of miners, the miner majority, in check?

If the market prefers BTC, thus choosing to hold or buy BTC and sell BTC-X, how would the miner majority react? They would be economically incentivized to mine BTC rather than BTC-X. Sure, their egos may be bruised by the fact that it would be an admission of defeat in the political battle over the chain split, but all that fades in the face of monetary incentives. As Voltaire put it: "When it is a question of money, everybody is of the same religion."

Facing substantial sunk costs in depreciating mining equipment and hefty electricity bills, miners will prioritize economics over everything else. Attacking BTC, such as attempting a 51 percent attack (discussed in chapter 6), would be extremely costly and economically irrational. It is not in their interests to bite the hand that feeds them.

The fact that miners will respond in this manner is not just theoretical. As we saw in chapter 3, it is in fact how the Bitcoin Cash (BCH) hard fork played out in 2017. This exemplifies how miners, constrained by their investments in rapidly depreciating assets and energy costs, are primarily motivated by the pursuit of profit, steering their hash rate toward the more economically advantageous chain.

The game-theoretic dynamics at play in bitcoin dictate that miners will take the most profitable course of action by directing their hash rate to the chain that offers higher returns and avoiding any actions that might jeopardize their revenue stream. Thus, the miner majority attack is doomed to fail.

HYPOTHETICAL SCENARIO 2: VALIDATOR ATTACK ON ETHEREUM

In this hypothetical scenario, a majority of Ethereum validators, (the validator majority) consider increasing the staking reward from a dynamically adjusted rate (currently around 5 percent) to a fixed rate of 10 percent. As mentioned, over 60 percent of staked ETH is controlled by only a handful of entities, so let us assume that this group proposes the reward increase. They argue that such a step will improve the decentralization of Ethereum because it will incentivize a greater amount of unstaked ETH (currently around 90 percent) to be staked, thereby increasing the number of validators and, purportedly, the decentralization of the network too.

Implementing this change will necessitate a hard fork, leading to the creation of two chains: the original ETH and a new chain, ETH-X. Similar to the bitcoin hypothetical scenario, the market will ultimately determine the dominant chain, with users choosing to buy, hold, or sell each chain.

Under a PoS consensus system, rational behavior would likely favor ETH due to ETH-X's significantly more dilutive impact on holdings. Therefore, users and holders of unstaked ETH (i.e., holders of 90 percent of ETH currently) would be at odds with validators because an increase in staking rewards benefits validators with staked ETH, thus economically incentivizing them to align with the validator majority and support ETH-X. This scenario mirrors the initial stance of the miner majority of bitcoin in hypothetical scenario 1, who might have initially pledged allegiance to mine only BTC-X until economic realities dictated a shift. With PoS, however, the absence of real-world sunk costs and operational expenses, coupled with the risk of being slashed if they make the wrong decision, changes the game-theoretic dynamics entirely.

Even if some validators believe ETH to be the better chain and expect it to be favored by the market, the PoS system discourages decisive action during a chain split. As Scott Sullivan points out, "If a chain split were to occur, then you should sit back and wait until a finalized block shows up somewhere, and once it does, then you know that's the 'correct' chain."[20] This is the result of the slashing mechanism in PoS, which serves as a deterrent against validating on the minority chain. When the majority, led by the validator majority, opts for ETH-X, any dissenting validators on the ETH chain risk having their holdings slashed. Economic incentives thus override political or ideological positions, making it rational for validators to wait, observe where the majority is heading, and then follow suit.

The majority validators (who control the most stake) always dictate the future course of events. No doubt the ETH staked by the validator majority is not all their own ETH but rather that of their customers. As discussed, however, any attempt by such customers to withdraw their support for the validators (for ideological or economic reasons) will take days or maybe weeks because of system-imposed throughput limitations on publishing entry and exit transactions to or from staking addresses. Contrast this to bitcoin, where a miner can switch mining pools instantly.

Any ETH holders not currently staking (thus not immediately threatened by slashing) who may theoretically wish to intervene and rescue ETH, will again face major barriers. Unlike PoW's permissionless system, where all you need to do is connect your ASIC machine to a power source, connect to the network, and begin mining, as mentioned above, the entry process to become a validator takes days or weeks. And once admitted, these validators will face a tyranny of the majority at the hands of the validator majority who have already endorsed ETH-X as the network's future and will not look kindly on new entrants in a competing chain.[21]

The critical point here is that, following the chain split, the validator majority remain the majority validator group in *both* chains. This means that they can censor the staking transactions needed for new validators to even enter. The very existence of such a possibility means you cannot rule out an adversarial situation where it is impossible to become a validator without the permission of the validator majority, thus making it a permissioned system.

The ultimate result is that dissent in PoS is not just challenging, it is virtually impossible: there is zero incentive for any validators to put their money at risk of being slashed in order to take a political stand, or even an economic stand, for that matter, because there is no greater downside risk than losing your money in a slashing event for voting on what turns out to be the 'wrong' chain. A rational participant will simply abstain because that is the correct game-theoretic decision. In short, the safest choice is to obediently toe the line laid down by the ruling class and avoid getting lashed (or slashed)! Thus, in this hypothetical scenario, the validator majority would succeed almost effortlessly in their endeavor.

These two hypothetical scenarios illustrate how there is no substitute for bitcoin's PoW-based consensus underpinned by a natural, voluntary, and freely formed economic incentive structure grounded in the real world. It is the only digital consensus system that operates in a truly trustless manner. PoS protocols may well have important use cases and applications (stablecoins, for instance), the discussion of which is beyond the scope of this book. However, with respect to the issue at hand—whether bitcoin should (or can) switch its consensus from PoW to PoS—the contention here is that it would be a futile and misinformed endeavor.

CHAPTER 5

Long-Term Security Budget

As discussed in chapter 3, bitcoin miners are essential to the security of the network. They contribute hash rate to the network by seeking to solve a computational puzzle as part of the mining process. The more computational power they contribute, the more secure the network becomes against attacks. This is because an attacker would need to amass more than half of the total network hash rate to probabilistically be able to execute a double-spend attack by solving the cryptographic puzzle before other miners and adding a fraudulent block to the blockchain. This makes such attacks highly expensive and difficult as the network grows stronger with more mining participation.

Miners are incentivized to contribute such computational power through a combination of the block subsidy and transaction fees:

1. **Block subsidy:** Each time a new block is mined, the miner receives a certain number of new bitcoins, referred to as the block subsidy. It serves as an incentive for miners to contribute their computational power to the network. The block subsidy started at fifty bitcoins per block and is halved approximately every four years in an event known as the *halving*. As discussed in chapter 3, this mechanism is designed to reduce the rate of new bitcoin creation gradually until the maximum supply of 21 million bitcoins is reached.

2. **Transaction fees:** Alongside the block subsidy, miners also collect transaction fees that users pay voluntarily to have their transactions included in a block. This fee is attached to their transaction when it is submitted to the memory pool (mempool) for processing. The fee amount can vary based on the network's congestion and the urgency of the transaction.

The block subsidy plus transaction fees is referred to as the *block reward*. This block reward is essentially the budget that is available to incentivize miners to secure the bitcoin network. It is consequently referred to as bitcoin's security budget.

Given that the primary motivation for miners is profit, it is naturally imperative that the block reward should outweigh the costs of mining, which include electricity, hardware, and maintenance expenses. The quadrennial halving of bitcoin's block subsidy brings into question the future incentive for miners because it directly affects their revenue. The block subsidy halves every four years, and if the price of bitcoin does not increase correspondingly, miners' earnings from securing the network would effectively be cut in half every four years, all else being equal.

Because of this reduction in revenue, the argument is that miners may be incentivized to contribute less hash rate as the profitability of mining decreases. Thus, halving of the block reward without a compensating increase in bitcoin's price could result in reduced overall hash rate, thereby lowering

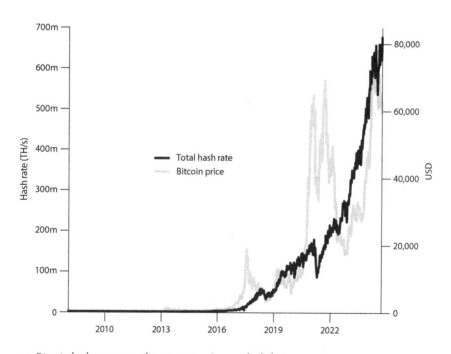

5.1 Bitcoin hash rate versus bitcoin price. *Source*: Blockchain.com, August 2024.

the network's security. This is referred to as bitcoin's long-term security budget problem. Although the block subsidy has been halved four times over the last fifteen years—from fifty bitcoins before 2012 to the current 3.125 bitcoins—the bitcoin hash rate has seen a relentless upward trajectory, reaching an all-time high in 2024.

This trend, in and of itself, manifestly challenges the notion of a long-term security budget problem. Therefore, the burden of proof should arguably rest on those claiming that such a problem exists because the evidence so far contradicts the proposition. In any event, let us assume this burden of proof and assess the merits of the concern.

TRANSACTION FEES

As discussed, the block reward comprises the block subsidy and transaction fees. Miners are incentivized to continue their operations if the transaction fee component grows sufficiently to compensate for the reduced block subsidy. The question of whether transaction fees will increase adequately to offset the diminishing block subsidy undoubtedly predates even the creation of the Genesis Block or the release of the Bitcoin Whitepaper. Presumably, it existed in Satoshi's head during the very design of the protocol. The premise that transaction fees would eventually supplant the block subsidy is mentioned in the whitepaper, where Satoshi states that "the incentive can transition entirely to transaction fees" over time.

The Fee Death Spiral

The debate over this aspect of bitcoin's design is not new either. As early as April 2011, BitcoinTalk user Vandroiy raised a concern:

> Any single small miner intends to maximize profit. His decision on what transactions to include doesn't create a big change in the height of fees. Thus, the miner will include all transactions that pay any fee, even very low fees, to have maximum profit. This results in the price for transactions dropping. In turn, those miners who already were hardly profitable have their earnings further

reduced and quit. This reduces hash rate, difficulty drops, and the circle repeats. By this reasoning, difficulty is likely to drop close to zero.[1]

Vandroiy was essentially saying that, because the marginal cost of including a transaction is near zero, the market would eventually clear at lower and lower prices, referred to as a fee death spiral. Mike Hearn, an early bitcoin developer, responded to Vandroiy's concern as follows:

> The death spiral argument assumes that I would include all transactions no matter how low their fee/priority, because it costs me nothing to do so and why would I not take the free money? Yet real life is full of companies that could do this but don't, because they understand it would undermine their own business.[2]

Hearn was saying that the death-spiral argument overlooks the strategic and long-term considerations that guide real-world business practices. There are many examples of this:

- Airlines could theoretically sell more tickets than there are seats on the plane, capitalizing on the assumption that some passengers will cancel or not show up. While overbooking is practiced to a degree, airlines manage it carefully to avoid the negative fallout of too many passengers and not enough seats, which can damage their reputation and customer loyalty. The long-term value of customer satisfaction outweighs the short-term gain from selling a few extra tickets.
- Online streaming platforms have the capability to host virtually unlimited content at little to no extra cost per title. Yet they curate their libraries carefully, removing titles that don't perform well and investing in those that do. This selective approach ensures that the platform's value proposition remains high, fostering subscriber loyalty and long-term revenue growth.
- Retailers sometimes sell products at a loss (loss leaders) to attract customers in the hope they will buy other, more profitable items. However, they do not make every product a loss leader because doing so would undermine their business. Strategic selection of loss leaders is crucial to ensure that these promotions contribute to, rather than detract from, long-term business success.

Increasing Demand for Blockspace

As the bitcoin network continues to grow and evolve, the demand for blockspace[3]—a finite resource in the network—is set to increase, leading to higher transaction fees. It is essentially based on the dynamics of demand and supply. By way of analogy, consider real estate in popular, densely populated cities. As more people desire to live in these areas, the limited available land means that property prices increase. As bitcoin's adoption grows and more transactions are made, the real estate on each block becomes more valuable, driving up the cost (transaction fees) for occupying this space. As the network grows, users naturally prioritize urgency and importance, paying higher fees to ensure that their transactions are confirmed swiftly.

We will discuss bitcoin's path to global adoption in chapter 11. If even a small fraction of the anticipated adoption takes place, it is a virtual certainty that demand for blockspace will cause vastly higher fees in the years and decades ahead. As awareness and acceptance of bitcoin expand, each transaction that requires blockspace, from small personal transfers to large institutional investments, will contribute to such fee growth.

The integration of bitcoin into mainstream payment systems and financial services will further fuel the demand. With major payment processors and financial institutions beginning to support bitcoin transactions, the ease of converting between bitcoin and traditional currencies is improving. This makes bitcoin more accessible to a wider audience and increases its utility as a payment method, contributing to higher transaction volumes on the blockchain.

The development of layer 2 solutions like the Lightning Network (discussed in chapter 3) are making bitcoin transactions faster, cheaper, and more scalable. While these innovations optimize the efficiency of blockspace usage, they also make bitcoin more appealing for everyday transactions, from buying coffee to paying for online services. As these solutions gain traction, they lower the barrier to entry, inviting more users to participate in the bitcoin network. This in turn will drive up the demand for blockspace for on-chain final settlements.[4] The burgeoning field of decentralized finance on bitcoin offers a wide array of financial services without the need for traditional intermediaries. As these platforms innovate and multiply and offer lending and borrowing opportunities, the need for blockspace will grow commensurately, with users engaging in more complex and frequent transactions.

During economic uncertainty and rampant inflation in many parts of the world, individuals and institutions may increasingly turn to bitcoin as a store of value to protect their wealth from diminishing purchasing power (see chapter 9). This flight to safety increases both the number of bitcoin holders and also the volume of transactions. Bitcoin's proposition of financial sovereignty—where individuals have full control over their assets without reliance on centralized authorities—will always create demand for on-chain transactions. This philosophical alignment may drive a conscientious wave of adopters as users seek to reclaim autonomy over their financial lives by self-custodying their savings on bitcoin's immutable blockspace.

Bitcoin is permissionless, censorship resistant, and immutable, and it has also seen several nonmonetary use cases evolve over the years. Many of these use cases have been controversial, resulting in cultural divisions within the bitcoin community. In recent years, these have included ordinals and inscriptions. Ordinals, a method to number uniquely and thus identify individual satoshis (the smallest units of bitcoin), allow for the association of specific data or digital artifacts with a particular satoshi (based on a theoretical framework known as Ordinal Theory). This has opened the door to inscriptions, wherein arbitrary data—ranging from images and texts to small programs—can be embedded directly onto the bitcoin blockchain by attaching them to a satoshi. These instances demonstrate bitcoin's use as an immutable repository able to preserve information beyond the reach of censorship or alteration. In addition, personal messages and tributes, ranging from marriage proposals to memorials, have been permanently recorded on the bitcoin blockchain.

These initiatives have occasionally resulted in surges in transaction fees, especially during periods when these inscriptions are created and accompanied by comprehensive marketing campaigns that lead to the emergence of a market for these digital artifacts. While nonmonetary applications of bitcoin are really a distraction from its true purpose (bitcoin was intended to be money, not a database), it is interesting to observe how users leverage a permissionless and censorship-resistant protocol for varied purposes. At the very least, this diversity of use cases illustrates the broad spectrum of factors that could drive demand for blockspace in the future. It lends support to the argument that it is almost impossible to imagine a future where bitcoin plays a significant role in public consciousness yet faces a lack of demand for its finite and limited blockspace.

MINING AS AN AUXILIARY TOOL

The utilization of nearly zero-cost stranded energy for bitcoin mining is discussed in chapter 16. This aspect presents a compelling solution to the long-term security budget concerns surrounding bitcoin. By tapping into stranded energy sources—such as surplus hydroelectric power, flare gas from oil extraction sites, or untapped geothermal energy—bitcoin mining can operate effectively with minimal operational costs. This approach ensures that there will always be an incentive for miners to contribute hash rate to the network, thereby securing it even as block rewards diminish over time. This strategy demonstrates how bitcoin can harness innovative energy solutions to maintain, and even enhance, its security mechanisms regardless of future block reward reductions.

Bitcoin mining is also increasingly serving as an auxiliary component to conventional industrial processes. Mining hardware machines produce significant amounts of heat during operation, a byproduct that has found innovative applications in other industries. For example, the heat generated can be harnessed to boil water, creating steam that can be condensed back into purified water, effectively subsidizing the process of water distillation with the energy expended in mining activities.[5]

The necessity to cool heat-generating ASIC machines introduces another opportunity for cross-industry collaboration. Industries that produce cool air, such as carbon capture facilities equipped with large fan banks for their operations, can benefit from integrating bitcoin mining processes. By utilizing the cool air generated from these facilities to offset the heat produced by ASICs, the operational costs associated with cooling mining equipment can be significantly reduced, providing a mutual benefit to both the mining and carbon capture sectors.

As bitcoin mining evolves, it will increasingly integrate with industries where it enhances profitability. Overlooking the opportunity to harness a business's excess heat or unused energy for bitcoin mining, or failing to utilize large-scale cooling systems for ASIC miners, seems imprudent. This evolution will lead to a greater number of miners incentivized by cost-effective energy use, ensuring the continued security of the network. As Philip Walton, cofounder of Gridless, observes: "ASICs will become an integrated component of any energy site . . . A turbine, a transformer, and a mining container. This is just what you will do. If you don't, you won't be competitive. You'll be wasting energy."[6]

ALTRUISTIC MINING

Altruistic mining refers to the practice of miners choosing to mine not primarily for profit but for other reasons that can be considered altruistic or community-oriented. This could involve mining at a loss or with minimal profit with the desire to support the network, enhance its security, or uphold principles like decentralization. Altruistic miners might prioritize the health and resilience of the blockchain over immediate financial gains. They could be individuals or organizations committed to the long-term success of bitcoin, believing in its value proposition and wanting to contribute to its security and viability. In some cases, altruistic mining could also involve mining transactions with low or no fees to facilitate the processing of small or noncommercial transactions, thus supporting users who might otherwise be priced out of the network during times of high demand.

We should also note that labeling such mining practices as purely altruistic overlooks a deeper, self-interested rationale, especially when miners are also significant holders of bitcoin. When miners invest their resources to secure the bitcoin network without direct profit motives, they are often safeguarding their own investments. Owning a substantial amount of bitcoin provides a strong incentive to maintain the network's security and functionality. In this light, altruistic mining can be seen as an enlightened self-interest strategy. You could compare it to a homeowner investing in the safety of her neighborhood: while her efforts benefit the community, the primary motivation is to protect and enhance the value of her own property.

Consider a world where bitcoin has achieved full monetization and widespread adoption over the next one hundred years. In such a scenario, the stakeholders, including those who have stored significant wealth in bitcoin, will obviously have a vested interest in its security and longevity. It is impossible to imagine a future where, after decades of contributing to bitcoin's success, these stakeholders suddenly abandon their commitment to bitcoin's security (effectively the security of their own stored wealth). Altruistic mining thus aligns with the long-term self-interest of miners who are also bitcoin investors. Their efforts to secure the network, even at a personal or immediate financial loss, are investments in their own financial future. This is yet another example of Satoshi's game-theoretic incentive structures at work.

CHAPTER 6

How Do You Kill Bitcoin?

How do you kill gold? No doubt, this question appears ludicrous. You will find that a deep understanding of bitcoin's permanence reveals an equally absurd idea regarding the possibility of its permanent destruction.

To kill gold, one might envision gathering every fragment of gold on the planet, placing it into a rocket, and launching it into the Sun.[1] Such an act would physically erase gold's value and existence. However, the feasibility of this endeavor is practically nonexistent. The logistical challenges of collecting every piece of gold are insurmountable given the vast amounts of gold stored in secure locations, personal collections, and even lost or undiscovered treasures around the globe. Despite the most coordinated efforts of global governments, the prospect of locating and destroying every last ounce of gold can only be a theoretical exercise rather than a practical possibility.

Bitcoin's existence is not tied to a physical form but to a ledger with over 100,000 copies spread out around the world, each being updated with the latest transactions in real time by each node. This number is, of course, always growing. Nothing stops anyone, anywhere, at any time from downloading and maintaining a new copy of the blockchain. North America is home to around 25 percent of bitcoin nodes, followed by Europe with 18 percent, Asia with 17 percent, and South America with 5 percent.[2] This means that, as long as a single copy exists anywhere in the world and at least one person is willing to maintain it, bitcoin continues to exist. An individual with nothing more than a laptop and an internet connection can continue to mine, transact, and sustain the network (just like Satoshi did on day 1 in 2009). It would therefore follow that the only conceivable way to shut down bitcoin would be to shut down the internet globally and permanently.[3]

The internet, much like bitcoin, is designed to be resilient, decentralized, and resistant to single points of failure. Efforts to censor or control the internet on a global scale face insurmountable technical, political, and social challenges. The key point to appreciate is that it is simply impossible to stop peer-to-peer transactions over the internet without shutting down the internet itself. Peer-to-peer transactions, a cornerstone of bitcoin, operate over Transmission Control Protocol/Internet Protocol (TCP/IP), which is foundational to the internet. Shutting down TCP/IP, and thereby the internet, would be not only technically infeasible but would also have catastrophic implications for the global economy, communications, and society at large.

This is the reason why bitcoin is often referred to as the internet's native currency. And this is why the internet changed money forever, and bitcoin is its natural offspring. With the creation of the Genesis Block in 2009, bitcoin and the internet were inextricably intertwined forever. They are united by a bond of enduring permanence, destined never to part for all eternity.

Notwithstanding the impossibility of shutting down the internet (with the aim of shutting down bitcoin), the reality is that bitcoin's resilience goes even further. While bitcoin is native to the internet, it does not strictly rely on the internet. Bitcoin transactions can be propagated by a variety of means outside the internet, including radio waves (e.g., ham radio), satellite networks (e.g., Blockstream Satellite), mesh networks (e.g., goTenna devices), or even SMS text messages. Thus, it may be argued that eradicating bitcoin is just as impractical as eradicating all gold from the planet. Gold and bitcoin embody the concept of permanence in their respective domains—physical and digital.

Notwithstanding its indestructibility, there are, of course, certain means by which bitcoin may be attacked and undermined. Let us analyze each of these.

FIFTY-ONE PERCENT ATTACK

A 51 percent attack refers to a potential attack where a single entity or group of entities gains control of more than 50 percent of bitcoin mining power (hash rate). This may result in the attacker double-spending bitcoin: they can make a transaction, then use their majority control to exclude or reverse it from the blockchain, essentially allowing them to spend the currency again. They may also prevent certain transactions from being confirmed, effectively stopping them from being completed.

The theoretical risk of a 51 percent attack is further accentuated in a scenario where the price of bitcoin drastically falls (in response to a public attack on the network by a nation-state, for example), the rewards (in fiat currency terms) for mining bitcoin also decrease. Because mining involves substantial electricity consumption, a lower bitcoin price means miners earn less for the hash rate they contribute. This reduction in earnings can deter miners from contributing hash rate to the network, making it easier to launch an attack. In reality, though, a 51 percent attack is impractical for several reasons:

Mining decentralization

Bitcoin's Proof-of-Work mechanism fosters multiple layers of decentralization, including, for example, on the geographic front and the temporal front.[4] This level of decentralization makes it extremely difficult for a potential attacker to amass the required hardware equipment to attempt an attack.

Geographic decentralization: With miners spread out in various global locations, the risk of a single entity or government gaining control over the majority of the network's hash rate is drastically reduced. This geographical spread ensures no single point of failure. Figure 6.1 shows the broad global distribution of bitcoin mining hash rate according to the Cambridge Bitcoin Electricity Consumption Index (CBECI).[5]

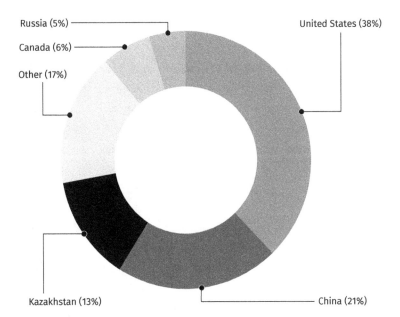

6.1 Global distribution of bitcoin mining hash rate. *Source*: Cambridge Bitcoin Electricity Consumption Index, 2022.

In 2021, China initiated a major crackdown on bitcoin, enacting an all-encompassing prohibition on bitcoin mining, trading, and related technological services. This was particularly significant given that China was a powerhouse in bitcoin mining, commanding around 45 percent of the global hash rate at that juncture (and up to 75 percent of hash rate at one point). The impact was immediate and stark: China's contribution to the global hash rate took a nosedive, plummeting to nearly zero as miners either ceased operations or migrated to more accommodating jurisdictions.

This migration created opportunities for other nations, with the United States, Kazakhstan, and Russia stepping in to fill the gap. The resilience of the bitcoin network was on full display as the global hash rate bounced back to levels seen before the ban in China by early 2022, and by March 2024, it had ascended to levels nearly 50 percent higher than those recorded in May 2021. China subsequently seemed to loosen its stance on mining once again, resulting in the return of some hash rate back to China.

The most significant consequence of this shift was the enhancement of bitcoin mining's decentralization. Prior to the ban, the concentration of mining power in China fueled arguments from bitcoin critics about the potential for a "China 51 percent attack"—whereby the majority of mining power, theoretically under Chinese government control, could enable an attack on the network.[6] The rebuttal of this argument (by virtue of its impracticality and technical infeasibility as a result of cost, hardware limitations, and other factors) has become moot because the ban's aftermath has paradoxically reinforced bitcoin's indestructibility. It is greatly ironic that the China ban itself has inadvertently dispelled a major criticism of bitcoin by further decentralizing its mining power.

Temporal decentralization: The requirement of specialized ASIC hardware for mining bitcoin introduces a significant temporal barrier to entry given that these devices are scarce thanks to production limitations. Setting up a mining operation large enough to threaten the network with a 51 percent attack would take considerable time, often years, during which the rest of the network can adapt or counteract the emerging threat. Changes in protocol (that could render such amassed hardware instantly redundant) or other coordinated responses by the community and miners can be implemented to safeguard the network.

The Proof-of-Work mechanism, by anchoring bitcoin in the physical world through the requirement of real-world resources (energy and hardware), introduces a layer of security that is difficult to compromise. The investment in time, money, and resources required to attempt a 51 percent attack, combined with the decentralized, global distribution of miners, creates a robust defense mechanism. The decentralized nature of bitcoin mining—both geographically and temporally—serves as an important defense against 51 percent attacks, making it prohibitively difficult for any single entity to gain control over the network. This resilience is a testament to the design principles of bitcoin, emphasizing security, decentralization, and adaptability.

Cheap Stranded Energy

Jeff Booth argues a counterpoint to the concern over network security falling in the face of price drops.[7] He suggests that miners can seek out and utilize the cheapest energy sources available worldwide. These energy sources are often in remote locations where energy would otherwise be wasted or not used. Booth argues that this capability to utilize low-cost energy ensures that there will always be an economic incentive to mine bitcoin even with much lower block rewards. This effectively means that the bitcoin network can maintain its security through a steady supply of hash rate. This low-cost stranded energy acts as a natural defense against potential attackers who may not have access to such cheap stranded energy.

The CBECI shows miners gravitate toward locations with cheap electricity like Kazakhstan, Iran, and the United States (Texas in particular). In June 2023, 37.23 percent of mining occurred in the United States, primarily because of abundant and cheap natural gas in specific regions. For example, bitcoin miners capture wasted natural gas from oil fields in North Dakota and use it for mining. Miners in Africa partner with mini-grid energy generators, which means that they have excess renewable energy (e.g., hydroelectric) that would otherwise be wasted. They use this stranded energy for bitcoin mining, generating revenue for the energy producer and promoting grid expansion.

A theoretical 51 percent attacker would find it nearly impossible to gain access to the required quantum of energy, even assuming they had the money to pay for it.[8] There probably are some power companies that can supply such an amount of power, but most power businesses are locked into long-term contracts. A short-term, intense burst of power for a week or two to perpetrate the attack is not practical. Factories, businesses, and homes rely on the electricity that these power plants supply to continue operating, and the supply cannot simply be turned off and diverted to a hypothetical attacker.[9]

An attacker would need an impracticably large supply of mining equipment (which is in limited supply and relies on time-intensive supply chains) and also an impracticably large amount of electricity. This means that they will likely need to produce their own mining equipment and possibly produce their own electricity. This likely requires years of lead time.

As bitcoin developer Jimmy Song notes, investing this much capital would only make sense if the attacker could profit enough from the attack and thus make the venture worthwhile. One could potentially enter into a short trade on bitcoin prior to a public attack (thus resulting in a price collapse and a profitable short position), but the perpetrator would require some off-ramp to take the money and run.[10] This is a lot harder in recent years because of anti-money-laundering (AML) and know-your-customer (KYC) laws surrounding most exchanges. Song also notes that getting an operation like this together means that the attacker has enormous revenue potential through honest mining. This is much less risky and requires much less capital investment upfront because they would not need 51 percent of the network.[11]

Even if the attacker somehow managed to achieve the impracticable, all they would achieve is a double spending that most likely causes financial damage to a cryptocurrency exchange. The attack does not destroy bitcoin. The rest of the network keeps moving along and can coordinate a response, including potentially updating the hashing algorithm, which would effectively render all the amassed mining machines useless instantly.[12] If it were a nation-state perpetrating this theoretical attack, imagine the global opprobrium that would result from this criminal act that affects an asset that is held by citizens of nearly all nations on Earth, including through pension funds and retirement accounts in the United States, among other nations.

DEVELOPER ATTACKS

> The nature of Bitcoin is such that once version 0.1 was released, the core design was set in stone for the rest of its lifetime.[13]
>
> —Satoshi Nakamoto, June 17, 2010

The above statement by Satoshi is backed primarily by game-theoretic dynamics, as explained in chapter 3. However, this statement should be contrasted with an observation by bitcoin technical expert Jameson Lopp: "99 percent of the code in Bitcoin Core was last edited by someone other than Satoshi. Software is never finished."[14]

While the core framework of bitcoin is set in stone, its ongoing evolution is akin to a living organism that sheds its old layers and regenerates continually, getting stronger with each iteration. Human participants in the ecosystem, that is, the developers, execute this ongoing metamorphosis and renewal process. Their actions or inactions, which may be intentional or unintentional, present certain attack vectors that warrant discussion here.

First, we should appreciate that the notion of bitcoin being "trustless" is not absolute. For the vast majority of users, node operators, and miners who do not have the ability to read or understand the code, there is an implicit trust in the developers. Developers are trusted to act in the best interest of the network, not introduce malicious code, and competently defend against external attacks. While this trust has generally been well placed, it does present some risks. This matter was highlighted in a *Wall Street Journal* article in 2023 entitled "Bitcoin's Future Depends on a Handful of Mysterious Coders" that unfortunately distorted the issue, consistent with the news media's typical analysis of bitcoin.

Developers no doubt play a crucial role in bitcoin's ecosystem. They maintain and upgrade the bitcoin software, identify bugs, propose improvements, and ensure the security of the network. While the open-source nature of bitcoin allows for transparency and the ability for changes to be reviewed by anyone, the reality is that the technical complexity of the subject matter means that only a relatively small portion of the user base has the expertise to review and understand the code thoroughly.

The bitcoin community mitigates the risks around this centralization and related trust concerns through several mechanisms.[15] First, the process for introducing changes to bitcoin's protocol is deliberate and transparent, involving extensive peer review, testing, and discussion before implementation. Proposals for changes are documented as Bitcoin Improvement Proposals (BIPs), which are publicly available and subject to community scrutiny. In addition, the decentralization of development—with multiple independent teams reviewing code and contributing to the software—reduces the risk of any single group introducing harmful changes.

The existence of multiple bitcoin *clients* (software applications that allows users to interact with the bitcoin network), with Bitcoin Core as the primary, but not exclusive, option, is another aspect of bitcoin's decentralized ecosystem. Users are not confined to using Bitcoin Core, thereby avoiding centralization around a single software client. They may choose from numerous other clients, including Bitcoin Knots, Libbitcoin, btcd, bcoin, and Electrum (light bitcoin wallet). As the *Wall Street Journal* article pointed out, the overwhelming majority of users use Bitcoin Core. But all it takes is one misstep, and users will migrate to other clients (in a manner similar to miners migrating away from China in response to the China ban). As the bitcoin meme goes, "everything is good for bitcoin." Such a theoretical attack by Bitcoin Core may cause short-term pain and loss of confidence, but it will ultimately serve to further decentralize and strengthen bitcoin for the long term. As Jonathan Bier observes in the critically acclaimed book *The Blocksize War*, "Control of a software repository, of course, does not mean control over bitcoin, as bitcoin users can run any software they like, from any repository they like. This misconception has lingered on for years."[16]

Also, updates within the Bitcoin Core software are *not* automatic; they require manual approval and implementation by users. This manual update process serves as a critical safeguard, significantly diminishing the risk that rogue developers could unilaterally introduce malicious updates with the intent of compromising the network. By requiring that users actively choose to adopt new versions, the ecosystem ensures a distributed form of oversight and consensus on software changes. Users can decide themselves on the software versions that govern their participation in the bitcoin network. By exercising this discretion, nodes effectively vote on the acceptance of new features or changes.

Bitcoin's code is arguably the most closely watched and monitored piece of software on the planet. This makes it virtually impossible to sneak in a malicious upgrade. And with each passing day, as bitcoin's user base and market capitalization grow, so does this scrutiny of the code. BIPs undergo rigorous analysis and discussion within the community. Developers, users, and miners must all agree on significant changes in a public manner, making it difficult for harmful proposals to gain traction. The lack of a central authority or leader in bitcoin's developer community (which is not true of any other cryptocurrency) further reduces the risk of targeted manipulation.

QUANTUM COMPUTING

The emergence of quantum computing presents theoretical challenges to bitcoin, particularly regarding its cryptography. Quantum computers leverage the principles of quantum mechanics to process information, potentially solving complex problems much faster than classical computers. Classical computing, based on Alan Turing's theoretical frameworks, operates with bits in states of 0's and 1's, forming the basis of today's digital technology. Quantum computing, on the other hand, leverages qubits, which can exist in multiple states simultaneously because of quantum superposition. This difference gives quantum computers the potential to solve certain problems much faster than their classical counterparts.[17]

As discussed in chapter 3, bitcoin's security relies heavily on cryptographic algorithms like elliptic curve digital signature algorithm (ECDSA) for digital signatures and secure hash algorithm 256-bit (SHA-256) for hashing. The concern is that quantum computers could potentially break these algorithms; specifically Shor's algorithm[18] could solve the discrete logarithm problem on which ECDSA is based. This would theoretically enable the derivation of private keys from public keys and allow a quantum attacker to sign transactions as if they were the owner of the bitcoin address.

Quantum computers could also significantly accelerate the mining process, potentially centralizing mining power. This could undermine the decentralized consensus mechanism of bitcoin if a quantum-enabled entity could outpace all other miners. The ability to mine quickly in a sudden quantum speedup could lead to destabilization of prices and control of the chain itself, potentially leading to 51 percent attacks.[19]

This potential threat is a topic of extensive debate in the bitcoin community, particularly because it is entirely theoretical and speculative. Large-scale quantum computers do not yet exist and it is not known when, or if, they may materialize. A computer powerful enough to break bitcoin's cryptographic defenses is a complex, resource-intensive endeavor facing numerous technical hurdles. Experts in quantum computing suggest that it could take decades before quantum computers can pose any potential threat.

In the hypothetical scenario that the threat does in fact materialize, how could bitcoin defend itself? First, the bitcoin protocol can be updated to adopt postquantum cryptographic algorithms that are resistant to quantum computing attacks. This would involve an upgrade of the cryptographic algorithms used for new transactions and addresses. Such a change can be implemented through a soft fork, requiring only miner consensus.[20] Upgrading to a quantum-resistant signing algorithm could be achieved this way with relative ease. In addition, users can already choose wallets that use cryptography believed to be more resistant to quantum attacks.[21]

While awaiting postquantum cryptography, increasing key sizes could be an interim solution to make it more difficult for quantum computers to break existing cryptographic algorithms. By increasing key sizes, the computational effort required to break the encryption increases exponentially, making it harder for quantum computers to crack.

Note also that only certain old forms of bitcoin addresses are at an increased risk of being hacked by a theoretical quantum computer.[22] These are addresses that use pay-to-public-key (p2pk), which reveal the public key directly when a transaction is made (both sending and receiving bitcoin), thus creating a vulnerability. According to Deloitte, approximately 25 percent of all bitcoins are potentially vulnerable in this respect.[23] Should a quantum computing threat ever become more likely in the coming years (or decades), steps may be taken by the public to safeguard their bitcoin.

Pay-to-public-key-hash (p2pkh) addresses are more secure because they do not reveal the public key when receiving bitcoin. In order to receive bitcoin, you only reveal an address that is created by taking the public key and hashing it multiple times using the SHA-256 and RACE Integrity Primitives Evaluation Message Digest 140 (RIPEMD-140) cryptographic functions (this generates a quantum-resistant bitcoin address). The public key is revealed, however, when coins are spent by these addresses. Reusing an address accentuates the risk because the public key is revealed repeatedly. Thus, a good practice to protect against potential threats is to avoid reusing addresses—each transaction should use a new address to minimize exposure of the public key.

With respect to the potential threat to mining, the most likely case is that future potential quantum computers will be treated like any kind of hardware advancement, similar to the transition between graphics processing units (GPUs), field-programmable gate arrays (FPGAs), and ASICs for mining bitcoin—a slow economic transition to better tooling, rather than a sudden revelation of a secret quantum supercomputer to the world, whose first priority is to attack bitcoin.

Note that this theoretical threat is not limited to bitcoin. These cryptographical vulnerabilities would affect the entire global banking and financial services industry, defense and military infrastructures, healthcare systems, telecommunications, and many other critical aspects of the global economy. If this ever became a realistic threat, it is likely to take the form of a global emergency warranting a multinational response, given the serious security risks involved. A soft fork to incorporate a quantum-resistant signing algorithm in bitcoin's protocol will be a relatively straightforward fix by comparison.

STATE ATTACKS

Regulatory crackdowns on bitcoin perpetually loom as a potential challenge. Such crackdowns could range from severe restrictions on bitcoin transactions to outright bans, encompassing a wide array of regulatory interventions. Governments might target the facilitation of bitcoin transactions by imposing legal barriers, effectively making it illegal for businesses and individuals to engage in buying, selling, or trading activities. A particularly impactful measure could involve prohibiting banks and financial institutions from processing cryptocurrency transactions, thereby severing the critical link between fiat currencies and bitcoin (referred to as fiat-crypto on-ramps and off-ramps), which would drastically reduce bitcoin's liquidity and utility.

Regulatory actions could also include the introduction of onerous taxation and reporting requirements for bitcoin transactions, thus imposing a heavy compliance burden. Governments could also target the mining sector, citing environmental concerns because of the significant energy consumption associated with the process. These concerns are addressed specifically in chapter 13.

DISRUPTION BY OTHER CRYPTOCURRENCIES

Several cryptocurrencies have emerged with the intention of addressing the perceived limitations of bitcoin. They offer enhancements in areas like scalability, transaction speed, energy efficiency, privacy, and programmability. Ethereum stands out with its claim to extend the utility of blockchain technology beyond mere value transfer. Introduced in 2013 and launched in 2015, Ethereum pioneered smart contracts and decentralized applications (dapps) with a view to enabling complex agreements and applications and thus operate autonomously on the blockchain.

Other cryptocurrencies have also positioned themselves as offering superior properties to bitcoin. For instance, Ripple claims to optimize cross-border payments, working directly with banks and financial institutions to facilitate fast, low-cost international transfers. Litecoin, created in 2011 as the "silver to bitcoin's gold," sought to improve on bitcoin's model by offering faster transaction confirmation times through a shorter block generation period. Monero offers users the ability to conduct transactions with a higher degree of anonymity than bitcoin. Polkadot is focused on blockchain interoperability and scalability and enables different blockchains to communicate and transfer value seamlessly.

The advent of alternative cryptocurrencies might be perceived by some as a potential challenge to bitcoin's enduring relevance. However, this view fails to appreciate that bitcoin represents a unique, path-dependent, once-in-history invention that simply cannot be duplicated or overtaken by a comparable technology. In chapter 7, we will delve deeper into the intricacies of this argument.

CHAPTER 7

Once-in-History Invention

It's genuinely surprising, but by all evidence it appears very hard to significantly improve Bitcoin's fundamental design. Most tradeoffs improving aspects make other properties worse. By curious happenstance, Bitcoin exists in a narrow optima in the near infinite design space.

—Adam Back

Is it possible to improve upon bitcoin's system for achieving decentralized consensus? Experts in the field, such as Adam Back, have noted that there is almost no room for further improvement of bitcoin's fundamental design.[1] However, any open-source technology, even if perfect, can always be copied. Does that mean it is possible to create an infinite number of new bitcoin networks? According to Jack Dorsey, founder of Twitter and Square, replication or replacement of bitcoin is "extremely unlikely since the conditions needed to create and sustain it were very special."[2]

To understand bitcoin's irreplicability, it is necessary to appreciate bitcoin as a "path-dependent one-time-invention."[3] Bitcoin is much more than the Bitcoin Core software that the protocol runs on, which is all too easy to copy. Bitcoin is the network of over 100,000 nodes, over 1 million miners, over 100 million users, and billions of dollars of mining equipment spread around the globe, built organically over fifteen years, and now securing over $1 trillion of wealth.

Path dependency means that the sequence of events matter as much as the events themselves: "You can take a shower and then dry yourself off, but you cannot dry yourself off and then take a shower."[4] Bitcoin's origin story, network effects, and application of Metcalfe's law (discussed in chapter 11) and the Lindy effect (discussed later in this chapter) are path dependent and cannot be replicated without the ability to travel back in time. Path dependency prevents bitcoin from disruption because the organic series of events that led to its creation and assimilation into the marketplace cannot be replicated.

IMMACULATE CONCEPTION

Let us consider bitcoin's origin story. During the global financial crisis, on October 31, 2008, a figure shrouded in mystery, known only by the pseudonym Satoshi Nakamoto, presented the world with the Bitcoin Whitepaper. He[5] posted it on a mailing list known as the Cryptography Mailing List on a platform called Metzdowd. His online profile stated that he was a male born on April 5, 1975, and listed his location as Japan. Beyond these few pieces of information, little else is known about his identity. The choice of details, including his nationality and age, has been subject to speculation and analysis, with some doubting their veracity considering the flawless English used in his communications and the fact that the timing of his email activity corresponded with the Pacific Time Zone rather than Japan's.

The origin of bitcoin was marked by the mining of the Genesis Block by Satoshi on January 3, 2009. Despite the global impact of bitcoin, Satoshi's identity has been kept a secret to this day, with his anonymity becoming a core part of bitcoin's lore and philosophy. Satoshi's anonymity was not just a personal choice but a statement on the principles of decentralization and privacy, ensuring that the focus remained on the technology rather than on its creator.

Numerous attempts have been made to unveil the person behind the pseudonym, ranging from linguistic analyses of Satoshi's writings to investigations into early bitcoin transactions. Speculations have pointed toward various individuals, from cryptographers to computer scientists, yet none have been proven to be Satoshi. In a twist, a Japanese American man named Dorian Satoshi Nakamoto was mistakenly identified as bitcoin's creator, leading to media frenzy and public speculation in 2014. Yet the true Satoshi remains elusive.

In April 2011, Satoshi posted his last public message on the BitcoinTalk forum, stating that he had "moved on to other things" in response to a question about the likelihood of him returning to the bitcoin community. This marked the end of his direct involvement. His true identity remains an enduring mystery.

To view bitcoin purely as a technology would be to miss the bigger picture—it represents a vision and a philosophy of decentralized governance that would have been impossible if the world knew the identity of its creator. Satoshi's anonymity highlights the ideals of privacy and autonomy in the face of centralized powers. The mystery of his identity encapsulates bitcoin's immaculate conception.

With this backdrop, consider that all cryptocurrencies created after bitcoin, regardless of their proclaimed technological advancements or innovations, emerge in a landscape already shaped by bitcoin's legacy, facing a world aware of cryptocurrency concepts and skeptical of imitators. The conditions of bitcoin's inception—technological novelty; historical context (introduction in the middle of the 2008 financial crisis as a solution to central banking excesses); and an anonymous, ideological founder—are a confluence that is practically impossible to replicate.

ORGANIC AND FAIR DISTRIBUTION

In the early days, bitcoin's introduction, through an obscure cryptography mailing list, invited open participation from anyone with an interest in digital currencies and cryptography. Those who got involved were, almost exclusively, technology enthusiasts ideologically and philosophically aligned with the cause espoused by the cypherpunk community (see chapter 18). This fostered a grass-roots level of growth, devoid of profit-driven centralized entities or venture capital-backed founders.

A crucial aspect of bitcoin's fair launch was the absence of a pre-mine. Satoshi did not reserve any coins for himself (or any Silicon Valley venture capitalists) before the network went live. Bitcoin's distribution began with the mining of the Genesis Block on January 3, 2009, and from that point, anyone with a computer could participate in mining and be rewarded with bitcoins in return. The mining *difficulty*[6] was much lower in the early days, allowing individuals to mine successfully with nothing more than a laptop or desktop computer. This accessibility meant that a wider range of people could contribute to, and benefit from, the network. The resulting distribution of coins was consequently fair and equitable. As bitcoin grew in popularity over the years, the mining process became more competitive and professionalized, leading to the creation of mining pools and the use of specialized hardware. However, the initial period of low difficulty and the lack of a pre-mine ensured that early adopters who took the risk and supported the network were rewarded when the bitcoin price appreciated.

Bitcoin's fair launch and distribution are in stark contrast with other cryptocurrencies that have been launched with significant portions of their supply allocated to the project's founders, developers, or early investors. Bitcoins that are assumed to have been mined by Satoshi himself would make him one of the top 20 richest people in the world, with a net worth of over $60 billion as of 2024. However, these bitcoins (closely monitored on the public ledger) have never moved since they were mined over fifteen years ago. Contrast this with Ethereum, where 60 percent of total coins were issued in a pre-mine to insiders and not through a public process like Proof-of-Work mining.[7] The founders have sold their pre-mined coins for personal profit over the years.[8] Pre-mining can lead to concerns over centralization and the potential for market manipulation. In contrast, the way bitcoin was introduced and distributed to the world stands as a testament to its foundational principles of decentralization, transparency, and fairness.

The valuation of bitcoin first took shape in a formalized context with the establishment of the New Liberty Standard, an early bitcoin exchange that, in October 2009, set the initial exchange rate of bitcoin to the U.S. dollar. By calculating the rate based on the electricity costs associated with mining, the New Liberty Standard pegged 1,309.03 bitcoins at $1. This rudimentary valuation method marked the first step toward bitcoin acquiring monetary value. Bitcoin's journey from $0.0008 to over $70,000 per bitcoin in 2024 truly boggles the mind.

Bitcoin first acquired transactional monetary value on May 22, 2010, a day now celebrated as Bitcoin Pizza Day. On this day, Laszlo Hanyecz, a programmer, made an offer on a bitcoin forum to pay 10,000 bitcoins for two pizzas. This transaction is recognized as the first time bitcoin was used to purchase goods in the real world. At that time, the value of 10,000 bitcoins was approximately $41, based on the agreement between Hanyecz and the individual who accepted the bitcoin payment in exchange for ordering the pizzas for him. This pegged the value of each bitcoin at a fraction of a cent ($0.004).

To encourage adoption and increase distribution, early adopters used online faucets that gave away free bitcoins to each visitor. This initiative played a significant role in getting bitcoins into the hands of many people and is remembered as a generous act that helped promote bitcoin's early use and distribution. This initiative is discussed further in chapter 11.

While initially a significant portion of bitcoin was held by early adopters and miners, often referred to as whales, over time, these whales have periodically distributed their holdings, generally by selling during market upswings, thus enabling a more equitable spread of bitcoin ownership. In recent years a new class of institutional investors have entered the stage. They include hedge funds, family offices, and publicly traded companies.[9] These entities, while potentially large holders, actually contribute further to the distribution of bitcoin because they typically represent a collective investment rather than an individual holding. cryptocurrency exchanges and financial products such as exchange-traded funds and trust funds also play a role in this redistribution process. These platforms and products lower the barrier to entry for individual and institutional investors alike, enabling those without the technical know-how to gain exposure to bitcoin's price performance. Bitcoin held in these funds and platforms is effectively spread across a multitude of individuals, further diluting the concentration of holdings.

There is a strong argument, no doubt, that holding bitcoin through these investment products and investment vehicles defeats the underlying purpose of bitcoin. The true benefits of censorship-resistant, unconfiscatable money are only achieved by the self-custody of bitcoin directly on the bitcoin protocol. However, the counterargument here is that such avenues of investment through financial products are incredibly effective at driving adoption. Individuals who gain financial exposure to bitcoin synthetically through an investment product are likely to educate themselves about it and try to understand its value, which they may not do otherwise. Once they do so, they may, of their own accord, choose to switch their holding from third-party custody to self-custody.

Bitcoin's initial landscape, dominated by a handful of early adopters and whales, is continuously transforming as the asset continues to attract a diverse range of participants. Bitcoin is steadily moving toward a future where its benefits and value are shared across an ever-expanding community, as shown in figure 7.1.

The largest group in figure 7.1, accounting for almost 60 percent of the supply of bitcoin, is represented by over 100 million people (some estimates are over 200 million) around the world. Among these individual holders, it is estimated that more than one-quarter own less than ten bitcoins each, and more than half own less than one hundred bitcoin each.[10] Large holdings are diluted continually over time. In 2012, it is estimated that over 60 percent of all bitcoins were held by individuals or entities with over one thousand bitcoins each. As of 2023, this

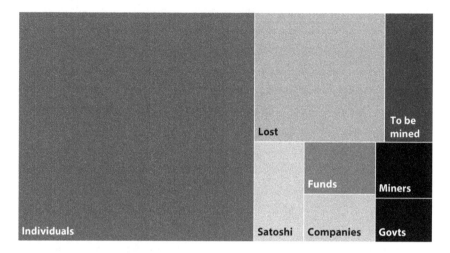

7.1 Bitcoin ownership distribution. *Source*: Bitcointreasuries.net, August 2024.

percentage has declined to less than 35 percent because large holders have gradually sold their holdings to smaller holders (the fastest growing cohort is that of holders with less than one bitcoin each).[11] This level of egalitarian distribution is beyond comparison within the crypto industry. The only reason this was achievable was because of bitcoin's evolution over several years through the collective psyche of humanity. This is path-dependent and irreplicable.

Given the crypto industry's shift to the "more energy efficient"[12] Proof-of-Stake alternatives,[13] one could anticipate that all potential future competitors will utilize a version of Proof-of-Stake. As a thought experiment, imagine if you were launching a new Proof-of-Stake coin. How would you achieve a fair distribution at issuance? With Proof-of-Stake, you would necessarily have to do a premine and issue the coins to a select group of initial holders (who are invariably going to be the founders of the coin and, depending on the coin, venture capital investors), who would then propagate the network by staking these coins. This initial nepotistic coin allocation is practically unavoidable with Proof-of-Stake. If the coin gains traction in the market and there are secondary buyers at high prices, these initial holders will subsequently receive a windfall when they sell their coins for cash. As a result, this move away from Proof-of-Work consensus to Proof-of-Stake consensus has permanently, and counterintuitively, closed the door to any possibility of a future challenger to bitcoin emerging with a more decentralized and fair distribution.

NETWORK EFFECTS

Network effects play a pivotal role in cementing bitcoin's status as a path-dependent, foundational invention, shaping its trajectory, and making it increasingly difficult for any subsequent technology to replicate its success. Network effects refer to the phenomenon where the value of a product or service increases with the number of users.[14] In the context of bitcoin, this means that as more people use, buy, and accept bitcoin, its utility, security, and value grow, creating a virtuous cycle that attracts even more users.

Bitcoin's inception came at a historically opportune moment, following the 2008 financial crisis, when the vulnerabilities and shortcomings of the traditional banking and financial system were on full display. Government bailouts, moral hazard, and systemic corruption were the biggest talking points around the financial world. In this environment, bitcoin was presented as the antidote. This timing was not just fortuitous; it was also irreplicable. It set the stage for certain unique circumstances that allowed bitcoin to establish a first-mover advantage. Bitcoin's technological and philosophical proposition quickly garnered attention from technology enthusiasts, libertarians, cryptographers, and those disillusioned with conventional financial systems.[15] This landscape seeded the initial network of users necessary to trigger network effects.

As the network grew, so did bitcoin's security. This in turn further enhanced the trust and reliability of bitcoin as a store of value and medium of exchange, attracting more users and miners to the ecosystem in a virtuous cycle. Bitcoin's burgeoning user base led to greater liquidity and market depth. The acceptance of bitcoin by merchants, payment processors, and even some governments further solidifies its utility and value, making it more attractive than newer cryptocurrencies that lack the same level of ecosystem development and recognition.[16] The interplay between bitcoin's timing, technological innovation, and growing adoption creates a virtuous cycle that is impossible to emulate. As more people join the bitcoin network, its advantages further solidify and are reinforced.

Figure 7.2 shows bitcoin's market capitalization compared to the next fifteen largest cryptocurrencies (from a universe of more than twenty thousand).[17] After over thirteen years of relentless attempts to create "the next Bitcoin," backed by billions of dollars of Silicon Valley venture capital money, the results speak for themselves. Aside from Ethereum (which has been examined in chapter 4

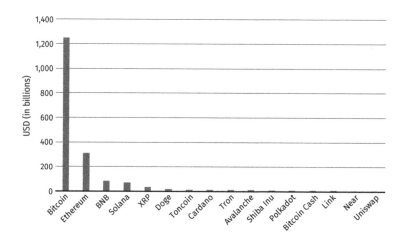

7.2 Market capitalization of the largest cryptocurrencies. *Source*: Coinmarketcap.com, August 2024.

in comparison to bitcoin), the relative sizes of "competing" cryptocurrencies are mere rounding errors. Does the chart make it look like bitcoin is at any risk of usurpation? As of 2024, bitcoin is four times larger than the second largest cryptocurrency, fifteen times larger than the third, forty times larger than the fifth, and more than 110 times larger than the tenth (excluding stablecoins, which are centralized and pegged to fiat and thus not relevant to the discussion).

It is also important to point out that none of these other cryptocurrencies even claim to be disrupting central banking and money. Their focus is more on smart contracting, programmability, scalable payment solutions, interoperability of blockchains, and other nuanced propositions. This makes it even harder to disrupt an incumbent monetary network like bitcoin, given that the network effects around money are arguably the strongest of all networks. Money is, after all, "the oldest social network in the world."[18]

LINDY EFFECT

Every day that goes by and Bitcoin hasn't collapsed due to legal or technical problems, that brings new information to the market. It increases the chance of Bitcoin's eventual success and justifies a higher price.[19]

—Hal Finney, June 4, 2011

The Lindy effect, a concept originating from the realm of technology and cultural longevity, posits that the future life expectancy of some nonperishable things, like a technology or an idea, is proportional to their current age.[20] In simpler terms, the longer something has been around, the longer it is likely to continue to exist. This concept offers an apt perspective on bitcoin's evolution and status.

Since its inception in 2009, bitcoin has more than survived; it has thrived in the face of a myriad of challenges, including regulatory scrutiny, market volatility, exchange hacks and frauds, and competition from newer cryptocurrencies boasting superior technological features. Each day that bitcoin continues to operate, gain adoption, and maintain or increase its value, it lends credence to the Lindy effect. Each challenge that bitcoin faces demonstrates the robustness of its architecture. This in turn increases the confidence of investors, users, and regulators in its longevity.

Much like the internet, which evolved from a fragile network of computers into the backbone of modern civilization, bitcoin has grown from a niche cypherpunk project to a global financial asset class today (and it still remains in the very early stages of global adoption). Bitcoin's trajectory mirrors that of the internet as it becomes increasingly woven into the fabric of global finance.

Another relevant analogy can be found in the story of gold as a store of value. Gold has been valued by humanity for thousands of years, and its history of enduring worth gives it a credibility that cannot be easily replicated by newer commodities. As bitcoin continues to exist and function as intended, it continues to accumulate a history as "digital gold." As its Lindy effect compounds with each passing day, it becomes increasingly impossible to destroy or supplant.

10× IMPROVEMENT RULE

According to Peter Thiel, a new entrant in a market must offer a solution that is not just slightly better but ten times better than the next best thing to be successful.[21] This is referred to as the 10-x improvement rule. The proposition that bitcoin is a foundational, once-in-history invention that no competitor can ever usurp is intrinsically linked to the notion of the 10-x improvement rule. For a competitor to dislodge bitcoin's position as the leading digital commodity, they would need to offer benefits that are orders of magnitude greater in value.[22]

Bitcoin's unique combination of attributes—scarcity, portability, verifiability, durability, divisibility, censorship resistance, and unconfiscatability—lay the foundation of its unmatched status. Each characteristic represents a critical aspect of bitcoin's value proposition as a digital commodity. Imagining a competitor that could offer a tenfold improvement over bitcoin's combined monetary properties is challenging. Such an improvement would, first, require the replication of the trust and security that underpin bitcoin (which are path-dependent, as discussed earlier) and, second, present a compelling reason for users to transition to a new system with potentially unproven security and lesser recognition.

The challenge of achieving a 10-x improvement is further compounded by bitcoin's first-mover advantage and the extensive infrastructure that has been built around it, including exchanges, wallets, and merchants worldwide that have integrated bitcoin or a bitcoin layer 2 payment technology. This ecosystem, developed over more than a decade, provides bitcoin with an unshakeable foundation that a new challenger would find impossible to replicate, let alone decimate, with a tenfold improvement in its foundational monetary properties.

The principle is that it is not just about introducing enhancements or improvements. The challenger would need to render bitcoin's near-perfect monetary attributes (as discussed in chapter 2) entirely obsolete. The likelihood of such a disruption appears increasingly remote. This analysis reinforces the view of bitcoin as an irreplicable, once-in-history invention. Its combination of technological innovation, economic principles, philosophical ideals, and widespread adoption sets an insurmountable hurdle for any sort of meaningful improvement, let alone a 10-x improvement.

SCHELLING POINT

The Schelling point, a concept introduced by American economist Thomas Schelling,[23] refers to a solution that people tend to choose by default in situations where they have to make a decision without communicating with others. It is based on the premise that individuals, when faced with multiple options and no way to coordinate their choices with others, gravitate toward an option that feels natural or prominent as a focal point.[24] The Schelling point is the option that people intuitively select because it seems obvious or significant to them, even when there are no explicit incentives or rational reasons to choose one option over another. For example, if two people are told to meet in a large city without being given a specific time and place, they might independently decide to meet at the most famous landmark at noon, assuming it to be the most logical choice given the lack of communication. The landmark, in this case, serves as the Schelling point.[25]

Multiple factors, already discussed, would make bitcoin the Schelling point of monetary assets within the crypto industry and beyond over time. We discussed in chapter 2 bitcoin's monetary properties that make a strong case for it being the best form of money ever created. In addition, bitcoin is a first mover in the cryptocurrency space, making it a natural focal point for both investors and developers. This early start has made bitcoin the primary digital asset around which discussions revolve.

In addition, bitcoin has unrivaled brand recognition. Bitcoin itself has become synonymous with cryptocurrencies for many people, both within and outside the crypto community. This widespread recognition acts as a Schelling point, attracting new users and investors to bitcoin as the default or safe choice. Its high liquidity and market capitalization also make it an attractive asset for investors, further establishing its position as the Schelling point.

PART III

The Economics

CHAPTER 8

Money and the State

In chapter 2, we discussed the distinction between commodity money (e.g., gold and silver) and fiat money. In the context of fiat money, a primary tenet of the distinction is that it is the exclusive creation of the state, while commodity money, by its nature, is stateless. A digital commodity, bitcoin, is commodity money and thus is stateless. Monetary history, as we shall see in this chapter, chronicles money's progression from commodity money to fiat money, with events of the twentieth century as a critical turning point in that journey. Any notion of a return to bitcoin as money heralds a transition back from fiat to commodity money. It would foreshadow a monumental shift (or reversion): the separation of money and state.

Today, the state's exclusive control over money is manifested through the concept of legal tender, which is typically defined and enforced by the government. Most countries mandate their state-issued currency as the sole legal tender, meaning that it must be accepted if offered in payment of debts. Correspondingly, most countries ban private money. In the United States, for example, issuing private paper currencies or minting metal coins intended for use as currency is illegal under 18 U.S. Code § 486, highlighting the government's monopoly on legal tender:

> Whoever, except as authorized by law, makes or utters or passes, or attempts to utter or pass, any coins of gold or silver or other metal, or alloys of metals, intended for use as current money, whether in the resemblance of coins of the United States or of foreign countries, or of original design, shall be *fined* under this title 1 or *imprisoned* not more than five years, or both.

Such laws effectively create monopolistic control over money that nearly all governments around the world today enjoy. This reality is so ingrained in our collective consciousness that people scarcely give it a second thought. Analyzing monetary history and thinking in first principles would reveal, however, that this is not a given. On the contrary, it has been a topic of great debate over centuries.

As discussed in chapter 2, Carl Menger in 1892 challenged the then-prevailing notion that money should be a creation of the state or the result of a legislative act. Instead, he argued that money emerged naturally and spontaneously through the self-interested actions of people. This process occurred as individuals sought a more efficient means of exchange than barter. He noted that no government compulsion was necessary to effect the transition from a condition of barter to a money-economy. To better evaluate Menger's narrative, it would be helpful to embark on a brief journey through monetary history to understand the events that led to the state's capture of money.

A (BRIEF) HISTORY OF MONEY

The history of money is intertwined with the evolutionary path of human civilizations. As societies evolved over thousands of years, they naturally sought more and more efficient ways to engage in trade and commercial activities. Consequently, money has had a huge influence on cultures and civilizations throughout history. A study of the history of money is thus a study of the history of civilizations.

1. From Barter to Gold

Before the advent of money, early human societies are said to have relied on the barter system for trade.[1] This direct exchange of goods and services required a double coincidence of wants,[2] making it efficient only within small, insular communities. As civilizations grew and diversified in the Neolithic period and beyond, the limitations of barter became evident, spurring the search for more flexible means of trade.

Every prudent man in every period of society, after the first establishment of the division of labour, must naturally have endeavoured to manage his affairs in such a manner, as to have at all times by him, besides the peculiar produce of his own industry, a certain quantity of some one commodity or other, such as he imagined few people would be likely to refuse in exchange for the produce of their industry.

—Adam Smith

With the domestication of cattle and cultivation of crops from 9,000 to 3,000 BCE, cattle and crops began to be used as money. They may have been the first forms of commodity money. The Sumerians in Mesopotamia may have been the first to use goods like barley as a form of money around 3,000 BCE.[3] Other civilizations followed suit; some, like the Incas in Peru, may have survived without money altogether. In ancient Rome, salt became a valued commodity money representing its utility in food preservation and seasoning. Shells and beads were used in many civilizations given their portability, durability, and aesthetic appeal. Cowrie shells were of particular importance as money in regions like China, Africa, and the Pacific Islands.

The perishability and inconsistency of items like grains and shells led to the use of metals, which provided a comparatively more durable, divisible, and portable form of money. Gold, silver, and copper emerged as preferred materials because of their malleability and intrinsic value. The Egyptians utilized gold bars of a set weight in trade.[4] A big breakthrough came from the Lydians in Anatolia around 700 BCE; they introduced the first minted coins.[5] Ancient Greek historian Herodotus (440 BCE), observed:

All the young women of Lydia prostitute themselves, by which they procure their marriage portion; this, with their persons, they afterwards dispose of, as they think proper . . .

. . . The manners and customs of the Lydians do not essentially vary from those of Greece, except in this prostitution of the young women. They are the first people on record who coined gold and silver into money, and traded in retail.[6]

According to Alexander Del Mar, it is possible, based on references to the Hindu epics, that coins were in use in India some hundreds of years earlier.[7]

This innovation provided nations and societies a standardized medium of exchange, significantly boosting trade efficiency and economic integration across regions.

With the advent of coins and their standardized issuance came arguably the first instance of monetary debasement. "Debasement" technically refers to the lowering of the value of a currency in real terms. In the case of coins, debasement involved the reduction of the amount of gold or silver that constituted the coin while keeping the face value of the coin constant. Under Emperor Nero around 60 CE, the Romans began debasing the currency by reducing the size of silver coins as well as their silver content. Through this process, the government was able to create more coins with the same amount of silver. Coin clipping was the act of shaving off a small portion of a coin to gradually accumulate quantities of the precious metal to make more coins. This practice became prevalent across Medieval Europe. In Britain, during the 1200s, it was estimated that most circulating coins had been reduced by as much as a third of their weight (this is not entirely attributable to governments—private citizens also engaged in clipping coins for their own enrichment). As a deterrent to rampant coin clipping, Isaac Newton, in his role as Master of the Royal Mint in 1699, introduced milling or reeding on the rims of coins that would be destroyed if the coins were clipped.

2. From Gold to Gold-Backed Paper

The transition from coins to paper money is a significant chapter in the history of money. The earliest known use of paper money may have been in China during the Tang Dynasty (618-907 AD).[8] In response to the cumbersome nature of transporting metal coins and gold bars over long distances, merchants began using paper notes as a promise for future payment in physical gold. During the subsequent Song Dynasty (960-1279 AD), the use of paper money became more widespread. The government issued the first true paper currency, known as *jiaozi*, around 1023 AD.[9] One of the main drivers of this shift may have been the shortage of copper for coinage. The government shifted first to iron coins and eventually to paper, due to its comparative ease of production.

The use of paper money spread throughout the Mongol Empire, including the Yuan Dynasty in China (1271-1368 AD).[10] Marco Polo famously documented the efficiency of the Mongol paper money system in his travels during the late thirteenth century. He marveled at the way Kublai Khan could move wealth across his vast empire using paper instead of precious metals:[11]

> All these pieces of paper are issued with as much solemnity and authority as if they were of pure gold or silver. On every piece a variety of officials, whose duty it is, have to write their names, and to put their seals. And when all is prepared duly, the chief officer, deputed by the Khan, dips in cinnabar the royal seal entrusted to him, and stamps it on the top of the piece of paper so that the form of the seal remains impressed upon it in vermilion; the money is then authentic. Any one forging it would be punished with death.[12]

In the Islamic world, particularly during the Abbasid Caliphate, promissory notes known as sakk were in use, and they were a precursor to paper money.[13] However, these were not as widely used as the paper currency in China.

Europe was relatively late to adopt paper money. The first European banknotes were issued in Sweden in 1661 by Stockholms Banco, a precursor to the Sveriges Riksbank, the central bank of Sweden.[14] The bank issued these notes as a promise against deposited coins. In 1694, the Bank of England was established and began issuing notes with a "promise to pay the bearer" a sum of money. These notes were initially handwritten and issued for the exact amount deposited. Over time, they became standardized and were printed in fixed denominations.[15]

After the establishment of the Bank of England in 1694, the evolution toward a formal gold standard had key milestones. In 1717, Isaac Newton set a price for gold that inadvertently established a de facto gold standard in Britain. In his book *A Treatise on Money*, John Maynard Keynes refers to this event: "Newton was a great scientist, but he was no financier, and his fixing of the guinea at 21 shillings and 6 pence in terms of gold, which undervalued silver, was the greatest mistake in his life, and led to the establishment of the gold standard."[16] Newton's "mistake," according to Keynes, was that setting the exchange rate of gold to silver at a certain level made silver coins more valuable as bullion than as currency, which led to silver coins being melted down and exported. This necessitated England's adoption of the gold standard.

The formalization of the gold standard in Britain took place in 1819 in the aftermath of the Napoleonic Wars. Thereafter, the idea of the gold standard started to take hold gradually across the developed world. Following the

Franco-Prussian War, Germany adopted the gold standard in 1871. The United States began its adoption in 1875.[17]

Adoption of the gold standard allowed paper money to be traded for its worth in gold, as mandated by the law of the land. In the United States, this period of adoption of the gold standard is known as the Gilded Age, an era when industrial output in the nation skyrocketed. The gold standard also operated in its purest form, with every piece of paper currency exchangeable for physical gold on demand. John D. Rockefeller, Thomas Edison, Andrew Carnegie, and J. P. Morgan created their famous monopolies, and the world watched as the United States emerged on the world stage as an economic powerhouse.[18]

Tying currencies to gold at a standardized rate produced a stable, worldwide exchange rate system. Trade and commerce boomed worldwide under this efficient new paradigm, with gold's portability and divisibility problems virtually eliminated by this ingenious invention of gold-backed paper. Because the money supply was correlated with the gold supply, inflation was usually kept in check. In 1914, fifty-nine countries used the gold standard. Backing a currency with gold signaled that a country was a serious player in the global economy.[19]

3. From Gold-Backed Paper to Just Paper

> Someone mentioned the philosopher's stone. To the surprise of all present, Law said he had discovered it. "I can tell you my secret," said the financier. "It is to make gold out of paper."
>
> —*John Law* by H. Montgomery Hyde[20]

Unfortunately, the rigidity of the gold standard brought challenges for governments (particularly the war-mongering ones). During World War I, the gold standard started to fall apart as nations sought more funds for war operations than they could have been supported from their gold supplies. As author Liaquat Ahmed observes in his Pulitzer Prize-winning book, *Lords of Finance*: "During World War I, the classical gold standard fell apart as European countries abandoned the standard to print money for war efforts. This abandonment marked the beginning of the end for the gold standard as it had been known."[21]

Many nations abandoned the gold standard during the war, and while some tried to resume its use in the interwar period, economic pressures and the Great Depression dictated otherwise. The gold standard was viewed as too financially constraining during the 1930s. Countries that dropped the gold standard—like Britain in 1931—appeared to bounce back from the depression faster than those that stayed on it.[22] In 1944, during World War II, the Allied nations gathered at Bretton Woods to design a new global monetary system. The U.S. dollar, pegged to gold, was established as the world's reserve currency, and other currencies were pegged to the dollar.

Pegging the U.S. dollar to gold did not sit very well with U.S. economic and foreign policies. With war raging in Vietnam and other extensive military expenditures overseas, the United States experienced persistent balance of payments deficits. This situation was exacerbated during the 1960s with the immense outflow of money from the country as U.S. dollars began to be held by nations and institutions abroad. Concerns grew in the international community about the U.S. capacity to redeem all these dollars for gold at the fixed exchange rate. With ballooning expenditures overseas as well as domestically, and with no corresponding tax increases, the U.S. economy began experiencing growing inflation in the late 1960s.[23] While the inflationary pressures devalued the dollar domestically, on the international stage, it was still pegged to gold at a fixed rate. This made the gold standard increasingly untenable for the U.S. economy.

In response to these developments, several European countries, notably France under Charles de Gaulle, openly criticized the U.S. dollar's privileged position. They began to demand gold for their dollar reserves.[24] It was quickly becoming clear that the economic risks of exposure to the U.S. dollar were unsustainable. In 1971, foreign central banks and governments held $64 billion worth of claims on just $10 billion of gold still held by the United States.[25] That August, French President Georges Pompidou sent a battleship to New York to collect his nation's gold holdings from the Federal Reserve.[26] The British also asked the United States to prepare $3 billion worth of gold held in Fort Knox for withdrawal.[27] Switzerland withdrew $50 million in bullion, and other foreign governments and investors added to the chorus, leading to a rapid depletion of U.S. gold reserves. Speculation mounted against the dollar, leading to a crisis of confidence in the U.S. ability to maintain the gold standard.

On August 15, 1971, in a historic move and in the face of the imminent threat of a collapsing U.S. economy, President Richard Nixon, advised by his Treasury Secretary John Connally and Federal Reserve Chair Arthur Burns, decided to suspend the convertibility of the dollar into gold. This action effectively ended the Bretton Woods system after only twenty-seven years of its existence. And it marked the transition to a regime of floating exchange rates that we see today. This momentous event in monetary history is known as the Nixon Shock. It marked the global transition to the fiat currency system that is still in place today, where the value of money is not backed by gold or any other physical commodity but rather simply by the faith and credit of the government that issues it.[28]

Under the gold standard, as you would expect from a piece of paper that is contractually backed by something of real value, U.S. dollar notes bore the words "The United States of America will pay to the bearer on demand." In 1963, these words were eliminated from all newly issued currency notes. In 1968, as a precursor to the Nixon Shock, redemption of pre-1963 notes for gold or silver officially ended.

> The abandonment of the gold standard made it clear that the value of a currency
> would henceforth be determined by the actions and policies of governments.
> The dollar, once anchored by gold, now floated on the confidence in American
> economic policy.
>
> —John Kenneth Galbraith

So, in a nutshell, thousands of years of monetary history may be summarized as humanity's progression from barter, to physical commodities, to paper backed by physical commodities, to paper partially backed by physical commodities, to just paper backed by nothing at all. What the world considers to be "money" is now issued by governments at will, in either paper or electronic form, with nothing backing it beyond the *perception* of the relevant government's economic policies and credibility on the world stage and in foreign exchange markets.

Monetary Monopoly

It is interesting to observe that while governments slowly but surely lifted all real-world constraints on their ability to issue limitless money, they also made sure to do something else: they eliminated all competition in the monetary department. As discussed earlier, this was achieved by virtue of the government retaining the sole power and authority to designate a certain money as legal tender. Today, in almost all nations around the world, governments have the exclusive power to pass laws regarding what constitutes legal tender. Violation of these laws is typically a criminal offence punishable by fines, imprisonment, or worse.

The notion of the state deeming a certain money or commodity to be legal tender may date back thousands of years. The precise moment in history when this initiative began is difficult to pinpoint. Some say it happened in the ancient city of Babylon, four thousand years ago, where the Code of Hammurabi enforced grain as legal tender:[29] "If a wine-seller gives 60 KA of drink on credit, at the time of harvest she shall receive 50 KA of grain."[30]

Several historical examples show that private money coexisted alongside state-issued money. For example, in colonial America, private banks, merchants, and even individuals issued their own forms of currency, known as bills of credit. This form of private money often circulated alongside official British, Spanish, and French currencies.[31] In his essay, "Unenumerated," Nick Szabo provides examples of nongovernment money through history, including private bank notes, copper coins issued by private merchants, and personal jewelry.[32]

In modern history, the first formal codification of legal tender laws giving the state exclusive authority over money may have occurred in the nineteenth century, when both the United States and the United Kingdom were grappling with financing wars and stabilizing their economies. It became clear to these governments that assuming full and exclusive control of the issuance of their nation's currency would be an invaluable tool in negotiating the different crises they were facing. They thus formalized the concept of legal tender through a series of legislative acts.

In the United Kingdom, the Bank Charter Act of 1844 banned private money and centralized the issuance of currency in the central bank. The Bank of England was given a monopoly over the issuance of banknotes in England and Wales. Until that point, commercial banks in the United Kingdom were allowed to issue their own banknotes. The act outlawed such activities. Private banknotes disappeared as a result, leaving the Bank of England with a monopoly over the issuance of new banknotes in England.

In the United States, Abraham Lincoln became president in 1860, and the U.S. Civil War began shortly after. The cost of the war had been hugely underestimated. In 1862, given the emergency of the ongoing war, the government proposed the Legal Tender Act to authorize the issuance of unbacked paper notes as legal tender. This caused tremendous controversy in Congress because until that point, the Constitution had been interpreted as not granting the government the power to issue a paper currency.[33] However, the bill was presented as an emergency wartime measure: Representative Elbridge G. Spaulding, who drafted the bill, stated, "These are extraordinary times, and extraordinary measures must be resorted to in order to save our Government, and preserve our nationality."[34]

The reverse of the notes were printed with green ink, which gave them the name "greenbacks." Most importantly, greenbacks were not backed by gold.[35] It is said that when Lincoln's cabinet asked if they should put "In God We Trust" on notes (as was engraved on U.S. coins), he responded in jest: "If you are going to put a legend on the greenbacks, I would suggest that of Peter and Paul, 'Silver and gold I have none, but such as I have I give to thee.'" This was the first time the U.S. government issued currency that was explicitly designated as legal tender. It marked the beginning of centralized currency issuance in the country. In 1913, the complete centralization of monetary policy came with the creation of the Federal Reserve as the central bank of the United States. It was vested with exclusive control over the country's monetary policy and the ability to issue Federal Reserve notes, which became the exclusive form of legal tender in the United States.

By defining legal tender and banning the private issuance of money, nations around the world effectively gained a monopoly over money and monetary policy. It was nothing short of a gradual, unassailable, and absolute coup d'état. In hindsight, it might appear that it was all somehow premeditated—a grand coordinated scheme by governments to seize control of money. But in reality, politicians, central bankers, and government bureaucrats are typically just regular people reacting to circumstances and playing the hand they are dealt. Ironically, it would be giving past governments too much credit to suggest that they masterminded a multidecade or multicentury plan to capture monetary policy. Rather than seeking to attribute blame, the above analysis is more useful in assessing historical events from first principles and understanding their underlying incentives. This may help to avoid similar pitfalls in the future.

MANIPULATION OF MONEY

> I don't believe we shall ever have a good money again before we take the thing out
> of the hands of government, that is, we can't take them violently out of the hands
> of government, all we can do is by some sly roundabout way introduce something
> that they can't stop.
>
> —Friedrich Hayek, 1984

Friedrich Hayek's quote is truly iconic to bitcoin. It describes uncannily what many believe to be bitcoin's ultimate purpose. That is, bitcoin perfectly fits the description of a "sly roundabout way."

As discussed in chapter 2, the state's dominion over the issuance of money is the specific problem that Satoshi set out to solve in the first place. This is clear from his writings as well as many references to Order 6102 in the design of the bitcoin protocol. The very first bitcoin block that was mined famously included a message containing a reference to a newspaper headline: "*The Times* 03/Jan/2009 Chancellor on brink of second bailout for banks." Satoshi was highlighting the state's intervention into the operation of free markets through selective and preferential treatment of banks. In February 2009, Satoshi commented on the BitcoinTalk forum (quoted earlier): "The root problem with conventional currency is all the trust that's required to make it work. The central bank must be trusted not to debase the currency, but the history of fiat currencies is full of breaches of that trust."[36]

The concept of debasing the currency to which Satoshi was referring is the ability of central banks to increase the money supply in the economy by expanding their balance sheets. When a central bank purchases an asset (e.g., a government bond, mortgage-backed security, or, in some instances, even public equity securities) and adds it to its balance sheet, it effectively creates new money used for the purchase. This money is usually (but not always) issued by crediting the reserve accounts of banks with the requisite purchase amount. This is effectively "new money" in the economy in the form of electronic deposits. The result is that banks have more reserves, and with more reserves, they can infuse more money into the economy through their lending operations. This process is referred to as quantitative easing (QE).

Although economists differ on this point, history shows rather undeniably (see chapter 9) that this expansion of the money supply results in a reduction in the purchasing power of the currency over time. This is what Satoshi was referring to as "debasing the currency" through the artificial and centrally controlled actions of a handful of unelected central bank officials. He was also expressing his concerns over bailouts of banks that are orchestrated by the government. This was very topical at the time in 2009 when governments around the world were taking unprecedented steps to prop up failing banks and financial institutions (which they determined to be systemically important in their discretion) through various means of financial support. Satoshi was alluding to the risks inherent in this practice of picking winners and losers via monetary policy and bailouts because it distorts the free-market economy.

Monetary expansion is only one of the measures that central banks have at their disposal for tinkering with the free market. They have several other powers to prop up a failing financial system:[37]

1. Interest rates: Lowering interest rates reduces borrowing costs for banks, companies, and individuals. If money were a commodity, its price would be its interest rate. By unilaterally altering this interest rate, central banks effectively manipulate the value of money.

2. Forward guidance: This involves the communication of the future direction of monetary policy to the market. It affects the value of money today by defining steps to be taken in the future with respect to interest rates.

3. Liquidity operations: To ensure that banks have adequate liquidity to meet their obligations to customers and financial counterparties, central banks might provide them temporary loans.

4. Capital injections: In severe crises, central banks or governments may inject money directly into banks and financial institutions to stabilize the financial system by boosting market confidence and deterring a run on the banks.

5. Yield curve control: This central bank strategy has the goal of controlling interest rates of government bonds of varying maturities. The central bank may achieve this by pledging to buy or sell as many bonds as needed to maintain the desired yield on the bonds. This in turn affects lending rates for all corresponding maturities in the economy.

The key issue, however, is that all the above artificial measures are departures from the sanctity of free-market economics. And such departures typically have unintended consequences.

Death of the Free Market

Free markets are driven by economic fundamentals. Prudent risk management is rewarded over time, and reckless risk-taking is punished. The process of death and renewal is a necessary part of the economic cycle. When market participants and the financial system are artificially propped up, however, it creates perverse incentives.

The antithesis of the free market is an environment wherein the pulse of the market beats in tandem with the actions of central banks rather than underlying economic fundamentals. Investment decisions are made based on one's expectations of how politicians and unelected bureaucrats will adjust the value of the money in the future. This Pavlovian conditioning was accentuated in the aftermath of the COVID-19 pandemic. In response to the total economic shutdown and disruption of global supply chains, central banks around the world instituted unprecedented QE measures by slashing interest rates to zero or near zero and exponentially increasing the money supply. In response, stock markets hit record highs, which was totally disconnected from underlying economic realities. This environment continued even after the pandemic. As far as the stock markets were concerned, it became an accepted principle that good news is bad news, and vice versa:

Stocks Post Broad Losses After Strong Economic Data.[38]

—*Wall Street Journal*, July 7, 2023

Markets today accept such headlines without any sense of irony—as if it were completely natural that strong economic data would cause broad losses in the stock markets! The underlying reason for the counterintuitive scenario, of course, is the fact that the stock market anticipates that bad economic data might result in the Federal Reserve easing monetary policy, which will in turn push up stock prices, while the opposite data would have the opposite effect. As Milton Friedman observed, "The government solution to a problem is usually as bad as the problem and very often makes the problem worse."[39]

What are the unintended consequences that might result from this collapse of free-market economics? Systemic risk resulting from moral hazard is one serious consequence.[40] The term "moral hazard" refers to the scenario where individuals or institutions take excessive risks in the knowledge that if things go wrong, they will be rescued anyway, regardless. "Heads, I win. Tails, you lose." Taxpaying citizens are the ones who lose in that coin toss. The concept of "too big to fail" that evolved out of the 2008 global financial crisis encapsulated this risk. Knowing that an institution is too big to fail, and therefore will be bailed out come what may, might encourage excessive risk-taking rather than prudent risk management.

The practice of maintaining low interest rates for extended periods of time (which was the case for well over a decade until significant hikes in 2022 to combat skyrocketing inflation rates) encourages banks, companies, and people to take on more risk than they would under normal circumstances.[41] Investors in search of higher returns are forced to move further and further out in the risk spectrum. This in turn fuels asset bubbles, dooming the system to inevitable collapse and corresponding central bank rescue measures, to repeat the cycle again.

The death of the free market at the hands of QE also makes price discovery difficult.[42] QE skews asset prices and market signals, making it nearly impossible to assess the fundamental value of investments, particularly riskier ones. An artificially low "risk-free rate" set by the Federal Reserve underlies all asset valuations. The lower the risk-free rate, the higher the valuation, encouraging further risk-taking. Investors face the impossible task of accurately evaluating investment risks, resulting in the misallocation of capital across the economy.

A critical implication of distorting the free market, most relevant to the discussion in this book, is inflation and currency debasement. Over the long term, aggressive monetary easing and monetary expansion can lead to inflationary pressures, eroding the purchasing power of the currency. While inflation may remain contained in the short to medium term, especially in a low-demand environment, persistent QE has been shown to cause inflation over time. This subject is analyzed in detail in chapter 9.

Systemic risk is embedded in the centralization of monetary control because it diverges from free-market economics. We live in a rather strange world where the health of the global economy and the value of people's savings are effectively determined by decisions made by a handful of bureaucrats—seven governors of the Federal Reserve[43] to be exact, rather than being the result of countless individual decisions made in a truly free market.[44] This distorts investment incentives away from long-term productivity and toward short-term speculation about what decisions these bureaucrats might make. This brings us back to the conceptual framing of this chapter: the economic justification for the separation of money and state. Chapter 9 will delve deeper into these arguments and further explain why our monetary system is broken.

CHAPTER 9

Inflation

The Hidden Tax

I do not think it is an exaggeration to say history is largely a history of inflation, usually inflations engineered by governments for the gain of governments.

—Friedrich Hayek

Inflation is the rate of increase in prices over a given period of time. It is typically a broad measure, such as the overall increase in prices or the increase in the cost of living in a country. The practical consequence of inflation is the erosion in the purchasing power of money. In other words, each unit of your money buys fewer goods and services over time. Inflation may be the result of several factors, including rising production costs; increasing demand; and, as we shall discuss in this chapter, an increase in the money supply.

The most widely used measure of inflation is the Consumer Price Index (CPI). To measure the average consumer's cost of living, government agencies conduct household surveys to identify a basket of commonly purchased items. They then track, over time, the cost of purchasing this basket of goods. Housing, food, clothes, health care, transportation, and so on, constitute the consumer basket in the United States. The cost of this basket at a given time expressed relative to a base year is the CPI, and the percentage change in the CPI over a certain period is consumer price inflation. For example, if the base year CPI is 100 and the current CPI is 110, inflation is 10 percent over the period.

CPI is only one manifestation of inflation. Asset price inflation is the rise in the value of financial and capital assets such as stocks, real estate, and certain commodities. Unlike CPI, asset price inflation affects portfolios of wealth and investment. CPI affects consumers with regard to their daily cost of living, while asset price inflation affects wealth and savings and is a major contributor toward wealth inequality. Those who own appreciating assets may see their wealth grow, while those without such assets may experience a declining ability to purchase and own such appreciating assets in their lifetimes.

How do central banks impact inflation? In the United States, the Federal Reserve's statutory mandate, as described in the 1977 amendment to the Federal Reserve Act, is to "promote effectively the goals of maximum employment, stable prices, and moderate long-term interest rates." Inflation, in particular, CPI inflation, is therefore a primary focus of the Federal Reserve. Other central banks around the world have largely similar mandates—the key focus being inflation. To meet this mandate, central banks use monetary policy to pull the different levers available to them. These levers include, in particular, interest rates and the quantum of money supply in the economy (as discussed in chapter 8).

Like many other central banks, the Federal Reserve is ostensibly an independent government agency. However, it is ultimately accountable to the public and to Congress. The chair and other staff testify before Congress, and the board submits extensive reports on its plans for monetary policy twice a year. It also makes public its independently audited financial statements along with minutes from its meetings. It would therefore be rather naïve to hold the view that central banks operate entirely independently, free from political pressures. Central bank actions around the world, especially in times of crisis, have been highly politicized.

This politicization manifests in many ways. As Joseph Salerno of the Cato Institute articulated in a 1982 policy paper, governments have an inherent incentive to use inflation as a means to meet political ends. He argued that the government (via the central bank) may inflate the currency because it allows them to fund their activities covertly compared to raising taxes, which is often unpopular and can provoke public unrest.[1] Inflation is often described by economists as a "hidden tax" because, in the words of Nobel laureate Milton Friedman, it represents "taxation without legislation." In other words, it reduces the savings of the citizenry without explicit legislation to that effect.[2]

By diminishing the purchasing power per unit of a currency, inflation silently operates akin to an implicit tax on people's wealth and income. Where the government has mounting debt obligations (denominated in its own currency, as is the case with the United States), devaluing its currency helps reduce its debt burden. As the Federal Reserve Bank of St. Louis notes on its website, "an increase in the price level [via currency devaluation] directly reduces the real value of government debt." Inflation increases gross domestic product (GDP) in nominal terms, thereby reducing the debt-to-GDP ratio. Through this method, the government reduces the real value of its own debt, paying back creditors with money that is worth less than it was at the time of borrowing. This is effectively a covert transfer of wealth from holders of the currency or of debt instruments (that pay out in the said currency) to the government. It indirectly operates as a tax on the holders of its currency and of its debt.

Money Supply

As discussed, central banks use several tools to manage inflation and influence economic activity, including adjusting interest rates (to either encourage borrowing and spending or to cool down spending) and conducting open market buying or selling of government securities and other assets, which has the effect of increasing the money supply in the economy. There is a long-standing debate in economic circles about whether the supply of money has an impact on inflation. For example, at a congressional hearing in 2021, Federal Reserve Chair Jerome Powell quipped: "When you and I studied economics a million years ago, M2 and monetary aggregates seemed to have a relationship to economic growth . . . Right now . . . M2 . . . does not really have important implications. It is something we have to unlearn I guess."[3]

Sadly, his self-assurance was remarkably short-lived. Following an unprecedented expansion of the money supply in 2020, a few months following his comments, CPI rose 7.0 percent year-over-year, marking the highest increase since 1982, peaking at 9.1 percent in June 2022, levels not seen since 1981. Figure 9.1 depicts a significant correlation between the increase in the money supply in the economy and inflation (CPI and asset price inflation). It should be acknowledged that correlation does not always imply causation. However, it should also be acknowledged that sometimes the correlation (as shown in the chart) is so strong and apparent that it is the most compelling explanation available. Even if it is not definitive proof, the correlation can be a critical indicator and the best evidence available to guide one's understanding.

Since the abandonment of the gold standard in 1971, there has been a marked increase in the money supply and monetary debasement globally. In 1971, money supply in the United States (M2, which is a broad measure of money

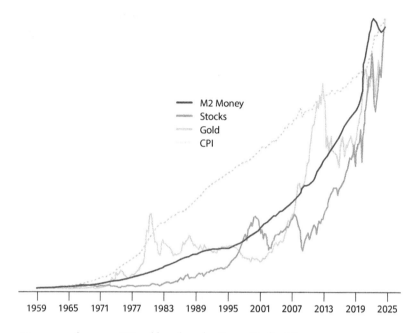

9.1 Money supply versus CPI, gold, and stocks. *Source*: TradingView.

that includes cash, checking deposits, savings deposits, small time deposits, and retail money market mutual funds) was approximately $700 billion.[4] The money supply in the United States as of this writing stands at over $20 trillion.[5] That is a thirtyfold increase since the country abandoned the gold standard. Since the global financial crisis in 2008 alone, the Federal Reserve's balance sheet has expanded from less than $1 trillion to $7.2 trillion in 2024, after peaking at almost $9 trillion in 2022.[6]

Given the trajectory of these exponential increases, it seems likely that anyone reading this chapter a few years from today will look back at these figures as representing the "good old days" before things *really* got out of hand. In his 1984 essay, Milton Friedman expressed his frustration about the Federal Reserve's unchecked powers over monetary expansion:

> I have found that few things are harder even for knowledgeable non-experts to accept than the proposition that 12 (or 19) people sitting around a table in Washington, subject to neither election or dismissal nor close administrative or political control, have the power to determine the quantity of money.

That power is too important, too pervasive to be exercised by a few people, however public-spirited.

If Friedman were alive today, he might well reminisce about the 1980s, when M2 was a mere $2 trillion—a rather quaint figure compared to today's $20 trillion. He might even find it amusing how little power, by comparison, central bankers appeared to wield when he wrote the essay.

Purchasing Power

According to the United States Bureau of Labor Statistics, $1 in 1971 had the same buying power as approximately $6 today. There has been significant inflation in asset prices, such as the stock market, with the S&P 500 index rising from 100 points in 1971 to over 5,000 points in 2024. Real estate prices have also seen considerable increases, with the median home price in the United States increasing from approximately $25,000 in 1971 to over $300,000 today. Figure 9.2 shows the precipitous decline of the purchasing power of the U.S. dollar over the last century.

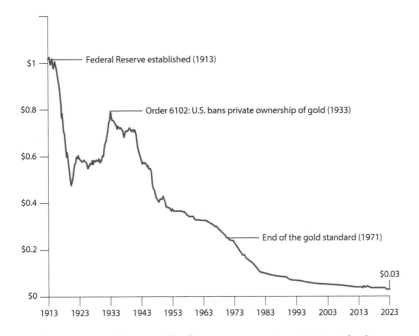

9.2 Purchasing power of the U.S. dollar from 1913 to 2023. *Source:* FRED, Federal Reserve Bank of St. Louis.

In addition to its impact on purchasing power, inflation redistributes income and wealth. Debtors benefit from inflation because the real value of their debts diminishes over time; creditors suffer a loss in real wealth as a result. Inflation thus exacerbates wealth disparities by favoring those with debt obligations (who may use the capital to make risk investments, causing asset bubbles) at the expense of savers and lenders. If your savings held in cash and debt instruments do not grow in value at the same rate as inflation, you are losing money. These effects are disproportionately felt by older savers and retirees. It diminishes the value of the wealth they accumulated over an entire lifetime of hard work and prudent saving in the hope of enjoying a comfortable retirement. They may find their savings increasingly inadequate to maintain their standard of living. This erosion of savings thus disproportionately burdens vulnerable segments of the population.

Hyperinflation

This phenomenon of central banks having an impact on the value of money through monetary policy is by no means unique to the United States. It is a global phenomenon that has been showcased across numerous economic crises since the very inception of the idea that monetary policy should be centralized in the hands of a few central bank bureaucrats. Several nations have experienced and continue to experience the adverse effects of such policies, affecting societies at various scales.

Venezuela's currency instability began in the 1980s and continues to this day. In 2018, inflation exceeded 1,000,000 percent and, in 2019, the International Monetary Fund (IMF) estimated that its inflation rate had reached 10,000,000 percent. Many economists attribute the country's hyperinflation to excessive money printing and deficit spending. When Nicolas Maduro first took office as president in 2013, the inflation rate stood at below 30 percent. During his presidency, the Central Bank of Venezuela drastically accelerated the increase in the money supply, taking the economy eventually into hyperinflation.

Zimbabwe's hyperinflation began in 2007. At its peak, the country's rate of inflation hit 80 billion percent month to month.[7] In 2009, the country's central bank stopped printing its currency, and currencies from other countries were used. In 2019, a new Zimbabwe dollar was introduced. The same year, the inflation rate of the new currency reached 175 percent. In 2020, inflation exceeded 700 percent. Experts attribute the main reason for hyperinflation in

Zimbabwe to the indiscriminate increase in the money supply in response to rising national debt.

Argentina, a Group of 20 (G20) nation with a population of over 46 million, experienced a significant crisis in 1989, with inflation reaching 20,000 percent at one point and then again in 2001, leading to a debt default.[8] In 2023, inflation rates exceeded 200 percent, and they are well over 100 percent in 2024. Perpetual budget deficits have led to the government printing money at an ever-increasing pace, which is said to have been the main cause of these hyperinflationary episodes.

Just over the last forty years, with the world on a fiat standard, Brazil, Argentina, Yugoslavia, Zimbabwe, Venezuela, Poland, Kazakhstan, Peru, Belarus, Bulgaria, Ukraine, Lebanon, Israel, Mexico, Vietnam, Ecuador, Costa Rica, Turkey, and several others have experienced hyperinflation or near-hyperinflation.[9] These countries represent almost 1 billion people whose savings have been obliterated and their lives plunged into chaos and poverty over a relatively short time. These examples from around the world illustrate that the implications of central bank actions for inflation, currency debasement, and market distortions are a global phenomenon. The Weimar Republic's hyperinflation episode in the early 1920s stands as a stark historical reminder of the havoc that hyperinflation can wreak on the lives of populations. In the aftermath of World War I, Germany faced enormous reparations payments alongside a struggling economy. To meet its obligations and stimulate economic activity, the Weimar government began to print money at an unprecedented rate. In 1922, 63 percent of Germany's total government spending was financed through money printing.[10] These steps led to hyperinflation. At its peak, prices doubled every few hours, rendering the German mark nearly worthless. In 1914, a U.S. dollar was worth 4.2 marks; in November 1923, a dollar equaled 630 billion marks. A loaf of bread cost 140 billion marks.[11] Savings were obliterated, leading to widespread poverty and social unrest, and eventually to World War II.

WAR FINANCE

Throughout history, nations have abandoned the gold standard in favor of fiat money to prolong expensive warfare. The motivation is quite clear—it allows governments to create money at will, primarily through central banks, to finance war efforts without immediate financial constraints. For example, during the

Napoleonic Wars, Britain suspended the gold standard in 1797 because of the financial pressures from the war. This allowed the Bank of England to issue more paper money to finance the war effort without the constraint of gold reserves. During World War I, many countries abandoned the gold standard to print more money to finance the war. Britain, Germany, France, and the United States all altered or suspended the gold standard during this time. In the United States, the Federal Reserve Act of 1913 allowed for a more elastic money supply, and the Gold Reserve Act of 1934 further detached the dollar from gold. During World War II, financial demands led to the de facto suspension of the gold standard in many countries as governments resorted to printing money to meet their massive military expenditures. And during the Vietnam War, skyrocketing expenses led President Nixon to end the direct convertibility of the U.S. dollar to gold in 1971.

Many academics and monetary historians have commented on the undeniable link between untethered fiat money and so-called forever wars. For example, as economist Saifedean Ammous explains in the context of World War I:

> Had European nations remained on the gold standard, or had the people of Europe held their own gold in their own hands, forcing governments to resort to taxation instead of inflation, history might have been different. It is likely that World War I would have been settled militarily within a few months of conflict, as one of the allied factions started running out of financing and faced difficulties in extracting wealth from a population that was not willing to part with its wealth to defend their regime's survival. But with the suspension of the gold standard, running out of financing was not enough to end the war; a sovereign had to run out of its people's accumulated wealth expropriated through inflation.[12]

Ammous goes on to point out that, while various governments involved in World War I were funding their war efforts through inflationary money printing, they began to witness significant declines in the value of their currencies. This is illustrated through a comparison of the exchange rates of the countries engaging in such inflationary policies with the Swiss franc, which was still on the gold standard at the time. Table 9.1 shows the change in the value of each national currency against the Swiss franc during World War I.[13]

TABLE 9.1 Change in national currency values compared to the
Swiss franc for various countries during World War I

Nation	Change in Currency Value (%)
Austria	–69
Germany	–49
Italy	–23
France	–9
United Kingdom	–7
United States	–4

The financing of warfare by governments through history offers a glaring reminder of the covert power of inflationary monetary expansion. As author Liaquat Ahmed observes, during World War I, currency in circulation doubled in Britain; tripled in France; and quadrupled in Germany, where this was particularly disastrous. Germany spent $47 billion on the war but raised only 10 percent of that amount from taxes.[14]

Inflation subtly diminishes the value of currency without the immediate notice of its holders, in contrast to direct taxation, which is a conspicuous charge on citizens' earnings. Whereas taxation is a transparent extraction of wealth usually subject to potentially contentious debate, inflation silently erodes purchasing power, often circumventing the need for democratic consensus.

> It's especially hard to sell to the public the idea that the government needs to raise
> domestic taxes to go fight a war between different foreign nations in foreign lands
> for some sort of vague national strategic advantage.[15]
>
> —Lyn Alden

This insidious nature of inflation serves as a potent tool for governments to finance extended military campaigns—forever wars—without facing immediate backlash from the electorate. The immediate burden of war costs is obscured because the government does not have to levy taxes directly, which could incite public opposition and act as a natural check on prolonged conflict. Inflation thus masks the true cost of war.

Britain's War Bond Cover-Up

In 1914, as World War I commenced, Britain sought to finance its military efforts by issuing war bonds. These bonds promised higher interest rates compared to standard government bonds and were met with widespread media acclaim, reported as being in high demand by a patriotically fervent public. However, this narrative of successful fundraising was later revealed to be an elaborate lie.[16]

A century later, in 2017, archival research exposed this as a deliberate cover-up: the historical recount, shared on the *Bank Underground* blog, detailed that capital inflows from the public were in reality, no more than a trickle.[17] This disclosure was presented in a document titled "Your Country Needs Funds: The Extraordinary Story of Britain's Early Efforts to Finance the First World War," which highlighted the truth behind the so-called amazing result of the bond issuance.[18]

It became evident that the funding gap was filled not by widespread public investment but rather through monetary expansion by the Bank of England itself. The central bank essentially printed the money to purchase a substantial portion of the war bonds and falsely claimed that the funds had generously poured in from the patriotic British masses. In the ensuing years, the result of this action was considerable inflationary pressure as both the broad money supply and consumer price index more than doubled within five years, destroying the public's savings and purchasing power.

The government's approach extended beyond monetary policy. In a bid to control inflation and direct resources toward the war effort, it imposed strict controls on industry, property, and trade. Private industries were coerced into producing war goods, rents were frozen to curb inflation, and foreign securities owned by British citizens were confiscated. In January 1915, the British Treasury banned the issuance and purchase of new private securities, a move that reflected a drastic shift from free-market principles to centralized control.[19]

The *Financial Times*, which in 1914 had helped spread the false news that the war bonds were oversubscribed, issued a correction in 2017 in response to the newly uncovered information:

> Clarification: On 23 November 1914, a piece published in the *Financial Times* claimed
> the UK government's War Loan was "oversubscribed," with applications "pouring in."

The item described this as an "amazing result" that "proves how strong is the financial position of the British nation." We are now happy to make clear that none of the above was true.[20]

THE DEBT DEATH SPIRAL

A debt spiral occurs when a person, company, or country borrows money to cover existing debt, leading to a cycle of increasing debt and interest payments that becomes unsustainable. New loans are taken out to pay off old ones, and the growing interest on the total debt acts like a quicksand, dragging the borrower deeper and deeper into insolvency with every attempt to escape. For instance, Greece experienced a debt spiral during the European debt crisis in the 2010s. The country borrowed heavily to fund public spending and then had to borrow more to pay off the skyrocketing interest. This led to severe economic and social collapse.

If something cannot go on forever, it will stop.

—Herbert Stein

The United States is currently navigating a precarious financial situation, marked by a spiraling debt crisis exacerbated by substantial interest service expenses and looming Social Security obligations. This situation has been decades in the making. Figure 9.3 traces U.S. government debt since World War II. There is an unmistakable uptick in the 1970s in the aftermath of the 1971 Nixon Shock (discussed in chapter 8), which marked the birth of fiat and the abandonment of the gold standard. However, the trajectory began to skyrocket in 2021, and it appears to have reached escape velocity in the aftermath of the COVID-19 pandemic.

The background to this recent further acceleration in debt is the Federal Reserve's unprecedented monetary expansion during the COVID-19 pandemic. The Federal Reserve's balance sheet increased from $4.2 trillion at the beginning of 2020 to just under $9 trillion in 2022. This expansion was aimed at stabilizing financial markets and injecting liquidity into the markets and economy. As discussed earlier in this chapter, contrary to the expectation of the Federal Reserve and many Keynesian supporters of its loose monetary policies, inflation surged in the aftermath of these liquidity injections. CPI peaked at around

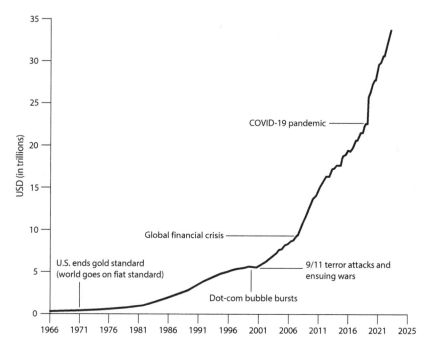

9.3 U.S. government debt, 1942 to 2024. *Source:* FRED, Federal Reserve Bank of St. Louis.

9 percent in June 2022, reflecting the highest inflation rates in several decades. Asset prices, including real estate, the stock markets, and cryptocurrencies, also experienced significant increases during this period.

Consistent with its historically reactionary policymaking, the Federal Reserve responded to this rising inflation by raising interest rates at an unprecedented pace to levels not seen in years. The idea is that, by raising the cost of borrowing (i.e., interest rates), economic activity is slowed, thus dampening inflation. On the flip side, however, rising interest rates correspondingly increase the cost of servicing new and existing debt, necessitating further borrowing, particularly for those heavily indebted—notably the U.S. government.

Given the current high interest rates and the federal government's continuous accumulation of approximately $2 trillion per year toward the national debt,[21] interest expenses are projected to skyrocket further. According to the Committee for a Responsible Federal Budget, the U.S. government's spending on net interest has surpassed both defense and Medicare expenditures. Interest expense in 2024 exceeds all the money spent on veterans, education, and transportation combined.[22]

This alarming trend reflects a significant increase from previous years, with net interest costs approximately doubling since 2020. According to Bank of America, U.S. debt is on track to reach $40 trillion by 2025.[23] This represents a *doubling* of the nation's debt burden over a period of just eight years ($20 trillion in 2017 to an expected $40 trillion by 2025). As of 2024, the debt is climbing at an astonishing rate of $1 trillion every one hundred days. Over a twenty-five-year span since 2000, this would represent a staggering 570 percent jump in the national debt.

The situation is further compounded by the impending surge in Social Security obligations as the United States faces demographic shifts with an aging population. In a 2023 interview, billionaire investor Stan Druckenmiller made a shocking observation: he noted that the headline U.S. debt figure ($35 trillion as of this writing and growing at an unprecedented rate) does not account for future entitlement payments. Accounting for the present value of that burden, the debt load is more than $200 trillion, he estimated.[24] The last sentence above perhaps deserves to be restated in bold:

Accounting for the present value of future entitlement payments, the United States debt load is more than $200 trillion.

As is abundantly clear from these statistics, the United States faces the undeniable risk of a debt spiral. Rising interest costs exacerbate deficits and debt. This continues the vicious spiral as the government is forced to pile on more debt. This cycle continues with the country's debt obligations taking up more and more of the federal budget. As entitlement obligations continue to skyrocket, the downward spiral further accelerates.

As Lyn Alden has observed, the Federal Reserve's strategy of raising interest rates to combat inflation, although aimed at tightening monetary conditions, paradoxically acts akin to quantitative easing.[25] A feedback loop develops, where rising debt levels lead to higher interest costs, necessitating more government borrowing. As the government repays these growing debt obligations, the money supply in the economy is projected to increase. This in turn contributes to higher inflation, potentially necessitating further interest rate hikes to cool inflation, thereby further increasing the debt load. The unstoppable spiral thus continues. The purported tightening policy inadvertently leads to an expansionary outcome. This is a glaring illustration of the complex dynamics between managed monetary policy and its unintended consequences.

The precarious fiscal and monetary situation in the United States is the 800 pound gorilla in the room (though perhaps the elephant in the room may be a more apt idiom accounting for size and seriousness). The implications of the situation extend far beyond the United States to the entire global economy and financial system. Yet the world seems largely ignorant of its inevitable consequences. The options available to the United States to tackle this situation are worryingly limited. Some commentators continue to call for fiscal cuts in the United States in order to curb the spiraling debt. However, a pragmatic analysis of this prospect demonstrates its infeasibility in the current sociopolitical environment. A Pew Research Center study from July 2023 reveals that only 4 percent of the U.S. population thinks the political system works very well. Trust in the federal government is among the lowest in nearly seven decades. In addition, 28 percent have unfavorable views of both major political parties. Cutting entitlements or government spending in this scenario is political suicide.[26] If anything, pressure is only increasing to expand social welfare programs and other government services rather than reduce them. The current environment is not unprecedented in history. Scottish historian and judge Alexander Fraser Tytler had some dire words of warning in the 1700s:

> A democracy cannot exist as a permanent form of government. It can only exist until the voters discover that they can vote themselves largesse from the public treasury. From that moment on, the majority always votes for the candidates promising the most benefits from the public treasury with the result that a democracy always collapses over loose fiscal policy, always followed by a dictatorship. The average age of the world's greatest civilizations has been 200 years. These nations have progressed through this sequence: From bondage to spiritual faith; From spiritual faith to great courage; From courage to liberty; From liberty to abundance; From abundance to selfishness; From selfishness to apathy; From apathy to dependence; From dependence back into bondage.

Putting aside cuts to entitlements, the government's other option is to cut defense spending. However, in the current geopolitical environment, which is characterized by U.S. involvement in the Russia-Ukraine and Israel-Palestine wars, tensions with Iran, and an ongoing arms race with China, it is quite clear that the United States is under pressure to sustain, or even increase, its defense spending. National security will always trump all other considerations. Thus, significant cuts in defense budgets are politically and strategically unpopular.

Faced with high debt levels and substantial fiscal obligations, the government faces a dilemma. Defaulting on the national debt is certainly not considered a feasible option because of the catastrophic economic, financial and reputational consequences that would ensue, including loss of confidence in U.S. debt securities, which would unquestionably trigger a global financial crisis of epic proportions. Therefore, the only viable option is to continue piling on debt in the unfolding of a classic debt spiral. But will the lenders that the United States has traditionally relied on continue to lend (i.e. purchase U.S. Treasuries (USTs))? As financial analyst Luke Gromen observes, "No one alive has ever seen a time where the 'risk free asset' underpinning the valuation of every other asset on the board—USTs—has risk."[27] Gromen notes that we may be witnessing the first global sovereign debt bubble in eighty to one hundred years. For over 120 years, this has been resolved via default restructuring or inflation (and hyperinflation, in some cases). Driven by perceptions of such risks coupled with recent geopolitical developments (see chapter 15), we are witnessing global central banks pivoting away from USTs in favor of the hard asset that the world is most familiar and comfortable with for historical reasons: gold.[28] Figures 9.4 and 9.5 illustrate the starkness of this trend.

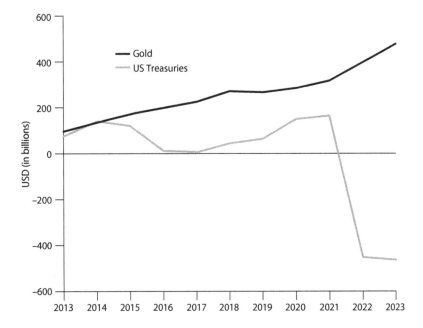

9.4 Central bank purchases of gold versus USTs. *Source*: United States Treasury, World Gold Council, FFTT, LLC.

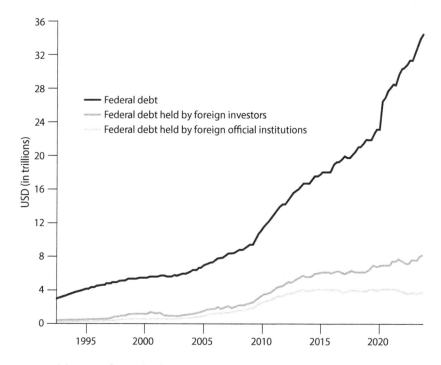

9.5 U.S. debt versus foreign holdings of U.S. debt. *Source:* FRED, Federal Reserve Bank of St. Louis.

As figure 9.5 illustrates, there is a clear lack of foreign appetite for the sky-rocketing borrowing needs of the United States. In this scenario, the primary long-term option for the government to fund its obligations is clear: the Federal Reserve's balance sheet (i.e., further monetary expansion).[29]

From a game theoretical standpoint, the decision to continue borrowing from the central bank to meet the government's obligations can be seen as the least bad option compared to the alternatives. The strategy may be chosen based on its outcome being less damaging than (1) the potential fallout from cutting entitlements, (2) real or perceived national security threats from cutting defense spending, and (3) an outright U.S. debt default. In this case, the decision-making process involves selecting the option that minimizes potential harm to the economy and political standing and also acknowledging the trade-offs and risks associated with increased monetary expansion, including inflation and devaluation of currency.

This analysis implies that, barring a significant shift in political willingness to embrace cuts in entitlements, a sudden decrease in geopolitical tensions that drastically reduces defense spending needs, or a sudden economic boom of unprecedented and unrealistic proportions, the United States may continue to rely on monetary expansion to manage its monetary and fiscal challenges. The normalization of this choice may begin with a shift in central banking and political narratives signaling acceptance of higher inflation rates as the new normal. Or perhaps it could be addressed more nefariously through changes in key methodologies for calculating CPI inflation, potentially portraying lower inflation than reality reflects.[30] Nevertheless, the end result—further currency debasement—remains the closest thing to a mathematical certainty as economic projections allow.

CONTRASTING ECONOMIC IDEOLOGIES

The post-1971 era of global fiat currencies has spurred significant discussions and debates on monetary policy and the schools of economic thought that either justify or criticize the prevailing monetary and fiscal situation in the United States and around the world. The centralization of monetary policy has always been a contentious issue going back over a century, and it has divided economists across various ideological lines.

On one side of the debate are the Keynesian economists, followers of British economist John Maynard Keynes, who is considered the founder of modern macroeconomics. In his influential work, *The General Theory of Employment, Interest, and Money* in 1936, Keynes advocated for the management of economic activity through government intervention.[31] His economic theory emerged in response to the Great Depression, with the backdrop of high and persistent unemployment. He challenged the classical view that economies are naturally self-correcting toward full employment. He advocated for active government intervention not just through fiscal policies (e.g., government spending and taxation) but also through monetary policy by lowering interest rates and increasing the money supply to stimulate borrowing and spending. While this approach did not constitute central planning in the way socialist or communist economies operate, the idea of government involvement to "manage" economic fluctuations was a significant departure from free-market principles. In a much-cited quote from his book, Keynes expressed his economic theory with remarkable cynicism:

> If the Treasury were to fill old bottles with banknotes, bury them at suitable depths
> in disused coal mines which are then filled up to the surface with town rubbish,

and leave it to private enterprise on well-tried principles of laissez-faire to dig the notes up again (the right to do so being obtained, of course, by tendering for leases of the note-bearing territory), there need be no more unemployment and, with the help of the repercussions, the real income of the community, and its capital wealth also, would probably become a good deal greater than it actually is.

His scenario is deliberately absurd to highlight the notion that the specific method of government spending is less important than the act of spending itself. He was proposing the idea that by simply injecting money into the economy, *even through obviously wasteful projects*, the government can create jobs and increase overall economic output. His thesis was that initial government spending leads to further economic activity as people spend their earnings, thus boosting aggregate demand and contributing to economic growth.

Keynesian economists believe that a troubled economy will continue struggling unless some form of government intervention drives customers to buy more goods and services. They focus on government spending to influence economic activity, believing that the solution to a recession is expansionary fiscal policy. Through government spending, they aim to increase consumer demand, thereby increasing inflation—which they view as a sign of a flourishing economy.

Today, Keynesian economists dominate global economic and monetary discourse, commanding an outsized influence. One of them is Paul Krugman, a 2008 Nobel laureate, well-known for his work on international economics, economic geography, and liquidity traps. A vocal proponent of Keynesian economics, he has discussed fiscal stimulus and monetary policy extensively in the context of economic recessions and crises. Joseph Stiglitz, also a Nobel Prize winner (2001), has been a strong advocate for government intervention in markets to promote economic stability, which also reflects Keynesian ideals. Lawrence Summers, a key figure in economic policy circles who has served in several high-profile roles in the U.S. government, writes and speaks extensively on issues related to economic stagnation and government intervention. Olivier Blanchard, former Chief Economist at the IMF, is known for advocating economic policies informed by Keynesian principles. And Janet Yellen, former Chair of the Federal Reserve and U.S. Secretary of the Treasury as of this writing, has often emphasized the importance of the government and central bank in stabilizing the economy. That is a substantial amount of firepower backing the Keynesian ideology and influencing global policymaking.

On the other side of the intellectual and philosophical divide are critics of Keynesian economics who have historically included economists subscribing to the Austrian School of Economics and monetarists like Milton Friedman. They have argued that excessive government intervention (particularly in the form of monetary expansion) can lead to long-term inflationary problems, distort market mechanisms, and encourage public- and private-sector debt.

Ludwig von Mises and Friedrich Hayek are associated with the Austrian School of Economics and have long been critical of central planning and the expansion of the money supply without the backing of tangible assets like gold.[32] Mises taught at the University of Vienna and New York University and published his renowned work *Human Action* in 1949. Hayek was an Austrian-British economist, philosopher, and 1970 Nobel laureate who had fought in World War I as a teenager and is best known for his highly influential books *The Road to Serfdom* (1944) and *The Constitution of Liberty* (1960). Both economists were advocates of free-market capitalism and staunch opponents of interventionism. They argued that government intervention in the economy could never reproduce the results of a free market. They believed that interventionist practices can lead to distortions in the economy, boom and bust cycles, and the erosion of savings because of inflation. They advocated for a more laissez-faire approach to economics, where the market is allowed to regulate itself with minimal government involvement. The notion of sound money—currency with a stable value that is not prone to debasement—was a centerpiece of their economic ideology.

A key insight of the Austrian School was to point out the impossibility of a central authority managing the complexity of market preferences and economic dynamics effectively.[33] Hayek famously criticized the hubris of policymakers who believe they can accurately predict and control economic outcomes. Upon receiving the Nobel Memorial Prize in Economic Sciences in 1974, Hayek delivered a seminal lecture titled "The Pretence of Knowledge" in which he noted: "I prefer true but imperfect knowledge, even if it leaves much undetermined and unpredictable, to a pretence of exact knowledge that is likely to be false. . . . To act on the belief that we possess the knowledge and the power which enable us to shape the processes of society entirely to our liking, knowledge which in fact we do not possess, is likely to make us do much harm."[34] In his work, *Individualism and Economic Order*, he expressed the sentiment more gravely: "The recognition of the insuperable limits to his knowledge ought indeed to teach the student of society a lesson of humility which should guard him against becoming an accomplice in men's fatal striving to control society—a striving which makes him not only a tyrant over his fellows, but which may well make him the destroyer of a civilization."[35] According to Hayek, such attempts at control often lead to worse outcomes than if the market were left to its own devices because the dispersed knowledge of market participants is far more effective at allocating resources than any centralized body.[36] The contrast with Keynes's ideologies discussed earlier could not be starker.

American economist Friedman was also known for his strong advocacy of free-market capitalism.[37] His primary thesis was that monetary policy is more important than fiscal policy, and that free markets trump government intervention. His views were considered radical by the Keynesian establishment at the time. In his view, "inflation is always and everywhere a monetary phenomenon, in the sense that it is and can be produced only by a more rapid increase in the quantity of money than in output." In other words, he argued that inflation was the result of too much money chasing too few goods.[38] He criticized Keynesian policies that encouraged inflation in the name of short-term gains in employment statistics, believing that such policies would lead to higher inflation rates in the long run. He emphasized the importance of expectations in the economy, arguing that temporary measures to stimulate the economy would be anticipated by businesses and consumers, thereby diminishing their effectiveness over time. He noted that people would adjust their behavior based on their expectations of future policy.[39]

The post–gold standard era's expansion of the money supply and corresponding monetary debasement has fueled the arguments of both Keynesian and Austrian economists. The former see monetary intervention as necessary tools for economic stability, while the latter warn of the long-term dangers of such policies and advocate for a return to sound money principles and minimal government intervention. The debate is, of course, highly politicized. Economists with a preference for a small role of government generally take the Austrian School position, and those preferring a larger role for the government tend toward the Keynesian side.[40] Needless to say, sitting governments around the world have naturally tended toward the latter over time.

Impact of Technology

Jeff Booth, technology entrepreneur and author of *The Price of Tomorrow*,[41] has highlighted the inherent contradiction between a rapidly advancing technological landscape, which is naturally deflationary, and Keynesian economic policies that contrive to maintain a certain level of inflation. Technological progress leads to increased efficiency that in turn contributes to reduced costs, that is, deflation. Technological advancements, including digitalization and automation in almost all industries, are driving down costs and increasing productivity. He argues that deflation is good and should be allowed to occur naturally because it would lead to lower costs, higher purchasing power for consumers, and improved standards of living. Deflation would drive an overall increase in societal wealth.[42] Yet central banks attempt to suppress it using quantitative easing and other means.

By contrast, inflation can be seen as an evil for several reasons, including distortion of true economic signals that prices are supposed to provide, which leads to poor investment decisions. Resources are allocated inefficiently, based on inflated prices rather than real demand and the true cost of production. The insistence on inflation in the face of technological deflation puts economic policies at odds with the natural progression of technology. This contradiction necessitates ever-increasing levels of debt to sustain inflationary growth, leading to economic fragility and catastrophic market corrections.[43]

Embracing technological deflation could instead lead to a future where economic growth does not depend on debt and inflation but on the real value generated by technological advancement.

> Prices falling by extension of the value we provide to others becomes natural. This accelerates as technology continues to do more of our work. Incentives become aligned as we look back with bewilderment that we ever lived in a system where prices were manipulated to rise. We realize a truth that was hidden from our view. *Abundance in money = Scarcity in everything else*, and conversely, *Scarcity in money = Abundance everywhere else.*[44]
>
> —Jeff Booth

Booth has argued that the ultimate deflationary hard money built for the digital era is bitcoin.

CHAPTER 10

A Store of Value

We have elected to put our money and faith in a mathematical framework.

—Tyler Winklevoss, 2013

The largest addressable market in the world is the market for the store of value. The market is currently served primarily by the asset classes represented in table 10.1 alongside their approximate market capitalizations. Total quantum of global wealth seeking a store of value currently stands in the region of $900 trillion (based on rough estimates in some cases). This represents the addressable market for a store of value. Gold, holding approximately 2 percent of the global store of value market, and bitcoin, with its market share currently at 0.12 percent at a valuation of $60,000 per unit as of this writing, present a striking contrast in the world of financial assets. This disparity might be perceived as an undervaluation of bitcoin, especially when considering its unprecedented monetary characteristics (discussed in chapter 2). This "mispricing" of bitcoin may stem from the widespread lack of comprehension of what it actually is within the global investment community.[1]

Determining the "right price" for bitcoin is a complex endeavor. If bitcoin were to reach gold's market capitalization, it would necessitate a fifteenfold increase from its current valuation. Given bitcoin's enhancements over gold's monetary attributes, it is arguable that bitcoin could be valued significantly higher than gold. In addition to its superior monetary attributes, bitcoin can be transacted easily across borders, giving it a powerful international network effect that is another major advantage over gold.[2] To illustrate the likelihood of bitcoin overtaking gold's market capitalization, consider the nine bitcoin exchange-traded funds

TABLE 10.1 Market Capitalization of Assets for Storing Value

Asset	Market Cap. (in $ trillions)	Market Share (%)
Real estate[1]	380	42
Debt[2]	315	34
Equities[3]	115	12
Cash[4]	90	9.9
Gold[5]	16	1.8
Art/collectibles[6]	1.7	0.18
Bitcoin[7]	1.4	0.12
Total	**919**	**100**

[1]Paul Tostevin and Charlotte Rushton, "Total Value of Global Real Estate," *Savills* (September 2023), https://www.savills.com/impacts/market-trends/the-total-value-of-global-real-estate-property-remains-the -worlds-biggest-store-of-wealth.html.
[2]BIS Data Portal, "Debt Securities Statistics," 2023, https://www.visualcapitalist.com/global-debt-hits -a-new-high-of-315-trillion/?utm_source=chatgpt.com; Institute of International Finance, "Global Debt Monitor," 2024, https://www.iif.com/Products/Global-Debt-Monitor.
[3]"Capital Markets Fact Book 2024"," SIFMA Research Quarterly, https://www.sifma.org/resources/research /statistics/fact-book/.
[4]"World—Major Central Bank M2 Money Supply," 2024, accessed July 15, 2024, https://en.macromicro.me /series/4675/global-money-supply-m2.
[5]World Gold Council—Gold Market Primer, https://www.gold.org/goldhub/research/market-primer/gold -market-primer-market-size-and-structure.
[6]Deloitte, "ArtTactic: Deloitte Art and Finance Report 2019."
[7]"Today's Cryptocurrency Prices by Market Cap," coinmarketcap.com.

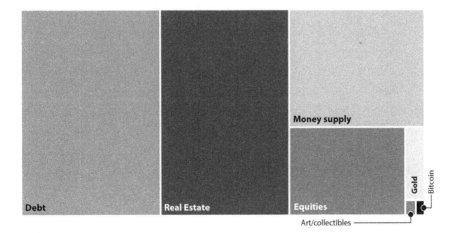

10.1 Global wealth allocation. *Source*: Author.

(ETFs) that were launched in the United States in January 2024. After just two months of their launch, the ETFs amassed approximately $60 billion in assets under management. It took gold ETFs fifteen years to achieve the same number.

TEMPORAL SALABILITY

As discussed in chapter 3, the salability of an asset refers to the ease with which it can be exchanged for goods and services over different measures of time and space without losing value.[3] *Spatial* salability is the ability of an asset to be transported and used over long distances without losing value, while *temporal* salability is the ability of an asset to be sold at an undefined time in the future without losing value. The latter is especially important for a good to function effectively as money in order to enable people to store the fruits of their labor for use in the future. It ensures that individuals can save today with the confidence that the value of their savings will not diminish over time.[4]

While gold has historically been prized for its temporal salability, it has faced significant challenges in terms of spatial salability. As we have discussed in chapter 2, gold is dense and heavy, and requires secure storage and transportation, making it less than ideal for many types of transactions, especially those requiring quick exchanges over long distances. Gold's portability constraints limited its effectiveness and efficiency as a medium of exchange, particularly in comparison to lighter, more easily transportable forms of money.

The limitations of gold on the spatial front led societies to innovate and develop more practical forms of money. As discussed in chapter 8, one of the most significant developments was the introduction of paper money, initially as gold receipts and ultimately as fiat. The invention of paper money represented a revolutionary improvement in spatial salability. Paper is lightweight, easy to transport, and can be used in a wide range of transactions, facilitating trade over long distances and at a larger scale than ever before. It allowed for the expansion of commerce and the economy by significantly reducing the costs and risks associated with transporting physical gold.[5]

As we have discussed, however, the move to paper money pegged to a hard asset ultimately and inevitably culminated in depegging from the hard asset to create fiat currency. And, as we have seen, fiat currency in turn has been responsible for monetary expansion and debasement at an unprecedented global scale over recent decades. Thus, we see how *the need for spatial salability ultimately resulted in the sacrifice of temporal salability.*

The feature most critical to temporal salability is the asset's scarcity. The relative difficulty of producing more of an asset determines the *hardness* of it. Money whose supply is hard to increase is known as hard money, while easy money is money whose supply is amenable to large increases. This fact is demonstrated throughout human history by what societies have attributed value to. Mark Twain described the relationship between scarcity and value when he observed: "Buy land, they're not making it anymore." It is a misconception that gold derives value from its use in making jewelry or industrial applications—in reality, its value is derived from its scarcity and market consensus of its role as a store of value.

We have discussed bitcoin's absolute scarcity based on its immutable cap of 21 million coins. We also recognize bitcoin's capacity for instantaneous transmission over the internet. These characteristics epitomize the pinnacle of spatial and temporal salability. Consequently, it may be argued that bitcoin obliterates most of the foundational justifications for fiat currency. In other words, the need to compromise temporal salability for the sake of spatial salability is now obsolete.

> Historically, people have taken up scarce commodities as money, if necessary taking up whatever is at hand, such as shells or stones . . . Until now, no scarce commodity that can be traded over a communications channel without a trusted third party has been available. If there is a desire to take up a form of money that can be traded over the Internet without a trusted third party, then now that is possible.[6]
>
> —Satoshi Nakamoto, May 3, 2009

The Fastest Horse

> At the end of the day, the best profit-maximizing strategy is to own the fastest horse. Just own the best performer . . . If I am forced to forecast, my bet is it will be bitcoin.[7]
>
> —Paul Tudor Jones

The horse race that renowned hedge fund manager and billionaire Paul Tudor Jones is referring to is the race to beat inflation. What makes bitcoin the fastest horse in that race?

Number-Go-Up (NGU) Technology is a comical bitcoin meme that is used to illustrate the argument that bitcoin is "engineered" for rapid price appreciation over time (albeit in a volatile manner) simply as a result of supply and demand. The core idea is that you have an infinite amount of fiat money on the one side and an absolutely scarce asset on the other. The latter hard asset will consume the former over time. In other words, when infinite demand meets a finite supply, the mathematical result is an upward explosion in price. This notion is what is satirically referred to as NGU Technology. It also leads to a related meme: bitcoin has no top because fiat has no bottom; that is, fiat can be theoretically printed to infinity, which could, as the meme suggests, push bitcoin's price to infinity.

On the fiat side of the equation, just looking at the relatively brief period since bitcoin was created in 2008, the money supply (M2) has gone from 8 trillion to approximately 21 trillion (see figure 9.1). That is a total supply increase of over 160 percent in sixteen years. What Jones is suggesting in his quote above is to think in first principles—an acute skew in supply versus demand leads to a corresponding impact on price action. If bitcoin is the only asset class with provable absolute scarcity,[8] then it should have the highest sensitivity to this acute skew over the long term. (It is possible, of course, that certain small cap stocks or cryptocurrencies might have short bursts of higher sensitivity, but the likelihood of sustaining this over years and decades may be questionable).

How has bitcoin fared in past periods of profligate monetary expansion by central banks? The COVID-19 pandemic provides a helpful illustration. In response to the economic downturn triggered by the global shutdowns as a result of the pandemic, governments and central banks across the globe launched an array of monetary and fiscal stimulus measures unparalleled in history. The objective was to mitigate the economic impact of the pandemic and government-imposed lockdowns, stimulate growth, and stabilize financial markets.

Throughout 2020, within a span of just eight months, these measures included setting interest rates at zero or near-zero levels, expanding the money supply through aggressive quantitative easing, and introducing a variety of new central bank lending programs. Following the March 2020 market crash that affected both equities and bitcoin, these interventions paved the way for bitcoin's extraordinary surge, climbing over 1,700 percent to reach a new all-time peak. Among major asset classes, bitcoin was unquestionably the fastest horse. Figure 10.2 shows bitcoin's historical performance versus the global money supply.[9] The correlation depicted is higher than that of any other major asset class.

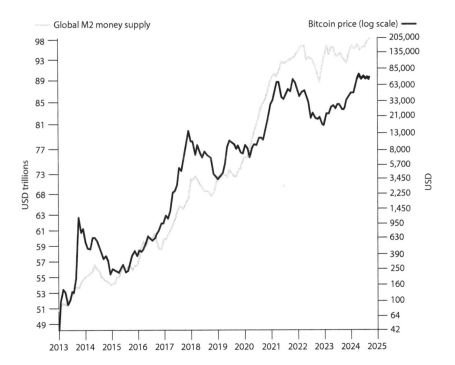

10.2 The global money supply versus the price of bitcoin. *Source:* TradingView.

While the stimulus efforts during the COVID-19 pandemic were initially effective in reviving economic activity, they had long-term consequences and contributed to the highest inflation rates seen in decades. In an attempt to control inflation, central banks around the world embarked on a path of steep interest rate hikes. Despite the initial adverse effect of rising interest rates on bitcoin's valuation, it demonstrated resilience. In 2024, it returned to its all-time high over $70,000 despite high interest rates. This effectively silenced many bitcoin critics who have argued throughout bitcoin's life that its rise is purely a symptom of a low interest rate environment. Bitcoin's resilience amid economic turbulence illustrates its evolving role as a major asset class.

Stock-to-Flow Ratio

The stock-to-flow (S2F) model is a popular quantitative framework used to evaluate the price of assets with limited supply. Based on the assumption that scarcity leads to higher prices, the model measures scarcity by comparing an asset's total stock (how much is currently available) to the flow (how much is produced in a year). A higher S2F ratio suggests a greater level of scarcity because it implies a lower amount of new supply entering the market, which, according to the model, could lead to a higher value of the asset. Gold has been the primary asset analyzed by the S2F model because of its long-standing role as a store of wealth with limited supply. Gold's high S2F ratio is driven by its significant existing stockpile relative to new yearly production. This inherent scarcity has maintained gold's value over millennia.

Analysis of bitcoin's absolute scarcity was discussed in chapters 2 and 3. Its capped supply of 21 million coins makes it a prime candidate for S2F analysis. As we have seen, its protocol dictates that the reward for mining new blocks is halved every four years. This process reduces the flow relative to the existing stock, thereby increasing bitcoin's S2F ratio over time. The fourth bitcoin halving in April 2024 put its S2F ratio ahead of the S2F ratio for gold for the first time.

Advocates of the S2F model argue that a statistically significant link exists between bitcoin's price and its scarcity, as indicated by the S2F ratio. Detractors argue that the model fails to account for demand, which they rightly see as a crucial determinant of price. Although bitcoin's major rallies in price have historically coincided with the quadrennial halving of its supply, attempting to predict its future prices based on this model may lead to disappointment. The model demonstrates correlation rather than causation. With over 92 percent of bitcoin's supply mined to date, perhaps a better approach is to assume simply that bitcoin's supply is already fully issued and to focus instead on its demand-side path to global adoption. In any event, what arguably has a much greater impact than the quadrennial supply reduction is the media hype that surrounds it, and the expectation of significant price jumps based on historical performance. This likely acts as a self-fulfilling prophecy.

"BITCOIN IS TOO VOLATILE"

The critique of bitcoin's volatility often overlooks the inherent nature of what bitcoin aims to achieve: a fundamental disruption of fiat money and monetary systems. This mission necessarily entails a departure from the status quo.

The path to disruption is never smooth and linear. It is chaotic; unpredictable; and, yes, volatile. It would seem rather absurd to expect bitcoin to somehow maintain a stable relationship with fiat currency while simultaneously disrupting it. The disruptor and the disrupted are, by definition, at perpetual odds with each other. If bitcoin were to achieve its stated objective, critics of its volatility should ask themselves: how else were you expecting things to play out other than through volatility?

> Ludwig Wittgenstein once asked a friend, "tell me, why do people say it is more natural to think that the sun rotates around the earth than that the earth is rotating?" The friend said, "well, obviously, because it just *seems like* the sun is going around the earth." Wittgenstein replied, "well, what would it *seem like* if it did *seem like* the earth were rotating?" If it seemed like a global, digital, sound, open source, programmable money was monetizing from absolute zero, it would seem a lot like [bitcoin].[10]
>
> —Allen Farrington

Bitcoin's volatility reflects its value proposition, which is entirely different from the traditional monetary system. It must be free to find its value independent of the system that it aims to supplant. Stablecoins are not volatile, but they do not challenge fiat money; they rely on it.

As observed by Fidelity Digital Assets,[11] volatility also arises from bitcoin's supply being hard-coded to remain constant, unaffected by fluctuations in its market price. Any shifts in demand, whether short term or long term, must be accommodated through price adjustments. There is no other outlet. The inelasticity of supply inherently leads to greater price volatility. Bitcoin's volatility is essentially a direct outcome of its core attribute: a predetermined, unchangeable supply.

Consider the adoption trajectories of transformative technologies like the telephone, steam engine, mobile phones, and the internet.[12] New innovations often undergo a baptism by fire, enduring a series of rigorous trials and skepticism before gaining acceptance by society. This is the case with bitcoin too, but with one critical difference. These historical innovations had no real-time metric to gauge public perception and acceptance. The volatility in their adoption played out in a more abstract manner over longer periods. Bitcoin, however, is a unique case where its adoption and the public's changing perceptions are immediately visible through its price.

Unlike traditional technologies and innovations, bitcoin's price provides real-time feedback on the global investment community's collective understanding, sentiment, and valuation of the asset. This immediacy is unprecedented in the history of technological adoption. Bitcoin does not have cash flows, dividends, or other traditional financial metrics that can be used to assess its value. Instead, its price is purely a function of supply and demand dynamics, influenced by perceptions, speculation, and investor sentiment. This makes its valuation highly sensitive to shifts in collective understanding of it. Human emotions are volatile.

The process of understanding bitcoin is complex and involves multiple disciplines, as elucidated in this book. This complexity, combined with the emotional nature of financial investment, contributes to the asset's volatility. As understanding deepens and adoption widens, the collective psyche may reach a more stable consensus on bitcoin's value, potentially leading to less volatility. This journey toward broader comprehension and acceptance is inherently volatile, echoing the tumultuous paths of major innovations throughout history.[13]

Investment Horizons

When viewing the price chart of an asset showing exponential growth, a linear price chart can be misleading. It presents a skewed image of price by magnifying near-term volatility. A logarithmic chart is often preferred for bitcoin because it offers a truer and more holistic perspective. For example, the linear price in figure 10.3 completely obscures bitcoin's price performance before 2017 because it is depicted as a flat line near zero. With the logarithmic price, you can appreciate the exponential growth that the asset experienced from 2010, when it was no more than a couple of cents, to 2017, when it exceeded $1,000.

An individual's investment horizon becomes a critical factor when assessing bitcoin's potential, especially as a long-term inflation hedge. Rather than focusing on bitcoin's daily price chart, Observing its four-year moving average illuminates a consistent upward trend, countering concerns about its volatility for those with a long-term investment horizon. When viewed through the lens of its four-year moving average (coinciding with its quadrennial supply-halving cycle), bitcoin's performance shows an uninterrupted upward trajectory over the years, despite periods of significant interim volatility. This perspective highlights the importance of a long-term outlook. This is particularly relevant for younger

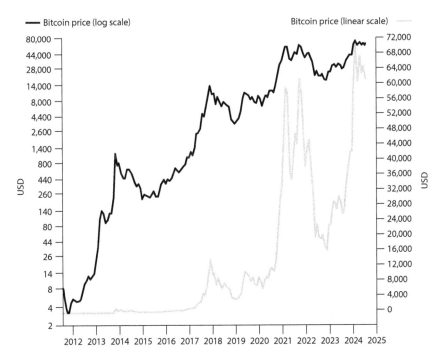

10.3 The price of bitcoin on a log scale versus a linear scale. *Source*: TradingView.

investors or investors not nearing retirement, who have the luxury of time to ride out the market's ups and downs.

Figure 10.4 shows the volatile daily price chart of bitcoin and a smooth upward ascending line that has never seen a period of declining value since bitcoin's inception. Taking a four-year investment horizon would have witnessed an investment appreciate nonstop from $0.01 to $37,000 (the four-year moving average as of this writing) over a fourteen-year period. There is no other asset in history that has shown a comparable performance over a comparable period.

Financial news reports often amplify the sense of panic during market downturns by focusing on short-term performance and neglecting the broader trend. This can skew public perception of bitcoin, deterring potential investors who do not take the time to research and understand the asset's underlying value and long-term prospects. By adjusting their time horizon, investors can make more informed investment decisions.

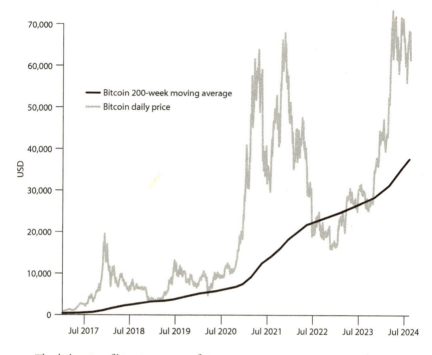

10.4 The daily price of bitcoin versus its four-year moving average. *Source:* TradingView.

The history of innovation is replete with instances when initial skepticism and volatility gave way to widespread acceptance and integration. Transformative innovations often face periods of volatility and criticism before their potential is fully recognized. The collective understanding and acceptance of a new technology (or investment opportunity) in society is a psychological, sociological, and philosophical process as much as it is an economic one.[14]

In any event, it is worth noting that bitcoin's annual realized volatility has lessened over time, reaching new all-time lows in November 2023, according to data provider Glassnode.[15] This is likely to continue as bitcoin's market capitalization grows along with its global adoption, further regulatory clarity emerges around the world, and investors gain a better understanding of its true investment thesis.

Finally, it is worth pointing out the cognitive error inherent in the perception of bitcoin's price volatility. Bitcoin is not volatile if your unit of account is bitcoin:[16] 1 BTC = 1 BTC, just like $1 = $1. But as long as bitcoin's value in *another* unit of account (i.e., dollars) is volatile, those on that other unit of account will necessarily perceive bitcoin as volatile. In chapter 11, we will discuss the progression of a monetary asset from a collectible to a store of value, then to a medium of exchange, and finally to a unit of account. As we shall see, bitcoin is in the very early stages of the second phase, where it is just starting to be accepted as a long-term store of value. It may take years and likely decades before it reaches the unit of account phase. Therefore, it is likely to be perceived as volatile from the standpoint of other units of account until that final phase comes to pass (at which point, presumably, dollars would be perceived as volatile in bitcoin's unit of account).

HOPE FOR THE UNBANKED

Having secure access to one's hard-earned money and savings in a bank account is the foundation of daily life and financial stability. According to the World Bank, over one-quarter of the world's adult population lacks access to basic banking services.[17] In other words, the financial industry, the backbone of our daily existence, does not engage with one in four of our fellow adult humans. The staggering statistic bears repeating: the number is one in four adults. The plight of the unbanked and underbanked populations is a story of hardship, resilience, and hope.

Sub-Saharan Africa is one of the regions most acutely affected by financial exclusion. Despite making significant strides in recent years, over half of all adults in the region are unbanked, relying on bills tucked in their pockets or stashed under their mattresses. In South Sudan, an astonishing 91 percent of the population is unbanked. In Nigeria, Africa's most populous country, inadequate infrastructure and economic instability has left over 60 million adults unbanked. For many in Nigeria, the informal financial sector has become a necessity. Informal savings groups, known locally as *esusu* or *ajo*, are widely prevalent.[18] However, participants are vulnerable to fraud. And the physical cash that members save can easily be lost, stolen, or eroded by inflation (over 40 percent p.a. in 2024 in Nigeria).

South Asia, another region with a significant unbanked population, faces its unique set of challenges. In India, the world's most populous country, over 200 million adults are unbanked. Its neighbor, Pakistan, is home to 2.8 percent of the global population and accounts for as much as 8 percent of the world's unbanked adults.[19] In rural areas, access to banking infrastructure is virtually nonexistent. Many villages lack a nearby bank branch, and even where branches exist, the cost of maintaining an account can be prohibitive for low-income individuals. In addition, societal norms often restrict women's access to financial services, exacerbating gender disparities in financial inclusion. As a result, women are more likely to be financially dependent and vulnerable to exploitation.

In Mexico, over 60 million people are unbanked. In Venezuela, the situation is exacerbated by the country's severe economic crisis. Hyperinflation, political instability, and the collapse of the banking system have left millions without any reliable means to save or transact. The bolivar has become practically worthless, pushing people to use foreign currencies or barter systems. Access to stable foreign currencies is limited, and the risks associated with holding cash, including theft and debasement, are ever present.

In the Middle East and North Africa region, conflict-affected countries like Syria, Yemen, and Iraq experience regular disruptions to the formal banking infrastructure, leaving millions without access to basic financial services, which compounds the difficulties faced by displaced populations and those living in conflict zones. In Egypt, a country with one of the largest populations in the region and where over half of the adults are unbanked, the informal economy (unregistered and unregulated businesses) plays a significant role in people's lives, providing jobs and services that the formal sector cannot. However, the informal nature of these arrangements means that individuals have no reliable means of saving or securing their earnings.

We live in a world where there is a 26 percent chance you could have been born into circumstances where you have no means to secure the fruits of your labor. One and a half billion individuals toil endlessly yet have no way to protect their earnings from the ravages of inflation or the grasp of corrupt regimes. They face a desperate plight, trapped in a cycle of poverty with no escape. Traditional solutions to this crisis involve massive investments to build financial infrastructure, requiring billions of dollars, extensive physical networks, and complex bureaucratic processes. Governments, often plagued by inefficiencies and corruption, are ill-equipped to address the needs of these underserved populations.

Now envision a revolutionary technology that transcends these barriers—a technology that requires no investment from any government, no elaborate physical infrastructure, and no burdensome paperwork. All it needs is an internet connection, (although ham radio or SMS messaging suffices, as discussed in chapter 6). Accessing financial services is as simple as going online, transacting, and saving, without the involvement of a single other third-party service provider or gatekeeper. Anyone anywhere can create a digital wallet, which functions like a personal bank account, where they may independently access and store an asset immune to corruption, debasement, and confiscation.

Certain parts of the world actually have higher internet penetration than financial inclusion. This is particularly true in Latin America and South Asia. For example, in Mexico, while less than 50 percent have access to a bank account, almost 80 percent have access to the internet. In such regions, bitcoin can be particularly transformative. Individuals can use bitcoin in a permissionless manner, achieving immediate financial inclusion and a secure savings tool. Simply by increasing internet penetration in these regions and by educating the masses about bitcoin, financial inclusion could be brought much closer to 100 percent without the need for billions of dollars of expenditure on banking infrastructure and investment. By capitalizing on the widespread use of mobile phones and growing internet access, bitcoin can enable a more inclusive financial system that offers secure, accessible, and affordable financial services to all.

Bitcoin can also facilitate low-cost, cross-border transactions, especially crucial in these parts of the world. According to the World Bank, the global average cost of sending $200 from one country to another is about $12.50, or 6.25 percent. The cost of sending $200 over the bitcoin Lightning Network (whereby the recipient receives U.S. dollars, not bitcoin—see chapter 3) is less than $0.01, or 0.005 percent. This capability is critical for remittance-dependent countries, where high fees can significantly reduce the amount of money received by families. By providing a secure and efficient means of transferring money, bitcoin can help unbanked populations participate in the global economy.

Bitcoin does not discriminate. For the first time ever, over one billion of the world's most marginalized individuals, some in the remotest parts of the planet, have a tool that empowers them to transact globally and independently, save for the future, and protect their earnings from the instability of their local economies.

CHAPTER 11

Global Adoption

Martti Malmi, a software developer from Finland, was one of bitcoin's earliest adopters. He became involved with bitcoin in May 2009 when he was still a college student, working on bitcoin's code directly with Satoshi, corresponding with him extensively over email. "Bitcoin is a great project, and it's really cool to participate!" he wrote to Satoshi.

He mined 55,000 bitcoins on his laptop in 2009 and 2010, which would be worth $3.3 billion today (at a price of $60,000 per bitcoin in 2024). In October 2009, he entered the first U.S. dollar–bitcoin transaction on the New Liberty Standard exchange by purchasing 5,050 bitcoins for $5.02 using PayPal. The bitcoins were used to seed the exchange, which was the world's first cryptocurrency exchange.

Malmi set up a bitcoin exchange of his own in 2010, and he operated it more with the intention of disseminating bitcoin than making a profit. He donated thirty thousand of his bitcoins (worth $1.8 billion today) toward the cause. In 2011, he sold ten thousand of his bitcoins (worth $600 million today) to buy a studio apartment in Helsinki for $200,000. In 2011, he offered one thousand of his bitcoins (worth $60 million today) as a reward to anyone who could convince a major business to accept bitcoin. The reward went unclaimed. He worked extensively on bitcoin's very first educational materials and frequently asked questions (FAQs) alongside Satoshi. In 2012, he sold most of his remaining bitcoins at a price of around $5 each when he had trouble finding a job. All these years later, Malmi simply says, "Perhaps owing to Finnish culture, idealistic mentality and lack of life experience, I never thought much about making money. It happened accidentally as a byproduct of Satoshi asking me to keep my node running so others could connect . . . You don't live forever. Pursuing something greater than yourself brings meaning in life . . . Thank you, Satoshi and others who have made

Bitcoin what it is today. May it bring peace and prosperity to the world. Long live Bitcoin."[1]

Money is typically the most powerful driver of adoption. As we shall discuss in chapter 20, however, philosophical narratives can also be just as strong a driving force. Not only was Malmi one of the earliest adopters of bitcoin, but his efforts likely onboarded thousands of other early adopters to the bitcoin network. It is difficult to fathom that bitcoin, even at a time when its monetary value was $0, had such a strong philosophical attraction to individuals like Malmi. Others similarly motivated included computer scientist Hal Finney, who received the first bitcoin transaction (long before it had monetary value) from Satoshi in January 2009.

Malmi's New Liberty Standard transaction set bitcoin's price for the first time at $0.0008. Bitcoin has grown from less than a cent to $60,000 today, and it has gained tens of millions of adopters along the way. This still represents no more than 3 or 4 percent of the global population, even by the most optimistic assessments. With a fixed supply of bitcoin, consider the price implications when adoption goes to 10 percent, 20 percent, or 50 percent. Most of the individuals who comprise the 3 or 4 percent own no more than $100 in bitcoin. Therefore, even within that cohort, the demand for additional bitcoin accumulation could increase substantially.

Despite bitcoin's trillion-dollar-plus market capitalization (which many still perceive to be unjustified and no more than a bubble), it is likely still in the earliest stages of global adoption. Bitcoin's success from this point on is primarily a story of demand-side growth. The drivers for this adoption could be philosophical, as was the case with Malmi, or economic, as investors start to recognize its superior long-term price performance versus any other asset class in history.

METCALFE'S LAW AND S-CURVE ADOPTION

Metcalfe's law states that the value of a network is proportional to the square of the number of its users. In its nascent stages of adoption, bitcoin's future value was purely theoretical. As more and more enthusiasts got involved, its foundations began to be laid. From that point on, every additional user, miner, node operator, and developer added to the network's value. The internet's adoption path offers an analogy demonstrating the operation of Metcalfe's law. In the early days of the internet, every new website, service, and user exponentially

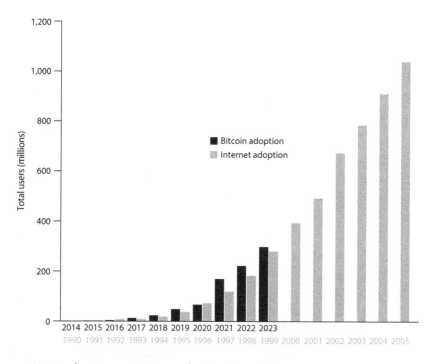

11.1 Bitcoin adoption versus internet adoption. *Source:* Crypto.com.

increased its utility and value. As seen in figure 11.1, we see a similar adoption path for bitcoin as its ecosystem grows with every new wallet, financial product, or layered solution that is built on top of it, thus enhancing its value, utility and society's perception of it.

The S-curve of adoption is a graphical representation of how a new product, technology, or innovation is adopted over time within a market or society. It illustrates the life cycle of adoption, starting slowly with early adopters, accelerating as the majority begins to adopt the innovation, and eventually leveling off as the market becomes saturated. The S shape comes from the sigmoid function, which reflects the cumulative growth of adoption.

The S-curve model has several historical examples. The adoption of electricity in homes and businesses starting in the late nineteenth century followed an S-curve. Adoption was slow initially because of the high cost and lack of infrastructure. But over time, as infrastructure improved and costs decreased, adoption accelerated, eventually becoming nearly universal in developed countries. The market for personal computers also experienced slow growth during the early years of its introduction in the 1970s and 1980s. Adoption rates soared through the 1990s as computers became more affordable and software applications increased. With smartphones, initial growth was slow in the early 2000s, but the introduction of the iPhone in 2007 and subsequent Android devices rapidly accelerated adoption. By the 2010s, smartphones had become ubiquitous in most parts of the world. Social media platforms also followed a similar path, with platforms like Facebook, Twitter, and Instagram initially attracting early adopters before exploding in popularity and becoming integral parts of daily life for billions of people globally. Surveys estimate that there are over 200 million bitcoin owners globally, most of whom own a tiny amount of bitcoin each.[2] It is thus arguable that bitcoin still sits in the early adoption phase of the S-curve as shown in figure 11.2.

Bitcoin's adoption, similar to the internet's, will be affected by its global nature (table 11.1). Its rate of adoption will vary across different regions depending on economic conditions, regulatory environments, technological infrastructure,

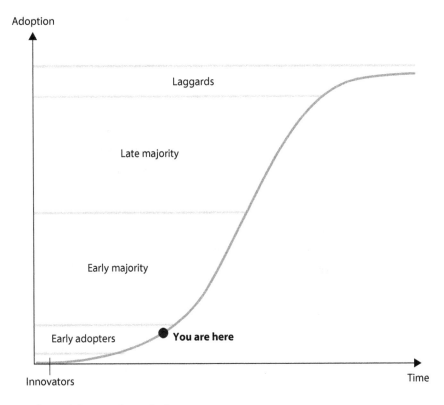

11.2 Bitcoin's S-curve. *Source*: Author.

TABLE 11.1 Respondents who either owned or used cryptocurrencies in 2023

Rank	Country	Adoption Rate (%)
1	Nigeria	47
2	Turkey	47
3	United Arab Emirates	31
4	Indonesia	29
5	Brazil	28
6	India	27
7	Argentina	26
8	Malaysia	23
9	Saudi Arabia	23
10 . . .	South Africa	22
21 . . .	United States	16
27 . . .	Russia	14
34 . . .	United Kingdom	12
38	China	10

Source: Statista, https://www.statista.com/statistics/1202468/global-cryptocurrency-ownership/, accessed June 30, 2024.

and cultural attitudes toward digital currencies and financial innovation. In countries with unstable currencies or financial systems, bitcoin may be adopted more rapidly as a store of value. Countries with favorable regulatory frameworks may see quicker adoption, and vice versa. The availability and accessibility of technology necessary to use bitcoin, such as internet connectivity and smartphones, will play a significant role. Societal and cultural openness to innovation and technology may also play a part. Thus, the global adoption of bitcoin will not be a uniform process but rather a patchwork of varying rates and patterns of adoption. As bitcoin continues to evolve, its adoption curve may exhibit multiple S-curves across different regions.

Generational Wealth Transfer

> The 21st century emergence of Bitcoin, encryption, and the internet are more than just [trends adopted by millennials]; they herald a wave of change that exhibits similar dynamics as the 16–17th century revolution that took place in Europe.[3]
>
> —Tuur Demeester

In October 2019, Coldwell Banker released a report revealing an unprecedented shift in economic power: millennials are set to inherit $68 trillion, marking one of the largest wealth transfers in history.[4] This demographic, born between 1981 and 1996, already accounts for nearly 620,000 millionaires in the United States, about 2.6 percent of the nation's millionaire population.[5] Their propensity toward the digital world and openness to new emerging avenues of investment is expected to herald a redirection of this vast amount of capital toward the digital realm in the coming years.[6]

This generational shift in attitude may be partly fueled by millennials' innate skepticism toward traditional financial systems—a sentiment that may emanate from their exposure to the 2008 financial crisis and its aftermath. The World Economic Forum's 2017 survey highlighted this distrust, with 45 percent of millennials doubting the fairness and honesty of banks.[7] This skepticism is echoed in an Edelman survey, which found that a majority of affluent millennials perceive the financial system as rigged in favor of the elite.[8] Gen Z, although less financially established, also exhibits propensities toward digital investments. Over half of Gen Z investors have chosen digital assets, with 20 percent investing exclusively in digital assets and NFTs.[9]

This generational pivot toward digital assets, supported by forthcoming wealth inheritance, signals a major transformation in the financial and investment landscape. The attraction of bitcoin to millennials and Gen Z members can be attributed to several key characteristics that align with their preferences and values, as highlighted by survey results indicating a shift toward bitcoin:

1. Both millennials and Gen Z members have grown up with the internet, making them more receptive to digital innovations like bitcoin.
2. Given their skepticism toward the traditional financial establishment, bitcoin offers an alternative that operates outside the conventional banking system.
3. Bitcoin provides a transparent ledger of transactions, appealing to those seeking transparency and personal control over their financial dealings.
4. Bitcoin can be accessed and used worldwide, appealing to younger generations with a global perspective and mobility and seeking borderless transactions.
5. Bitcoin offers a degree of privacy and security not always available in traditional financial systems.

6. The perception of bitcoin as a store of value and its historical price performance have showcased its potential for significant returns. Millennials and Gen Z members, facing economic uncertainties and seeking alternative investment opportunities, find bitcoin's potential for growth attractive.

This is why the views of septuagenarian, octogenarian, and even nonagenarian[10] critics of bitcoin should be appropriately weighted in the context of investments in disruptive technological innovations. The younger generations who will command future global wealth have a different mindset. It would be wise to pay close attention to assets that better reflect their worldviews, technological comfort levels, and aspirations.

GRESHAM'S LAW VERSUS THIERS'S LAW

Gresham's Law

Gresham's law, a principle in economics named after Sir Thomas Gresham, who advised Queen Elizabeth I, states, "Bad money drives out good." In simpler terms, when there are two forms of currency in circulation that are accepted by law as having similar face value, the more valuable, or "good," money tends to disappear from circulation because people prefer to hoard the valuable currency and spend the less valuable one. This was observed when coins made of precious metals were debased, or reduced in purity, by governments seeking to stretch their finances (discussed in chapter 8). Citizens would hoard the older, more pure coins and spend the newer, less valuable ones, leading to the good money disappearing from the market.[11]

When we relate Gresham's law to bitcoin and its adoption path, it is possible that people may consider it good money because of its limited supply, decentralization, and resistance to censorship, standing in contrast to fiat currencies, which are subject to inflation and government control. According to the principles of Gresham's law, one might expect bitcoin to be hoarded rather than spent because it represents good money in comparison to fiat currencies' bad money.

This analogy holds true to a significant extent. Many early investors in bitcoin are indeed hoarding it, viewing it as a store of value akin to digital gold rather than a currency to be spent on everyday transactions. They anticipate that its value will continue to rise as it becomes more widely accepted and its supply remains capped. Consequently, the circulation of bitcoin for everyday transactions is less common than might be expected for a currency. Instead, it is often held as a long-term investment or hedge against inflation and currency devaluation. To illustrate this point, for most of 2022 and 2023, when cryptocurrency prices were depressed (in the aftermath of certain monumental scams perpetrated in the centralized cryptocurrency industry), the percentage of the total supply of bitcoin that had not moved in six months exceeded 70 percent.[12] This depicted an incredibly high degree of unphased conviction and resilience among long-term holders of bitcoin who clearly appreciated its underlying potential, notwithstanding the short-term turmoil unrelated to its fundamentals.[13]

Thiers's Law

Thiers's law is somewhat of a counterpoint to Gresham's law and states, "Good money drives out bad" under certain conditions. This economic principle, named after the French economist and politician Adolphe Thiers, suggests that when people have confidence in the value of a particular form of money and prefer to use it over others, the more valued, or "good," money can actually come to dominate and replace the "bad," or less valued, money in circulation. This typically occurs in environments where there is a free choice of currency and where the intrinsic or perceived value of the good money leads to widespread acceptance and use.

While the use of bitcoin as a store of value is paramount, numerous layer 2 solutions have been developed that make faster and cheaper payments possible; that is, they address bitcoin's scalability challenges.[14] The Lightning Network (discussed in chapter 3) is one such example. It is relatively widely adopted, particularly in the developing world. The Lightning Network allows for off-chain transactions, meaning that transactions can occur without being recorded on the blockchain immediately. This reduces the time and fees associated with transactions, making them more practical for everyday use. In essence, these solutions enhance bitcoin's credence as a medium of exchange in addition to being a store of value. Under Thiers's law, this could lead to a scenario where bitcoin becomes more widely used for transactions, effectively driving out traditional fiat currencies. Lightning Network fees, for example, are orders of magnitude cheaper than Visa, Mastercard, or Western Union fees. As bitcoin transactions become cheaper and faster, more people and businesses might prefer to use it over other forms of payment that are slower, more expensive, or less secure.

Furthermore, the global and open-source nature of bitcoin and its layer 2 solutions contrast with the national or regional restrictions and controls often associated with fiat currencies and the closed-source nature of payment service companies. There is a growing recognition of these aspects at a global level. Thus, we might witness a natural shift toward the increased use of bitcoin, reflecting Thiers's law in action in the digital age.

Reconciling the Laws

Clearly, Gresham's law and Thiers's law are seemingly at odds—one suggesting that bad money drives out good and the other that good money drives out bad. Gresham's law suggests that bitcoin would be hoarded, which is inherently contradictory to it serving as a medium of exchange benefiting from Thiers's law. How do we reconcile the two?

The answer is that it is a matter of timing. Vijay Boyapati, in his influential 2018 paper, "The Bullish Case for Bitcoin,"[15] describes the path of global adoption of an asset. He notes that adoption typically starts with society being drawn to bitcoin as a collectible, and then it gradually becomes accepted as a store of value. Once that process is complete, only then does it start gaining acceptance as a medium of exchange. The final stage of adoption is when it is deemed a unit of account.

Applying this framework to bitcoin, we can see that we are still early in the process of the second phase. Fifteen years after its appearance on the world stage, bitcoin has now passed the phase of being deemed a collectible and is rapidly gaining acceptance as a store of value. Figure 11.3 illustrates where we might be in the path of adoption.[16]

The evolution of bitcoin mirrors the historical journey of gold from a collectible to store of value, then to a medium of exchange and finally to a unit of

11.3 Bitcoin adoption path. *Source:* Anil Patel.

account, with Gresham's and Thiers's laws playing crucial roles at different stages. Bitcoin, much like gold, traverses through these evolutionary phases of adoption in the global financial system. Much like bitcoin was initially a technological novelty, valued by a small group of enthusiasts, gold in its earliest days was likely no more than a shiny, rare object perhaps valued by only a few collectors. In this stage, neither Gresham's nor Thiers's law applied because bitcoin was not yet widely used as money but was collected and discussed for its future potential.

As awareness and understanding of bitcoin continues to grow, it is now becoming recognized for its inherent properties that align it with what makes gold a reliable store of value, that is, scarcity. Gresham's law becomes relevant as people start to see bitcoin as good money because of its deflationary nature and potential for appreciation. People start to hoard bitcoin and spend their fiat currency for daily transactions.

Over time, as technological scaling solutions like the Lightning Network are introduced that make bitcoin transactions faster and cheaper, we may witness the beginning of its transition to a medium of exchange. As more businesses and services begin to accept bitcoin and as it becomes easier to use for everyday purchases, bitcoin's role in the economy may shift. The good money now would not just be hoarded but would be actively used because of its practicality and growing acceptance. It may begin to circulate more widely, demonstrating Thiers's law. Bitcoin may start to drive out bad money (the less efficient, more inflation-prone fiat currencies) because people prefer using it for its benefits.

The adoption process may culminate in the acceptance of bitcoin as a unit of account, when industries and communities fully adopt it, and its use in international trade and remittances grows and bypasses the traditional banking systems' inefficiencies and costs. Bitcoin thus highlights how perceptions of value and utility at different points of time in the adoption curve, could drive its function and appeal.

PART IV

The Politics

CHAPTER 12

The Surveillance State

Most people think of money as merely a store of value and a medium of exchange. In reality, it is so much more than that. Money is a vessel of empowerment and freedom for humanity. Today, citizens around the world have come to accept the fiat monetary system as a given, not realizing the ease with which it may be weaponized against them. The fiat system concentrates power in the hands of a few, enabling them to censor transactions, freeze accounts, and regulate the movement of people's wealth. The ostensible justification for this increasingly unfettered control is to fight crime and protect the population. The problem, however, is that as long as humans wield this enormous power, history has shown that they invariably tend to abuse it.

The risk of such abuse is, of course, most accentuated for people living under authoritarian governments where financial surveillance and control are used as weapons of oppression. Governments may easily freeze the assets of dissidents, deny financial services to minority populations, or place wholesale restrictions on cross-border transactions or movement of people's wealth altogether. Cases of this abound around the world and throughout history.

This brings us to bitcoin and its political implications. For reasons we will discuss in part IV, bitcoin might well be the only antidote that has ever been available in this respect. It can fundamentally alter the relationship between money and state. Bitcoin is a tool of financial empowerment, enabling people to control their economic destinies, thereby resisting government overreach. The idea harks back to a bygone era when the state and money were independent rather than insidiously intertwined. To appreciate the enormity of its political significance fully, it would be useful first to gain a historical perspective of the evils of centralized financial power and the instances of its abuse.

HISTORICAL PERSPECTIVES

Medieval England

Long before our modern conception of the surveillance state, the Exchequer in Medieval England was an early pioneer in using financial supervision as a means of exercising government power and control. Acting as the Crown's treasury, the Exchequer handled the kingdom's accounting and revenue management function, overseeing tax collection and other financial operations. The unusual name Exchequer came from the checkered fabric on which he meticulously audited the finances of wealthy English barons.[1] He was effectively the financial nerve center of the kingdom and unsurprisingly wielded enormous power.

The detailed records that he maintained on nearly every citizen of moderate financial means were tools by which the Crown exercised financial oppression. Through these records, the monarchy could keep an eye on the financial activities of the clergy, nobles, and newly formed merchant classes, therefore ensuring that taxes were paid and financial responsibilities to the Crown were met in a timely manner.[2] These records covered property ownership, trade incomes, and other "useful" information about the activities of the monied nobility. This information gave the Crown tremendous influence over its vassals and subjects.

Under William the Conqueror's rule in 1086, one of the main tools of financial management used was the "Domesday Book."[3] This record was seemingly a mere survey to evaluate and chronicle the riches of the kingdom and its inhabitants for tax assessment. It also had a darker purpose, however, whereby it was used to gain insights into and exercise control over the financial and economic activities of the masses.[4]

The records were used to enforce the will of the Crown through fines and penalties, which were imposed on people as punishment for misdemeanors and violations of the royal peace. The Exchequer maintained a register tracking these fines and made sure to extract the monies by whatever means necessary. The records were regularly used to pressure powerful members of the aristocracy to do the Crown's bidding. Using the proceeds of these penalties, the sovereign bestowed favors, lands, and titles honoring allegiance and service. The Exchequer was also in charge of the gift-giving ceremonies (with the gifts being methodically recorded and tracked, needless to say). Every transaction was registered and tracked. The monarchy's great authority and influence over its people derived from this capacity to provide or deny such financial benefits and served as a tool to ensure loyalty and compliance.

The introduction of scutage is also relevant in this context because it marked an important turning point in the financializing of the surveillance state. Scutage was a charge paid by vassals as a substitute for military duty. While citizens were mandated to serve in the military, scutage let them pay money rather than serve. This gave the monarchy a significant income stream that could be used to employ professional soldiers. This had the effect of reducing the military power of the kingdom's nobility and centralizing it under the Crown.

The financial surveillance exercised by the Exchequer often led to tension between the monarchy and its subject. These tensions led to a political crisis culminating in the Magna Carta in 1215, which aimed to restrict the Crown's capacity to impose taxes without the "common counsel of the realm."[5] This revolution was a manifestation of people's palpable frustration with the level of financial surveillance and oppression that was perpetrated by the British Crown. Centuries before the advent of a surveillance state with various technological powers of oversight, the Exchequer's position in Medieval England and his manual record-keeping demonstrated the immense potential of financial control as an instrument of administration.

Soviet Union

The Soviet Union's exercise of control over the nation's economy and finances is a striking example of the perverse extent to which such powers may be taken. It depicts how financial monitoring and centralized economic planning can be used as part of a larger framework meant to guide the behavior of people toward certain ideological ends. Centralized planning was the centerpiece of the Soviet economic system since its inception. The state set out objectives for every area of the economy, distributing funds, and setting prices. The State Planning Committee, or Gosplan, was responsible for these activities.[6] From industrial production to the distribution of consumer products, the culture of control permeated nearly all economic activity.

Money in the Soviet Union had a different meaning and function compared to free-market-based systems. Although it was still a medium of exchange, it was not of much help as a store of value or unit of account.[7] Wages and prices were all regulated by the state with little regard for market dynamics. Resources were allocated and distributed based on Gosplan's own centrally managed goals, with no input for true market forces. This invariably led to extensive inefficiencies, shortages, and a lack of innovation.[8]

The state bank of the Union of Soviet Socialist Republics (USSR), Gosbank, was the central bank of the country, and the financial regulator of the entire banking sector. It controlled monetary policy, the issuance of new money, and the fixing of interest rates. It was also responsible for the supervision of all banking operations. Through these means, the state monitored and controlled all financial activities of citizens who had not even the slightest expectation of financial privacy or autonomy.[9]

Financial surveillance was used to suppress criticism and enforce conformity with official programs. Those seen to be a danger to the government's socialist ideology found themselves without jobs, cut off from financial resources, or subject to random property seizures.[10] The fact that the state was the only employer and supplier of goods and services left people with no means of escaping financial ruin—compliance and conformity seemed the only options.

But where there is a will, there is a way. These unprecedented economic restrictions imposed by the state led to one of the most notorious black markets in history.[11] In reaction to the inefficiencies and shortages brought about by centralized control, a parallel system emerged outside government boundaries. It offered the only means of accessing numerous commodities and services that were either unavailable, rationed, or prohibited by the state. Participating in this black market posed grave dangers. If caught, one could face fines, arrest, imprisonment, or far worse. Secrecy and trust were therefore the core tenets of its operation. The system relied on trusted networks to enable transactions. With the continual fear of getting caught, trust was a currency as important as the rubles or items being traded.

The centrally planned economy proved untenable, resulting in the collapse of the Soviet Union and its economic experiment.[12] The inefficiencies of the system as well as the absence of incentives for innovation and output were the primary cause of its demise. Yet the era serves as a reminder that the state can use its control over economic affairs to coerce a population to align their ideologies and behavior in certain ways. It showed that such suppression of the freedom and creativity of a people is unsustainable in the long term.

Nazi Germany

There are few examples in history that rival the depravity of the state-sponsored persecution of its citizens by the Nazi government in Germany throughout the 1930s and 1940s. Most tend to focus on the physical violence and atrocities, often overlooking the vast economic plunder that preceded Nazi rule and occurred in parallel. The government implemented a well-thought-out strategy to isolate, disenfranchise, and plunder the Jewish community. The economic mission of so-called Aryanization was vital in laying the foundation for the Holocaust that followed. It showcased the weaponization of economic policies to further the state's murderous goals.

With the passage of the Nuremberg Laws in 1935, the economic and financial attack on the Jewish people, as well as other communities deemed undesirable, started in earnest.[13] This legislation implemented the financial marginalization of the Jews, depriving them of their citizenship and civic rights. Jews were essentially cut off from Germany's economic life and were barred from practicing certain professions, owning businesses, or engaging in other forms of commerce. The clear policy objective of Aryanization was to drive all Jewish-owned businesses under Aryan ownership. In April 1938, a regulation was passed that required the registration of all assets owned by Jews above a certain value. This obviously made them easy targets for seizure. The wealth extracted from the Jewish community through these measures flooded the Nazi government coffers and enriched many loyal private citizens. By 1939, more than 100,000 Jewish companies were either shut down or transferred for virtually nothing to non-Jewish Germans.[14]

The law known as the Reich Flight Tax of 1931, which was initially intended to tax wealthy Germans who moved their assets abroad, was repurposed as a punitive tool against the Jews attempting to flee the Nazis.[15] Those caught had up to 90 percent of their assets seized on the spot. Operating in tandem with laws requiring Jews to disclose all their domestic and international assets, this legislation enabled the regime to amass vast amounts of Jewish wealth and belongings.

The November 1938 pogrom known as Kristallnacht marked a dramatic escalation of physical violence against the Jewish people.[16] To add insult to injury, the Jews were fined 1 billion Reichsmarks for the damages and devastation that resulted.[17] Authorities went even further and seized insurance payments that were paid to the Jews. The wealth stolen from the Jewish population through these measures greatly supported the Nazi war effort.[18] Germany's military growth was largely funded by seized assets, thus drawing a direct link between economic and financial persecution and the Nazi state's military ambitions.

The reaction of the global community to the plight of German Jews at the time was, at best, lukewarm. The Evian Conference of 1938, which was convened to address the situation in Germany, did not result in any noteworthy increase in support or assistance. This apathy was partly because of economic stresses and pressures experienced in other parts of the world at the time. This lack of international action indirectly facilitated the Nazi regime's continued assault.

The economic persecution of Jews in Nazi Germany shows the efficiency of financial mechanisms as agents of oppression. By means of laws, levies, and decrees, the Nazi government deprived Jews of their economic power and wealth, thereby funding its expansionist and homicidal objectives. This dark chapter in world history shows how quickly and viciously the state can turn its centralized financial, economic, and military might on its citizens.

United States: The McCarthy Era

From the late 1940s to the late 1950s, the United States underwent a great degree of anxiety about communism—a period known as the McCarthy era (named for Senator Joseph McCarthy). During this period, the government launched several initiatives to identify and disclose the identity of individuals who it claimed to be communists or Soviet spies within American society.

In Hollywood and the larger entertainment industry, blacklists were prevalent, targeting individuals thought to have communist affiliations or histories.[19] The House Un-American Activities Committee (HUAC) held several hearings exploring communist connections and affiliations within the film industry. People suspected of having ties to communism were placed on a blacklist, which prevented them from finding employment. They were often subjected to public humiliation and scorn. Important personalities in the entertainment business, including writers, directors, and actors, as well as educators, authors, and government officials outside Hollywood, suffered significantly as a result of these actions.[20]

Personal bank accounts and financial transactions of suspects were rigorously surveilled for any evidence of support for communist activity. Fearing retribution, many self-censored and decided against supporting progressive groups and causes. There was great apprehension over the prospect of being seen as a communist sympathizer in any shape or form.[21]

Those who were suspected of such Soviet affiliations, whether justifiably or not, had their lives ruined. Once on a blacklist, you were most likely unemployable. Many fell into financial hardship and even destitution. Even when the anticommunist fervor subsided, many of the victims in the years that followed were still unable to restore their professional or social status because of their former real or alleged affiliation with communism.[22] The lasting impacts of the McCarthy era warn us about the dangers of economic control and surveillance even within a democratic nation like the United States.

WHAT IF?

It is interesting to ponder the role that a censorship-resistant, permissionless, unconfiscatable, and uninflatable money might have played in each of these regimes. How might it have helped mitigate state control and provide a layer of financial autonomy and privacy previously unattainable? The mental image of the Rock of Centaurus, discussed in part I, might help with the exercise, particularly where it is hard to imagine something like the internet playing a part centuries ago. The idea is that of a scarce physical asset that could be turned invisible and transported at the speed of light.

Imagine such an asset in Medieval England, where it might have been seen as a hidden treasure, its value immune to the grasp of the British Crown. Unlike gold or land, which could be seized, this invisible treasure would remain hidden in plain sight, accessible only to those who knew the secret magic words. For the merchant wary of the Crown's prying eyes or the noble seeking to safeguard their fortune from royal decrees, it would have offered a sanctuary of wealth:

untouchable and unseen, its value preserved beyond the reach of feudal power. Would a middle-class Medieval Englishman have found value in such an asset?

In Nazi Germany's era of terror, it would have represented a sliver of hope, a form of wealth that was impossible to confiscate. It would have been a means of preserving wealth that bore no mark of identity, no Star of David. As families fled in search of safety, their fortunes could have traveled with them, invisible, as a silent companion that required no suitcase—just the knowledge of a few secret words. How would this magical and powerful tool have changed the fate of millions of innocent, persecuted Jews?

In the Soviet Union, it might have served as the currency of resistance. Just as *samizdat* literature circulated covertly, spreading banned ideas and forbidden knowledge, it could have enabled a parallel economy beneath the surface of state control. This *samizdat* money, flowing through the digital underground, would have empowered dissidents and reformers, allowing them to support each other without fear of interception.

During the McCarthy era in the United States, it might have served as a financial lifeline, a means of circumventing the blacklist that sought to starve suspected communists and Soviet spies into submission. With this invisible and uncensorable currency, the accused could have continued to earn, spend, and support their families. Their transactions would have been shielded from surveillance. It would have been a money of privacy and dignity in an age when both were under siege.

In each of these historical moments, the potential of a powerful tool like bitcoin to act as a bastion of economic freedom and resilience against the overreach of oppressive powers shines through. While these are thought experiments, we should remember that there are millions around the world today who continue to experience persecution at the hands of authoritarian regimes at an equivalent or even greater degree than these examples from history. These examples may seem distant for those living in free societies, but they should serve as a stark reminder of the precarious geopolitical situation we live in, exacerbated by the interconnectedness of global economies and supply chains. The idea that such turmoil and abuses of power could never unfold in free societies in the future is dangerously naïve.

In sum, the primary takeaway here is the inherent vulnerability of physical assets and fiat currency given their susceptibility to surveillance, confiscation, and manipulation by the state. It is a useful mental exercise to ponder bitcoin's powerful and unprecedented properties in this light.

CONTEMPORARY PERSPECTIVES

Venezuela under President Nicolás Maduro is a modern illustration of a surveillance state in operation. It demonstrates how the state can use various means at its disposal to oppress a population during a time of economic and political turmoil. The state has used a variety of technology-based tools to impose financial and economic restrictions aimed at preserving power and stifling its opposition.

Venezuela's economy has been hyperinflationary, with inflation figures peaking recently at unprecedented heights. The government responded by imposing stringent currency controls and limiting access to foreign currencies, thus depriving residents of any capacity to safeguard their money or transact abroad.[23] The Carnet de la Patria system is a key component of the state's financial censorship.[24] Using a government-issued ID, the system controls citizens' access to basic needs like food subsidies, health care, and fuel. The system has been criticized as effectively establishing a social credit system wherein benefits may be denied to anybody not aligned with the government.[25]

Remittances from abroad, a primary source of household income in many cases, have also been a target of surveillance. The government has tried to monopolize control over remittances, imposing hefty fees and unfavorable exchange rates, thus drastically reducing the amount of funds sent back home by Venezuelan nationals abroad.[26] International sanctions impose further restrictions and impediments on sending economic support to residents, thus isolating them even further.

Against this backdrop of hyperinflation and economic collapse, bitcoin has offered some respite. With access to U.S. dollars tightly limited, bitcoin has created a zone of autonomy wherein people may transact outside official oversight.[27] In many cases, it has proven to be the only tool available to Venezuelan people to receive donations from abroad and also transact with the outside world to import much needed goods and services.[28]

The Islamic Republic of Iran offers another case in the study of state-sponsored censorship and financial control with a view to retaining power and quelling opposition. The government restricts the flow of information and uses economic means to thwart opposition parties. Many of its measures affect personal freedoms, particularly with respect to women. International sanctions pertaining to the government's nuclear program and support for terrorism make matters much

worse for residents. Several crucial industries, including banking, financial services, and oil exports, are subject to sanctions by the United States, European
Union, and United Nations. The sanctions have crippled Iran's economy, pushing
inflation rates to over 50 percent, and devaluing the Iranian rial. In response, the
government has implemented capital controls and stepped up financial surveillance. The result is that residents are further marginalized and isolated.[29] In 2018,
following a major devaluation of the rial, there were widespread protests across
Iran reflecting the people's frustration with the economic mismanagement of the
nation's currency.[30] In response, the government imposed further capital controls
and restrictions on foreign currency holdings by citizens.

In this context, bitcoin provides many Iranians with a way out. For most Iranians, bitcoin presents an unprecedented means of interacting with the global
economy on their own terms. It offers a way to save money as the value of the
rial continues its decline and sanctions restrict access to conventional financial
services. It also provides a censorship-resistant method for remittances. Bitcoin
is often the only means by which donors and Iranians living abroad can send
money into the country. Bitcoin facilitates transfer almost for free, when all
other avenues are choked by sanctions, impose outrageous fee and exchange
rates, and involve severe delays.[31]

Beyond personal financial security, bitcoin's value to the Iranian people is
impossible to exaggerate. It continues to prove a lifeline to entrepreneurs, and
business owners trying to bypass restrictions to procure necessities to make a
living.[32] Navigating economic barriers is a way of life for Iranians—bitcoin offers
them hope.

Russia, in keeping with its Soviet era history, continues its long tradition of
extensive financial surveillance of its citizenry. The government achieves this
through a sophisticated network that tracks financial activities inside and outside
the country. Laws passed by the government mandate that banks and financial
institutions provide comprehensive details of account holders and transactions to
federal authorities. This enables the state to monitor the financial operations of
people and companies considered antagonistic or dangerous to the government.

The government has several levers it may pull to cut off financial support to
opposition parties, thereby restricting their ability to organize protests or put
up any meaningful opposition to the regime.[33] Laws mandate that nongovern-
mental organizations (NGOs) and media outlets disclose all foreign financing,
which serves to stigmatize and restrict their effectiveness. The government also

frequently freezes bank accounts and assets of those suspected of extremism, a phrase subject to liberal interpretation.[34]

The impending arrival of the digital ruble will only serve to extend these surveillance powers of the state into the financial and economic affairs of the population. A digital ruble would provide the government unmatched access to financial data, enabling real-time surveillance of economic activity, including daily transactions. Russia is also working to establish a "sovereign internet" in response to sanctions from the West.[35] This would provide the Kremlin unfettered access to cross-border data flows and financial activities. All these actions help to aggregate and concentrate power at the center. In this context, bitcoin gives Russian citizens a semblance of financial autonomy from state control, enables access to international markets, and allows the transfer of remittances in order to make ends meet.[36]

China's approach to censorship and surveillance is incredibly sophisticated. The state deploys a combination of cutting-edge technology and legislation to achieve its supervisory objectives. Its central banking digital currency, the digital yuan, advances the government's capabilities on this front. The nation's central bank issues and controls it, thus giving the state extensive control over the people's financial activities.

China has tight currency controls in place and closely monitors all cross-border transactions. It thus controls all investment activity and restricts the outflow of capital. These measures are meant to bolster the country's economy and the currency. The state's all-encompassing financial surveillance system shows the government's focus on controlling the social and economic life of the nation. In a system that values conformity and control, bitcoin offers an avenue for direct participation in international markets, in a private and self-sovereign manner.

A Global Trend

There is an unmistakable and disturbing trend of governments around the world using digital platforms and financial systems to stifle dissent and control narratives. They may vary in degree across regions, but their underlying objective remains constant—the preservation of power by thwarting the freedom of expression. Governments often achieve these ends through economic control by leveraging the latest technologies at their disposal. These developments present some of the biggest challenges to human rights in the digital era.

The Freedom House "Freedom on the Net" report, which surveys freedom on the internet, recently found an increase in the use of digital technologies to oppress and exert control over people around the world.[37] The study found that more and more governments use advanced techniques to track online financial activities. This is an increasing trend and shows no signs of abating. Usually justified under the cover of national security or fraud prevention, these measures are invariably used against political opponents, activists, and journalists.

The Committee to Protect Journalists (CPJ) offers another lens through which one may view this problem. It is clear that journalists, especially those covering delicate subjects or working in repressive environments, are experiencing financial retaliation and retribution.[38] CPJ documents numerous cases where, immediately following some form of critical reporting, bank accounts are frozen, and financial transactions are halted. Facing such threats on their livelihoods, journalists have no option but to self-censor or completely quit investigative reporting.

For instance, authorities in nations like Russia, Turkey, and several other Group of 20 (G20) nations have been known to target media outlets and reporters with economic penalties, fines, and other financial restrictions as payback for critical coverage.[39] These actions affect not just the reporters but also the larger media industry, discouraging investigative journalism or any sort of critical coverage.

Early in 2022, truckers in Canada staged protests and demonstrations against overbearing COVID-19 rules and restrictions. The administration used the Emergencies Act—a potent weapon intended only for times of national crisis—to quell the demonstrations. They used the emergency legislation to freeze the personal bank accounts of the protestors and other participants. These freezes occurred without any prior warning to the account holders or as the result of any court order. The actions led to extensive debate about whether such actions violated the fundamental rights of the people. A Canadian court subsequently ruled that these government actions under the Emergencies Act were unlawful.[40]

With this backdrop, bitcoin offers a new paradigm. As a monetary asset free from censorship, it has helped NGOs in authoritarian governments and opposition groups around the world. For instance, in Belarus, bitcoin donations have supported striking workers and protesters against the government of Alexander Lukashenko.[41] Ukraine requested bitcoin contributions on Twitter early in 2022 and received over $100 million in cryptocurrency. In these cases, bitcoin shows its ability to enable safe, anonymous transactions outside the reach of repressive regimes. It is arguably the most powerful financial tool available to facilitate political protests and civil disobedience in authoritarian regimes.

According to the Economist Intelligence Unit (an affiliate of *The Economist*), only forty-three of the more than seventy elections in 2023 were fully free and fair. It also found that fewer than 8 percent of people worldwide live in complete democracies; and 39.4 percent are under authoritarian control—a rise from 36.9 percent in 2022.[42] The Human Rights Foundation paints an even more grim picture. According to recent reports, it estimates that 54 percent of the world's population lives under some form of authoritarian regime. In other words, one in two people experience some or all the hardships we have discussed in this chapter. It is estimated that 3 billion people live under fully authoritarian regimes across fifty-five countries, "where there are no free and fair elections, no separation of state powers, no independent media, no vibrant civil society, and no civil liberties." An additional 1.2 billion people live under competitive authoritarian regimes across another forty-one countries—places where "opposition parties are allowed to exist but suffer pervasive harassment and judicial persecution."[43]

Bitcoin offers a path to reclaim the human right to economic self-determination. It envisions a future where financial independence is available to all, regardless of the whims of monarchs, tyrants, or despotic governments who control money as a method of controlling the citizenry. Bitcoin's global and borderless nature challenges the very concept of financial censorship. It reimagines a world where money flows as freely as information on the internet.

Central Bank Digital Currencies

The discussion of the surveillance state would be incomplete without mention of a new technological innovation on the horizon: Central bank digital currencies (CBDCs). A CBDC is a digital form of money issued directly by a central bank and made available to the public. Fiat money today typically exists in two forms: physical currency issued by the central bank, and digital reserves held by commercial banks at the central bank. A CBDC represents a novel change to this dichotomy—it would be issued directly to the public by the central bank (like cash) but in digital form. The digital currency would be a direct liability of the central bank, rather than of a commercial bank.

The U.S. Federal Reserve published a paper titled "Money and Payments: The U.S. Dollar in the Age of Digital Transformation" in 2022 discussing the pros and cons of a CBDC.[44] However, no decisions have yet been made on whether to launch one. CBDCs are often touted for their potential to enhance the efficiency, security, and inclusivity of financial systems. By providing a digital form of cash, CBDCs could reduce transaction costs and settlement times. They may help financial inclusion by offering the unbanked direct access to digital money without the need for commercial banks as intermediaries. They may enhance the ability of central banks to implement monetary policy by interfacing directly with the masses. As programmable money, they may reduce illicit financial activities through traceability.

While none of these factors are untrue per se, the flipside of these benefits is that a CBDC further strengthens the state's unfettered control and influence over money. Many mistakenly group bitcoin and CBDCs under the same "crypto" or "blockchain" umbrella, not appreciating that such an association could not be more misplaced. Bitcoin and CBDCs stand as polar opposites, embodying fundamentally opposing values. Where bitcoin is based on decentralized consensus, CBDCs epitomize centralization and concentration of power within the state, granting it unparalleled authority over the financial system. Where bitcoin offers a fixed, unalterable supply, CBDCs make it even easier for the state to inflate the money supply with a keystroke. Where bitcoin offers permissionless access and censorship resistance, CBDCs impose layers of permission, placing the ability to access and spend one's own money at the discretion of the state. Where bitcoin defends privacy through pseudonymity, CBDCs eliminate even the pretense of transactional privacy, exposing every interaction to potential scrutiny. Where bitcoin is unconfiscatable, CBDCs make the seizure of funds seamless and at the mercy of the state.

Imagine a world where the money in your account comes with an expiration date, vanishing if not spent within a specified time frame (Keynesians might rejoice at the idea). Imagine fines, taxes, or penalties deducted from your balance instantly and without prior consent, leaving you powerless against the whims of state authorities. CBDCs represent the final stage in a quiet coup d'état, where the state seizes absolute control over the financial system, transforming money into a weapon of surveillance, control, and coercion—all under the guise of innovation and efficiency. Far from belonging to the same technological lineage, bitcoin and CBDCs are diametrically opposed: one champions individual freedom and financial autonomy, while the other advances state control and oversight.

> It is impossible to grasp the meaning of the idea of sound money if one does not realize that it was devised as an instrument for the protection of civil liberties against despotic inroads on the part of governments. Ideologically it belongs in the same class with political constitutions and bills of rights.[45]
>
> Ludwig von Mises

CHAPTER 13

"Governments Will Ban Bitcoin"

There is great irony in the concern that governments will ban bitcoin. Remember the original intention behind Satoshi's invention: to withstand and survive a coordinated attack by centralized authorities. He made this objective clear on multiple occasions:

> Governments are good at cutting off the heads of centrally controlled networks like Napster, but pure P2P [peer-to-peer] networks like Gnutella and Tor seem to be holding their own.[1]
>
> —Satoshi Nakamoto, November 7, 2008

> A lot of people automatically dismiss e-currency as a lost cause because of all the companies that failed since the 1990's. I hope it's obvious it was only the centrally controlled nature of those systems that doomed them.
>
> —Satoshi Nakamoto, February 15, 2009

Based on Satoshi's stated objective, the notion that bitcoin can be shut down by a government is to say that bitcoin has not functioned as intended. In other words, there is an irony in evaluating whether governments will allow bitcoin to exist when it was created specifically to resist such an existential threat. Satoshi's assumption was that certain governments (particularly authoritarian ones) or perhaps even all governments would inevitably see bitcoin as a threat to their control over the financial system and attempt to ban it. Bitcoin's properties of immutability and censorship resistance are only real if they hold true in the face of such attacks.

Satoshi draws a distinction between centralized networks, which can be easily targeted and shut down by governments (as exemplified by Napster), and decentralized peer-to-peer (P2P) networks, which have proven to be more resilient (such as Gnutella and Tor). This distinction is a critical feature of bitcoin's architecture and its ability to withstand government bans or attempts at control.

A HYPOTHETICAL BAN

A centralized system has a single point of failure that can be shut down through coercion (which may be legal or illegal). Decentralized systems are more resilient because they have no single point to attack. This formed the basis of Satoshi's thinking in creating a system sufficiently resilient to withstand coordinated government efforts to control or ban it.

Nothing like bitcoin has ever existed in the traditional financial system. Governments and authorities have always had the power to shut down a bank or financial institution by targeting its C-suite executives, board, management team, employees, physical office space, and so on. With bitcoin, no such options are available to governments. While they may block access to cryptocurrency exchanges or disrupt the conversion of fiat currency (which is their exclusive domain) into bitcoin, their ability to attack the actual bitcoin network is very limited. Because bitcoin transactions are pseudonymous, it makes enforcement against specific users resident in the jurisdiction complicated and nearly impossible. As a result, even in countries where bitcoin is officially banned, P2P trading and the use of virtual private networks (VPNs) have allowed users to continue accessing the network.

To understand how a ban on bitcoin might be ineffective, let us walk through a hypothetical scenario in a given country. This scenario draws on real-world examples from countries like Nigeria and China, which have attempted to regulate or restrict the use of bitcoin.

Step 1. Government announces a ban: The government, without warning, introduces a ban on trading or possessing bitcoin. This would be similar to Nigeria, where the central bank banned banks from servicing cryptocurrency exchanges in 2021. China has repeatedly gone back and forth with bans on bitcoin mining and trading.

Step 2. Banks and exchanges comply: Banks and cryptocurrency exchanges (being centralized institutions) have no choice but to comply with the ban. They either cease operations or block local residents from operating on their platforms. In China, following the government-imposed ban, local exchanges were forced to restrict user access in response to regulatory pressure.

Step 3. Shift to P2P and decentralized platforms: Bitcoin users show their resilience; they quickly adapt by moving to P2P trading platforms and decentralized exchanges that do not have a centralized authority. On these platforms, they can continue engaging in direct transactions with other users, beyond the reach (or even knowledge, if done correctly) of authorities. In Nigeria, for example, bitcoin usage (via P2P trading platforms) surged after the ban.

Step 4. Use of privacy tools: VPNs and other privacy-enhancing tools are used to circumvent surveillance and to access restricted platforms. VPNs are used extensively by citizens of most authoritarian regimes around the world, and they allow users to mask their Internet Protocol (IP) addresses, making it challenging for authorities to enforce effective bans on internet usage.

Step 5. Adaptation of transaction methods: As long as restrictions remain on the connectivity of fiat currency to bitcoin, it is always possible for users to survive in a bitcoin-only ecosystem. Individuals might start using bitcoin for direct transactions for goods and services, and use paper wallets and cold storage to hold bitcoin offline, away from surveillance. These methods are hard to trace and shut down.

Step 6. International transactions and remittances: For a country with a significant diaspora or reliance on remittances, like Nigeria, bitcoin becomes an invaluable tool for cross-border transactions. Friends and relatives abroad continue sending bitcoin remittances to support residents. This form of remittance is seen as more desirable than traditional systems, given lower fees, convenience, anonymity, and censorship resistance.

The specific features of bitcoin that make it resistant and resilient against a government ban are the following:

1. Decentralization: True decentralization (i.e., not just distributed nodes and miners but the absence of a leader, foundation, etc., that can

exercise any form of control over the network) limits any single points of attack or control.

2. Pseudonymity: While not completely anonymous, bitcoin transactions can be conducted in a way that does not disclose the true identity of transactors (pseudonymity, though not anonymity), which greatly limits the ability of a government to bring enforcement actions against specific users.

3. Borderless: Just like the internet, bitcoin is borderless and does not require authorizations to cross state lines. No physical or digital checkpoints can override its censorship resistance. This enables international transactions independent of local restrictions.

4. P2P: The ability to transact directly with others without a centralized platform—akin to transacting in physical cash in the real world—means that even if exchanges are banned, individuals can still trade and use bitcoin.

Despite the ban, Nigeria ranks second globally in terms of cryptocurrency adoption based on Chainalysis' 2023 Global Crypto Adoption Index.[2] In a survey conducted by Kucoin, nearly two-thirds of Nigerian cryptocurrency investors surveyed used fiat to buy cryptocurrencies on P2P exchanges.[3] They rely on P2P platforms as an on-ramp for bitcoin and use it as a tool for receiving remittances and engaging in commercial transactions, according to Chainalysis. It is also used as a store of value. For background, the Nigerian naira has fallen almost 90 percent against the U.S. dollar since 2014, and annual inflation currently stands at over 33 percent (inflation in food prices is over 40 percent) according to the Central Bank of Nigeria.[4]

The scenario in our hypothetical country (inspired by real-world examples) illustrates the significant challenges governments face in enforcing bitcoin bans. The decentralized, P2P, and borderless nature of bitcoin, combined with the adaptability of its users, renders such bans largely ineffective. While governments can create hurdles and discourage mainstream adoption, the very design of bitcoin ensures that it can continue to operate and thrive even in hostile regulatory environments.

THE PSYCHOLOGY OF A BAN

A government's act of banning bitcoin, besides being ineffective, could also prove counterproductive. A decision by the state to ban something sends many powerful signals. For one, it highlights the authority's perceived threat from the banned object, which might inadvertently validate its significance and potential. This phenomenon has been observed across various domains, including technology, literature, and social movements. Let us consider a few examples.

In the United States, the government banned the production, importation, and sale of alcoholic beverages during the 1920s. This period is referred to as the Prohibition Era. Did these measures, introduced by an amendment to the U.S. Constitution, eliminate liquor consumption? The Prohibition Era saw the rise of bootlegging and speakeasies. It made alcohol consumption more appealing than ever before to many because it was viewed as an act of rebellion against authority. The ban and related constitutional amendment were repealed in 1933, making Prohibition Era speakeasy-inspired bars a cultural mainstay of nightlife across the United States and beyond to this day.

The Streisand effect demonstrates the unintended consequences of attempts to hide, conceal, or censor information. It is named after Barbra Streisand, whose attorney attempted in 2003 to suppress the publication of a photograph showing her clifftop residence in Malibu (which had been taken to document coastal erosion in California). The attempt inadvertently drew far greater attention to the photograph, which might otherwise have remained obscure. The attempted censorship led to greater dissemination, with millions viewing it despite legal efforts.

This phenomenon can be seen in various other cases through history where bans on books or films have inadvertently increased their popularity, readership, or viewership. The dystopian novel by George Orwell, *1984*, and *Brave New World*, a science fiction novel by Aldous Huxley, are two examples in literature. The books have been banned all over the world, especially in classrooms. However, the attempts at suppression have only fueled curiosity. The "forbidden fruit" becomes far more desirable than it may have been in the absence of the bans. Today, the books are regarded as classics and continue to be widely read and discussed.

By attempting to ban bitcoin, governments inadvertently draw tremendous attention to it. And bitcoin thrives on such attention. As P. T. Barnum noted, "There's no such thing as bad publicity." A ban and the ensuing attention can drive people to understand what it is and why it is perceived as a threat to the government in question. Just like banned books, photographs, and substances have a way of attracting more consumers, a ban on bitcoin can spur greater interest. Some may be attracted to it out of curiosity, and some out of sheer defiance.

Another inadvertent consequence of a government ban may be that it simply sparks more innovation to circumvent the ban. Developers and users may be motivated to create more robust privacy tools and decentralized exchanges. "Everything is good for bitcoin." The mythical monster, Hydra, is a serpentine creature with multiple heads—chopping off one head results in it growing two more in its place. In a similar vein, a bitcoin ban might cause an acceleration of innovation in the bitcoin ecosystem, making the network stronger than before.

POLITICAL GAME THEORY

In a scenario where various governments contemplate the prohibition of bitcoin, analyzing the situation through the lens of game theory presents interesting dynamics that would come into play. Let us consider a scenario where several governments around the world (perhaps all, hypothetically) are deliberating a blanket ban on bitcoin. Following a great deal of thought, they have concluded that bitcoin presents too much of a risk to their sovereign control of the monetary policy, and therefore the threat must be eliminated. Now it is time to come to global consensus regarding the implementation and execution of the worldwide ban.

But here lies the problem. In this geopolitical game, there will likely be holdout countries that recognize an opportunity to differentiate themselves by adopting a more bitcoin-friendly stance. Many such countries already exist, and it would be almost inconceivable for them to join any such global coalition against bitcoin. For example, El Salvador has adopted bitcoin as legal tender, and is unlikely to ever ban it. The last presidential election in El Salvador took place on February 4, 2024, when Nayib Bukele, who was responsible for the adoption of bitcoin as legal tender, claimed a landslide victory, securing over 80 percent of the votes. The proverbial genie is long out of the bottle as far as that nation's relationship with bitcoin goes.

Other similar countries might anticipate the economic benefits of attracting bitcoin businesses, innovators, and investors seeking refuge from restrictive regimes of the anti-bitcoin coalition. By positioning themselves as sanctuaries for digital assets, these nations could gain a competitive edge in digital finance. This would act as a major deterrent to participation in the bitcoin ban. This divergence in strategy would create a global patchwork of policies.

The conflicting incentives on the international stage present a classic prisoner's dilemma. Each government faces a choice: ban bitcoin and risk losing potential technological and economic benefits, or embrace it and potentially undermine one's control over monetary policy. The fear of being perceived as a technological laggard and missing out on an influx of money from rich bitcoiners from around the world may push more countries to adopt a friendly stance toward bitcoin. They may choose to accept the potential downside of diminishing influence over monetary policy rather than lose to their neighboring countries that may choose to open their doors to the asset.

Similar dynamics have played out historically with the advent of new technologies or financial systems. Countries or regions that were early adopters of the internet and related technological innovations (e.g. Silicon Valley in the United States) have reaped significant economic rewards. Conversely, nations that resisted technological changes often found themselves playing catch-up. We see this psychology at work in the cryptocurrency industry with countries like Singapore, United Arab Emirates, Ukraine, Portugal, Switzerland, the United Kingdom, and several others having declared their intention to become the "crypto capital of the world" at different points in time. In July 2024, former president Donald Trump, called for the United States to be the "crypto capital of the planet."[5]

This analysis resonates with the broader historical context of technological adoption and economic competition among nations. The Age of Exploration was a period in history that began in the early fifteenth century and lasted until the seventeenth century. During this period, European seafarers explored the world by ship in their quest for knowledge and wealth. The pioneers of these endeavors ruled the world for the centuries that followed. Today, a similar dynamic is potentially playing out with bitcoin. Those that adapt and integrate it stand to gain, while those that resist may find themselves at a strategic disadvantage.

TROJAN HORSE

Bitcoin has surreptitiously infiltrated and interwoven itself into many systems that would typically have resisted or rejected it altogether because of the threat it poses to them. It does indeed seem to be that "sly roundabout way" that Friedrich Hayek talked about all those years ago, in 1984.[6] The remarkable strategic cunning of bitcoin's design, and its implications for authoritarian regimes in particular, is worth discussing here.

The Trojan horse, as recounted in Virgil's *The Aeneid*, serves as an apt metaphor for bitcoin's entry into the global financial ecosystem. The Greeks, unable to breach Troy's formidable defenses through conventional means, resorted to subterfuge. They embedded their warriors within a seemingly innocuous gift—a wooden horse that the enemies willingly wheel past their defenses into their city. Bitcoin, under the guise of a lucrative investment opportunity—digital gold, has made its way into the vaults of individuals, corporations, and even governments, many of whom may not fully appreciate its revolutionary potential to undermine centralized control.

As discussed earlier, bitcoin is already past the point of no return in many nations. Even in the United States, bitcoin's journey toward mainstream acceptance was marked by a pivotal moment when the U.S. Securities and Exchange Commission (SEC) approved spot bitcoin exchange-traded funds (ETFs) in January 2024. This regulatory endorsement effectively signaled bitcoin's legitimacy as an investment suitable for the general populace, thus embedding it deeper within the financial system and rendering any attempts at prohibition futile.

With this level of broad distribution, it is safe to say that it is no longer politically tenable to ban an asset that people of all walks of life have invested their hard-earned money into; an asset that has found its way into retirement savings accounts and pension funds. The SEC's approval is a modern-day equivalent of the Trojans pulling the wooden horse within their city walls, beyond which point the process of transformation of the monetary system (for the better, no doubt, unlike with the Trojans horse) becomes irreversible.

Authoritarian regimes traditionally opposed to any form of decentralization that could undermine their control find themselves in a paradoxical embrace of bitcoin. Attracted by the potential for economic gain and the allure of being seen as forward-thinking and innovative, these regimes inadvertently promote the very forces of decentralization and freedom they typically suppress.

As wealthy individuals, institutions, and governments continue to invest in bitcoin, they become stealthily co-opted. Economic incentives trump all others and make them defend their investment. To quote Voltaire (again): "When it is a question of money, everybody is of the same religion." People with an authoritarian history find themselves preaching the virtues of decentralization and challenging the centralized status quo. Bitcoin's rise thus signifies a quiet and nonviolent revolution operating through peaceful economic incentives.

LEGALITY OF A BAN

For the purposes of this discussion, we shall look at the legal implications of a potential bitcoin ban in the world's largest economy—the United States. Bitcoin adoption in the United States has seen significant growth over the years, reflecting its increasing acceptance among the general public, businesses, and institutional investors. Surveys and reports indicate that 20 to 40 percent of adult Americans (approximately 45 to 90 million people), have traded in bitcoin and/or other cryptocurrencies.[7]

This adoption is not just limited to individuals; a growing number of businesses, from small enterprises to large corporations, have started accepting bitcoin as a form of payment. There are estimated to be around 30,000 bitcoin automated teller machines (ATMs) across the country.[8] Institutional adoption has also surged, with major financial institutions and investment funds incorporating bitcoin into their portfolios. The Commodity Futures Trading Commission (CFTC) regulates the trading of bitcoin futures contracts. The SEC has approved ETFs for bitcoin (allowing for the mass offering of bitcoin linked securities to the general public). In such circumstances, a government ban on holding or transacting in bitcoin would undoubtedly face legal challenges on several grounds:

1. Due process under the Fifth Amendment: The Fifth Amendment of the U.S. Constitution says to the federal government that no one shall be "deprived of life, liberty or property without due process of law." A sudden attempt to ban or confiscate bitcoin belonging to people could be seen as a violation of this right without due process. Given the legitimization of bitcoin by the SEC and the CFTC, such a move by the government would be even harder to justify. Investors could claim that they have a legitimate expectation of the continued legality of their investments.

2. Takings clause under the Fifth Amendment: The Takings Clause of the Fifth Amendment of the U.S. Constitution prohibits the government from taking private property for public use without "just compensation." This would certainly present grounds to challenge a bitcoin ban or confiscation, which could be argued to be a form of "taking" by the government and requiring just compensation.

3. The First Amendment: The First Amendment to the U.S. Constitution protects freedom of speech and expression. Bitcoin, in essence, is no more than lines of code. This may be argued to be a form of speech or expression, warranting protection under the First Amendment. Bitcoin transactions are merely alphanumeric text sent from one consenting party to another.

4. The Fourth Amendment: The Fourth Amendment to the U.S. Constitution protects against unreasonable searches and seizures. The government would likely need to engage in some form of digital surveillance or physical searches to obtain private keys in order to access people's bitcoin. Such actions could potentially be challenged under the Fourth Amendment.

5. Reasonable expectation of privacy: The reasonable expectation of privacy is a legal doctrine also arising from the Fourth Amendment to the U.S. Constitution, which individuals may rely on to resist the government seeking to gain access to their digital wallets and transactions. Such intrusive actions by the government without a warrant or probable cause could be argued to be unconstitutional.

The specifics of any legal challenge would depend heavily on the exact nature of the government's actions and the reasons given for them.

Comparison with Executive Order 6102

In April 1933, President Franklin D. Roosevelt passed the infamous Executive Order 6102 forbidding the "hoarding of gold coin, gold bullion, and gold certificates within the continental United States." The penalty for violation included fines amounting to $10,000 or ten years of imprisonment or both. The order operated as a de facto confiscation of gold holdings belonging to American citizens. This obviously draws into question the earlier analysis regarding the legal basis for such confiscation of property in the United States. Could a scenario similar to Executive Order 6102 occur in relation to bitcoin? An executive order like 6102 (or legislative act with similar effect) being implemented today or in the future to confiscate bitcoin seems unlikely for several reasons, mainly relating to the nature of bitcoin versus gold, the legal and economic context of the 1930s compared to today, and the evolution of financial systems and technologies.

First, Executive Order 6102 was issued in the context of the Great Depression, a time of great economic strife: desperate times call for desperate measures. Its intended purpose was to stabilize the U.S. banking system and economy. Today's economic conditions and the role of bitcoin in the economy are very different. The internationalization of the financial system and investment landscape mean that bitcoin is part of a broader, more complex, and interconnected environment. This would make an attempt to confiscate holdings of American residents alone almost impossible to implement.

Second, as discussed earlier in this chapter, confiscation of a digital commodity is difficult. It is inherently harder for a government to seize bitcoin compared to gold given that bitcoin's storage simply involves a set of words on a small piece of paper (or committed to memory) rather than having to transport and secure heavy pieces of metal in a safe or vault. In the face of a coercive attempt at confiscation, one could always claim, as a last resort, to have lost their private keys and therefore their bitcoin. One could also shard, or split up, their private keys and physically store a fragment of the key in a foreign country, thereby making it much harder to gain access to it.

Thus, it may be said with a reasonable degree of certainty that an executive order like 6102 would be extremely unlikely to succeed in any meaningful way in the context of bitcoin in the twenty-first century.

CHAPTER 14

Law and Regulation

"BITCOIN IS FOR CRIMINALS"

Cars do not cause accidents, drivers do. While bitcoin can be used for illicit activities, it is not inherently illicit or criminal. If critics actually took the time to peel back the onion, they might be surprised to note that over 99.6 percent of bitcoin transactions are perfectly legitimate, whereby it is used as a revolutionary financial instrument by millions to transact worldwide with self-sovereignty. The association of bitcoin with criminal activity is not entirely surprising. One of its earliest uses was on Silk Road, an online illegal black-market platform that was launched in 2011 and eventually shut down by the authorities in 2013. The site used bitcoin as its primary currency, allowing users to buy and sell illegal goods and services anonymously.

The reality is that criminals are typically the earliest adopters of new technologies. We have seen this with the dark web and encrypted communication tools. New technological vulnerabilities are often discovered and exploited by cyber-criminals before being patched by security specialists. The ability to transact in a private and peer-to-peer manner attracted a large proportion of criminal activity in the early years of bitcoin. As Tom Lee of Fundstrat Global Advisors has noted, "Pirates were the first people that liked gold, so we knew gold was valuable . . . criminals don't trust anybody, but they trust bitcoin."

The claim that bitcoin is a haven for criminal activities is often a dramatic cudgel in the hands of certain politicians as they try to spotlight bitcoin's darker associations in its early years. Foremost among them may be U.S. Senator Elizabeth Warren, who introduced a bill in 2023 to purportedly mitigate risks associated with money laundering, financing of terrorists, and operations by rogue nations using cryptocurrencies.[1] Key components of the proposal included extending know-your-customer (KYC) requirements to wallet providers, miners, and validators.

The bill received sweeping criticism. The extensive KYC requirements demonstrate a lack of understanding and appreciation of bitcoin's foundational principles of autonomy, privacy, and decentralization. Critics of the bill have cautioned that such steps could push innovation and economic activity related to bitcoin outside the United States, to jurisdictions with more favorable regulatory climates. As discussed in chapter 13, many of the proposals in the bill would also most likely be unconstitutional and would undoubtedly be litigated in the unlikely event that the bill ever became law.

For the purposes of this discussion, however, let us focus on Warren's underlying rationale for proposing the bill: the claim that bitcoin and other cryptocurrencies facilitate illegal activities, such as drug trafficking, ransomware attacks, and evasion of sanctions, by entities in countries like Iran, Russia, and North Korea. Despite the sensationalism, the reality tells a different story. Bitcoin accounts for a tiny portion of global criminal activity. The notion that cryptocurrencies are used primarily for illicit transactions is not supported by facts. According to Chainalysis, $24 billion worth of cryptocurrency was received by illicit addresses in 2023, accounting for just 0.34 percent of all transaction volume.[2] The figure is nearly 40 percent less than that of 2022.[3] For context, the United Nations estimates that $800 billion to $2 trillion is laundered each year through the traditional banking system.[4]

An important consideration in this analysis is that the proportion of transactions linked to illicit activities has not been increasing over the years, notwithstanding bitcoin's rapidly growing adoption and market capitalization. This trend may be attributable to enhanced regulatory frameworks, more stringent KYC and anti-money-laundering (AML) practices by cryptocurrency exchanges, and more sophisticated tracking and analysis tools. It is increasingly difficult for criminals to use bitcoin for illicit purposes (the counterpoint to this is that privacy of legitimate users is affected by these surveillance measures). In any event, even if cryptocurrency crime hits all-time highs, it remains a drop in the ocean compared to the vast sums laundered through banks and financial institutions.

Contrary to what certain politicians and many misinformed news outlets will have you believe, bitcoin's public blockchain ledger makes it a far-from-ideal tool for criminals.[5] The distributed *public* ledger is a bit of a giveaway in that regard. Every single transaction is there for the world to see (albeit in a pseudonymous manner). The inherent traceability of transactions has been on display in numerous high-profile law enforcement cases. One notable instance involved Heather Morgan and Ilya Lichtenstein, who tried to launder $4.5 billion in stolen bitcoin. Their attempts to hide the stolen funds through a series of complex transactions were thwarted because authorities were able to trace the digital trail back to the source of the theft.

In 2017, a significant amount of bitcoin was seized from cybercriminals who had infiltrated Bulgaria's customs office. Bitcoin's traceability was leveraged by the authorities, enabling the Bulgarian government to retrieve approximately 213,519 bitcoins (an amount valued at close to 18 percent of the nation's debt at the time). Another example is the U.S. government's landmark seizure of $3.36 billion in bitcoin tied to the Silk Road marketplace. These examples demonstrate how bitcoin's transparent and immutable ledger acts as a natural deterrent to criminal activity.

Many technological and societal advancements have come with trade-offs. Automobiles have significantly improved our ability to move from place to place, although they have come at the cost of traffic accidents causing injuries and deaths, as well as air and noise pollution. Medications have been developed to cure various health conditions, but they may occasionally have serious side effects. Nuclear energy, while a cleaner alternative to fossil fuels, carries the risk of radioactive waste and the potential for catastrophic accidents. Each of these advancements has brought considerable benefits, yet they also come with notable drawbacks. In each case, the broader benefits have justified the acceptance of certain downsides. Bitcoin deserves a similarly holistic and balanced evaluation.

REGULATORY FRAMEWORKS

Different jurisdictions around the world continue to create different approaches to regulating bitcoin and other cryptocurrencies. Each approach reflects the varying levels of understanding of the subject as well as the unique legal, economic, and security concerns of each country.

Legal Classification

The legal classification of bitcoin in a given jurisdiction is often a window into the diverse perceptions of regulators and lawmakers of what bitcoin represents to them. This classification in particular affects consumer protection rules relating to its sales as well as taxation of transactions and holdings. Most regulators around the world agree that bitcoin is not a security. While other cryptocurrencies continue to be the subject of debates on this front, bitcoin has rarely been drawn into question. That leaves commodities and currencies as the two remaining buckets into which bitcoin is typically placed:

Commodity: In most countries, bitcoin is classified as a commodity or similar to a commodity. In the United States, the Commodity Futures Trading Commission (CFTC) has classified bitcoin as a commodity, placing it under a regulatory framework similar to that of gold, oil, and so on. The United Kingdom, Canada, Australia, Brazil, India, and many other countries also classify bitcoin as a commodity, subjecting it to capital gains taxes and potentially income tax if it is received as payment for goods or services. Classification as a commodity also usually means that the sale of it to the general public is subject to consumer protection laws. Sellers need to be licensed, and investors must be furnished with risk disclosure regarding the asset.

Currencies: The recognition of bitcoin in some jurisdictions as a currency facilitates its use in everyday transactions. This entails the acceptance of bitcoin as being similar to fiat currencies, subjecting it to similar regulations. El Salvador made headlines in September 2021 by becoming the first country to adopt bitcoin as legal tender. This means bitcoin may be used in the settlement of debts and for the payment of taxes, as well as for daily purchases and transactions. The primary benefit of this classification is taxation. If bitcoin transactions are not subject to capital gains taxes, bitcoin becomes much more viable for everyday use. Many countries, including the United States, are exploring de minimis exemptions (i.e., transactions in bitcoin below a certain value will be exempt from capital gains tax). As bitcoin adoption increases around the world, we may start to see regulations move in this direction as users and the general public demand it.

Licensing and Compliance

Many regulators require cryptocurrency vendors, exchanges, and other related service providers to obtain licenses to operate. The objective is to protect the general public against fraud and negligence. Vendors are required to maintain certain minimum standards of security, transparency, and financial integrity. In the United States, exchanges are required to register with the Financial Crimes Enforcement Network (FinCEN) and to comply with local money transmission laws as money service businesses. Licensing regimes aim to legitimize the market by weeding out fraudulent and unreliable operators. Unfortunately, they also impose significant compliance costs, potentially limiting market entry to the larger and better funded players.

Money laundering is also a primary focus of these regulations, echoing politicians like Senator Warren. Cryptocurrency businesses are required to implement AML measures to detect, prevent, and report suspected criminal activities. The Financial Action Task Force has issued global guidelines on this front, including measures to report detailed information about bitcoin withdrawals by customers from exchanges and vendors. Compliance with AML regulations requires the implementation of customer due diligence, transaction monitoring, and reporting of suspicious activities to relevant authorities. Counterterrorism financing regulations, closely aligned with AML regulations, focus on preventing the use of bitcoin for the financing of terrorist activities. These regulations require the monitoring and reporting of transactions that are suspected to be related to terrorist financing.

The approach to regulating bitcoin varies widely across countries. Some regulators have tailormade regulatory regimes that largely address the specific nuances of bitcoin and encourage its growth and adoption. Others have adapted existing financial regulations to cover the cryptocurrency industry. The global and decentralized nature of bitcoin poses significant challenges for regulation, particularly in terms of enforcement. Regulatory arbitrage will also be an issue that regulators will have to be mindful of, particularly in the context of political game theory (as discussed in chapter 13).

Bitcoin Investment Products

Exchange-traded funds (ETFs) have long been viewed as a sort of "gateway drug" for the trillions of dollars housed in the traditional financial system to gradually find their way into bitcoin. ETFs are financial products, (that is, securities), that track the price of bitcoin and are traded on traditional stock exchanges. They allow investors to gain investment exposure to bitcoin through their brokerage accounts (where they may also hold shares of Apple and Amazon, for example) rather than purchasing it through a cryptocurrency exchange and holding it either on the exchange itself or in a digital wallet. This improves the ease with which investors may reallocate a portion of their capital to bitcoin without having to go through the onboarding process on a cryptocurrency exchange and the learning process of operating a wallet.

As financial products offered to the general public, all ETFs are required to be approved by the U.S. Securities and Exchange Commission (SEC) before they can be listed on a stock exchange. The approval process is intended to assess the product's suitability for retail investors and to ensure investor protection, market integrity, and financial transparency. Approval involves rigorous scrutiny to ensure that the ETF complies with securities laws, including risk disclosure, the ability to track bitcoin's price accurately, and safeguarding against manipulation and fraud. In 2013, the Winklevoss brothers, Cameron and Tyler, filed for SEC approval to launch the first bitcoin ETF; however, the SEC rejected the application in March 2017. The primary reasons provided by the SEC for rejection included concerns over the lack of regulation, the potential for fraud and manipulation within bitcoin markets, and the ETF's reliance on cryptocurrency exchanges that were unregulated.

The ensuing years, particularly 2021 to 2023, showcased a rather dark side of the U.S. financial regulatory landscape, notably, its propensity toward heavy-handed arbitrariness and, even more concerningly, its apparent politicization. In 2021, a perverse, obscure, and highly legalistic distinction began to be drawn between a bitcoin ETF that reflected the bitcoin spot price versus a bitcoin ETF that reflected the price of bitcoin derivative instruments (futures contracts). In the SEC's eyes, the former presented an unacceptable degree of risk to investors, while the latter did not (despite historical data unequivocally, and unsurprisingly, showing both prices to be virtually identical).

The ostensible rationale for the different treatment was that bitcoin futures contracts were regulated by the CFTC, while spot bitcoin markets had no equivalent regulated venue. In 2021, the SEC began approving bitcoin ETFs that linked to the price of bitcoin futures, while continuing to reject ETFs linked to the spot price of bitcoin. In 2023, the judicial system thankfully weighed in.

The U.S. Court of Appeals for the DC Circuit found that the SEC's distinction between the two products was "arbitrary and capricious." This highly publicized decision was a major vindication for the numerous ETF applicants and an ignominious defeat for the eminent U.S. securities regulator.

After this judgment, the SEC finally granted approval for several spot bitcoin ETFs in January 2024, marking the end of a long and highly political path to its full-fledged entry into the global financial system. We now have the world's largest asset managers, including Blackrock and Fidelity (that manage $15 trillion in assets between them), offering the product in the United States and around the globe.

Thus, the Winklevoss brothers' initial application sparked a decade-long journey marked by rejections, legal battles, political interjections, and finally the SEC's acceptance of the inevitable. In 2013, *Mad Magazine* listed the idea for a bitcoin ETF at number 5 on the list of the "20 Dumbest Things of 2013."[6] Blockrock's bitcoin ETF launched in 2024 was the fastest ETF in history to reach $10 billion in assets under management. Prior to this, the fastest time to reach this mark was around two years. It took the bitcoin ETF seven weeks to break the record, making it the most successful ETF launch in history.

CHAPTER 15

Bitcoin and Geopolitics

It costs only a few cents for the Bureau of Engraving and Printing to produce a $100 bill, but other countries had to pony up $100 of actual goods in order to obtain one.

—Barry Eichengreen

EXORBITANT PRIVILEGE

Former French finance minister Valéry Giscard d'Estaing coined the expression *privilège exorbitant* ("exorbitant privilege") in the 1960s in relation to the United States. He was not referring to U.S. military power (that is exorbitant indeed). Rather, he was pointing to the role that the U.S. dollar plays as the global reserve currency. Nearly 90 percent of foreign exchange transactions involve the U.S. dollar. Sixty percent of foreign exchange reserves are held in U.S. dollars; almost 40 percent of the world's debt is issued in U.S. dollars; and most commodities, including one of the most economically vital ones—oil, are priced in dollars. This is despite the fact that the United States today accounts for only around 20 percent of global gross domestic product (GDP).[1] Because of this dominance of the U.S. dollar, U.S. monetary policy affects not just the United States but the entire planet. The Federal Reserve's interest rate hikes or cuts affect loans denominated in U.S. dollars, making them more or less expensive, respectively, to repay. This is, without question, an exorbitant privilege that the United States has enjoyed for several decades.

Closely tied to this privilege of the U.S. dollar, is the Society for Worldwide Interbank Telecommunication (SWIFT) system used for the settlement of U.S. dollar transactions. SWIFT is an organization that provides efficient communication among financial institutions in relation to dollar payments. SWIFT does not process transactions or hold any currency; it is a messaging service that enables financial institutions worldwide to transmit information and instructions securely through a standardized system of codes. It connects to well over ten thousand financial institutions in more than two hundred countries.

The privilege of the U.S. dollar combined with the influence that the United States has over the SWIFT system enable the United States to impose economic sanctions on countries, entities, and individuals. Sanctions can restrict access to the international financial system if they cut off SWIFT, making it exceedingly difficult to access global markets and acquire foreign currency. As a result, most countries do not dare violate U.S. sanctions. The possibility of losing access to the U.S. dollar and the SWIFT system acts as a looming and imminent threat to most nations and institutions that might consider violating U.S. sanctions.

But necessity is the mother of invention. As Keith Rockwell of the Wilson Center has noted, the "weaponization of the dollar has been a wakeup call for many emerging countries and calls for 'de-dollarization' have grown louder in recent years."[2] In response to the threat of sanctions, several countries have sought ways to reduce their reliance on SWIFT and the U.S. dollar. At a Brazil, Russia, India, China, South Africa (BRICS) summit in 2022, leaders proposed the development of a new international reserve currency. Several Association of Southeast Asian Nations (ASEAN) countries have discussed using local currencies for intraregional trade. In 2023, Brazil's President Luiz Inacio Lula da Silva stated: "Every night I ask myself why all countries have to base their trade on the dollar. Why can't we do trade based on our own currencies? Who was it that decided that the dollar was the currency after the disappearance of the gold standard?"[3]

In a 2023 visit to China, Malaysian prime minister Anwar Ibrahim proposed the establishment of an Asian monetary fund to reduce reliance on the U.S. dollar.[4] The Indian Ministry of External Affairs has also announced that trade between India and Malaysia can be settled in Indian rupees in an attempt to de-dollarize. Russia and China have actively sought to de-dollarize their trade relationships for years.[5] They have signed multiple agreements to increase the use of the Russian ruble and the Chinese yuan in bilateral trade. These two countries have proposed alternatives to SWIFT. Russia's System for Transfer of Financial

Messages and China's Cross-Border Interbank Payment System are aimed at reducing reliance on SWIFT.[6] Iran and India have explored mechanisms to trade outside the U.S. dollar framework, especially for oil transactions. Turkey and Venezuela have engaged in trade agreements that utilize currencies besides the U.S. dollar (both countries face economic challenges and sanctions). Brazil and China, two of the largest economies in the BRICS group, have agreed on several occasions to use their local currencies for trade settlement. The Eurasian Economic Union (EAEU), which includes Russia, Belarus, Kazakhstan, Armenia, and Kyrgyzstan, has been exploring the use of local currencies for intra-union trade to reduce dependence on the U.S. dollar and euro.

The economic sanctions imposed on Russia in the wake of its invasion of Ukraine in 2022 were a pivotal moment on this front. The U.S. government took a number of steps to sanction Russia—most notable among them was the act of freezing the assets of the Russian Central Bank, comprised primarily of U.S. dollars and U.S. Treasury securities held in the United States.[7] The result was that the Russian government was prevented from accessing a significant portion of its own foreign currency reserves. While this step was deemed necessary in the context of Russia's attack on Ukraine, its implications continue to reverberate through the geopolitical landscape. The action has been perceived as setting a precedent that could be applied to other nations in the future. This is likely already having an impact on the way central banks around the world manage their foreign reserves. Several countries continue to look for ways to insulate themselves from the reach of sanctions.

These murmurs of discontentment with the dollar's exorbitant privilege are obviously not new given the French minister's coining of the term as early as the 1960s. But it has certainly been widely telegraphed in recent decades, too. For instance, China's intention to move away from the U.S. dollar has been articulated for well over fifteen years. As early as March 2009, in an essay posted on the People's Bank of China's website, Zhou Xiaochuan, the central bank's governor, said that China's goal was to create a reserve currency "that is disconnected from individual nations and is able to remain stable in the long run, thus removing the inherent deficiencies caused by using credit-based national currencies.[8] Zhou's statement reflected a recognition of the fact that no fiat currency can replace the dollar. While he may not have appreciated that his description of such a non-credit-based asset disconnected from any individual nation echoes bitcoin, he likely had bitcoin's analogue version, gold, in mind.

Today, there is a rapidly growing recognition of bitcoin as gold 2.0. For better or for worse, it is undeniably being seen as a potential avenue for countries to pursue transactions outside the U.S. dollar and SWIFT framework. This is not an endorsement of countries evading U.S. sanctions or of the usurpation of the U.S. dollar as reserve currency but rather an objective recognition of hard realities. For example, Iran's interest in bitcoin in recent years stems from its need to bypass U.S. sanctions. The country has actively encouraged the mining of bitcoin, seeing it as a strategic asset that can be used to trade internationally, particularly for importing goods and services that have become difficult to access because of sanctions.[9] Russia has shown interest in using bitcoin and other cryptocurrencies for similar reasons.[10] China has shown a rather ambivalent approach to bitcoin, but its intentions to take itself out of the SWIFT system are quite clear. These developments signify a potential shift in the global financial landscape in which bitcoin could play a more significant role. This could lead to a multipolar financial system and introduce new dynamics in geopolitics.

As discussed in chapter 14, it is important to reiterate that just because a tool is used in a manner that may be reprehensible to some does not make the tool itself reprehensible. Bitcoin can be used to undermine the force of U.S. sanctions against Iran and Russia, among others, but so can cash in a suitcase. The justifications for the continued existence of cash in the physical realm should apply to bitcoin in the digital realm. Cash is not deemed reprehensible despite its utility for such purposes. Seventeenth-century pirates of the Caribbean loved gold. They sailed across the seas and killed thousands to capture it, and they traded and transacted in it. None of this ever questioned the legitimacy of gold.

The United States may just have to come to terms with reality: the very utility of sanctions as an instrument of U.S. government power is likely to diminish as more and more countries employ various strategies to move away from the U.S. dollar. In statements to Congress in July 2024, Janet Yellen, secretary of the U.S. Treasury, acknowledged that the efficacy of sanctions depends on the U.S. dollar retaining its position of dominance in international transactions.[11] She noted that the more the United States has used sanctions, the more countries look for ways to engage in financial transactions that do not involve the U.S. dollar. In other words, sanctions tend to undercut the efficacy of sanctions themselves.[12]

BITCOIN NEUTRALITY

Bitcoin is apolitical money. It is a bastion of neutrality, akin to gold. In a 2013 speech, early bitcoin pioneer Andreas Antonopoulos describes this feature as follows:

> Bitcoin neutrality means being able to adopt bitcoin in any culture, any language, any religion, any geography, but also any political or economic system. So, bitcoin neutrality is about making bitcoin a standard that is independent of your desires and expectations. This isn't a libertarian currency any more than it's a communist currency. It is a currency. And it can be applied to any political system whether it is the political system you like, or not. It is a neutral currency.[13]

Just as gold has no allegiance to any flag, bitcoin represents an apolitical currency. Just like gold, bitcoin does not shift with the political winds, nor does it take sides in the affairs of nations. And like the internet, it is borderless. It cannot be co-opted like the SWIFT system as a tool by which one nation exerts control over another. Its decentralized nature insulates it from the influence of any single entity. It is an equitable financial tool accessible to anyone, anywhere, without prejudice. It symbolizes neutrality in an increasingly polarized world. The profound geopolitical and economic implications of a politically neutral currency cannot be overstated. As Saifedean Ammous observes:

> Bitcoin consumes so much energy because it uses a fully mechanical and digital process to ascertain truth. It doesn't rely on the authority of anyone. It isn't a more energy-intensive way of doing consumer payments; it's a less energy-intensive way of achieving consensus than war.
>
> Bitcoin replaces the need for strangers to have to be subject to the same government and central bank in order to trade internationally, which necessitates one government imposing its will on the rest of the world, which can only be done with war. Under the gold standard, it was the Bank of England that provided the global payment settlement platform. Under fiat, it's the Fed.
>
> Every other form of money, physical, governmental, or digital . . . relies ultimately on the authority of someone to move. Everyone wants to be that

someone and the stakes are so high, they'll fight for it. War is the only working alternative to bitcoin. We can keep using barbaric manual ways that rely on the authority of violence, causing endless conflict and politics. Or we could upgrade to a peaceful software solution that runs on electricity and cannot be corrupted by politics or violence. That's why bitcoin is worth it.[14]

BITCOIN AND AMERICA

The Age of Enlightenment was an intellectual movement that occurred in Europe in the seventeenth and eighteenth centuries. Individual liberty as opposed to absolute monarchy was a core principle of this philosophical revolution. America's Founding Fathers were greatly influenced by these Enlightenment ideas, as reflected in key documents like the Declaration of Independence and the Constitution, which seek to protect individual rights and establish a government accountable to its citizens. Many of these same ideas also echo bitcoin's core political ideology. The principles of liberty and freedom to transact peer to peer in private, without external intervention, are deeply interwoven with historical ideologies of the Age of Enlightenment and the American Revolution. On numerous occasions, America's forefathers have cautioned against the encroachment of government power and emphasized individual responsibility to resist.

> The natural progress of things is for liberty to yield and government to gain ground.
>
> —Thomas Jefferson

> It is the first responsibility of every citizen to question authority.
>
> —Benjamin Franklin

Bitcoin, in many respects, is inherently aligned with American values. The Founding Fathers believed in the power of individuals to make decisions for themselves, and to retain control over their own financial destinies, free from oppressive external forces. Bitcoin breathes new life into these beliefs.

Self-custody of one's bitcoin without needing to depend on intermediaries and centralized authorities echoes the American Revolutionary spirit that fought the British Crown's control of all economic and financial affairs, and taxation without representation. The Declaration of Independence enshrined the principles of liberty, self-determination, and the pursuit of happiness. By enabling people to secure their wealth independently, bitcoin exemplifies these principles.

Another example is the ability to transact in bitcoin on a peer-to-peer basis without external interference. The Boston Tea Party of 1773 was a political protest against the Tea Act, which restricted the freedom of Americans to trade freely. In protest, the Sons of Liberty, disguised as Native Americans, destroyed an entire shipment of tea sent by the East India Company to Boston. In line with that ideology, bitcoin provides a decentralized platform that allows users to engage in transactions independently and peer-to-peer, without the interference of banks or governments.

The notion of self-sovereignty that is core to bitcoin is reflected in the principles of the Bill of Rights. James Madison, who studied the deficiencies of the Constitution, crafted a series of corrective amendments that sought to guarantee civil rights and liberties to the individual. These rights are based on the philosophy of natural rights—all humans are given certain rights by God, and the government cannot take those rights away. The First Amendment, for instance, guarantees freedom of speech, while the Fourth Amendment protects citizens from unreasonable searches and seizures. By design, bitcoin is built around the concept that individuals should have sovereignty over their own financial transactions, protecting them from unwarranted surveillance and government overreach.

The Federalist Papers were a series of eighty-five essays written by Alexander Hamilton, James Madison, and John Jay with the aim of persuading the public to support the ratification of the U.S. Constitution. These papers provide insights into their philosophy of decentralized power in order to prevent the abuse of power by the centralized government. James Madison in particular emphasized the importance of a system of checks and balances to guard against the state's tyranny. (The American system of checks and balances was created to prevent any single branch of government from becoming too powerful.) In Federalist No. 51, Madison argues for a structure of government that ensures no single branch can dominate. He emphasized the need for the separation of powers to create a balance between the different branches of state. When he stated, "Ambition must be made to counteract ambition," what he was essentially arguing for was a system that, through incentive structures, decentralizes power at the top. This, he argued, was crucial to ensure a free and liberated society.[15]

In another striking parallel with bitcoin, the Federalist Papers were published pseudonymously (under the pseudonym, Publius). Similar to Satoshi's objective, Hamilton, Madison, and Jay chose to publish the essays pseudonymously to allow readers to focus on the material rather than the author.

There is an undeniable correlation between the foundational principles of American political history and bitcoin's architecture. It is hard to conceive of a more explicit technological manifestation of these ideologies than in bitcoin's decentralized network composed of nodes and miners spread around the globe, reflecting the system of checks and balances proposed by the framers of the U.S. political system. Bitcoin's protocol ensures that no single entity can control or manipulate the network. By decentralizing power and limiting external intervention, bitcoin represents a digital embodiment of the American spirit.

Global Reserve Asset

This confluence of ideologies may turn out to be more than a mere coincidence. It could prove to be a matter of great national significance. With the global geopolitical landscape evolving into a multipolar world, the dominance of the U.S. dollar as the global reserve currency is increasingly under threat. With the dollar's hegemony waning, there is a global quest for a replacement. Different rival currencies are being considered, either individually or as part of a basket of currencies. In such a scenario, the rise of currencies of nations that are hostile toward the United States poses significant economic and political risks.

Faced with these realities, what if the United States pursued a strategy of embracing bitcoin as the future reserve currency? While such a prospect may seem outrageous and unsettling to some readers, let us take a brief moment to evaluate with an open mind the benefits of such a strategy. A progressive and adaptive mindset is always helpful to challenge assumptions and respond to the rapidly changing circumstances facing the world.

First, by adopting bitcoin as a reserve asset, the United States can preempt the risk of an adversary establishing its currency as the global reserve and wielding undue influence. As a new "digital gold standard," bitcoin's political neutrality could be the perfect apolitical successor to the U.S. dollar. This may be the best possible outcome for the world with geopolitical tensions mounting by the day.

Second, bitcoin's borderless and inexpensive transactions could simplify international trade and finance, reducing barriers for cross-border payments. Imagine a global financial system devoid of counterparty risk, where final settlement is achieved globally every ten minutes. Imagine the trillions of dollars of efficiencies that would accrue through the disruption and elimination of the global payment systems that are built around managing counterparty risk. A digital bearer asset allowing for instant final settlement disrupts the legacy system entirely.

Third, bitcoin's permissionless nature could provide financial inclusion to hundreds of millions of unbanked people worldwide. People in even the most remote parts of the world may enter the financial system and transact independently with no more than a cell phone and an internet connection. The United States could be seen as an early pioneer in this revolution, championing freedom and equality, and reinforcing its global standing as a beacon of hope.

Fourth, bitcoin is a scarce commodity and thus offers a robust, long-term hedge against inflation and debasement of fiat currency. Adopting bitcoin as a reserve asset ahead of most other nations would potentially reap outsized financial rewards and enhance the country's strategic global influence. As more nations recognize the value of bitcoin, early adoption by the United States would set a powerful precedent. It would encourage other countries to follow suit, creating a domino effect and ushering in a new global financial order rooted in decentralization and fairness, reflecting the democratic principles that the United States has long pioneered.

On July 27, 2024, Senator Cynthia Lummis announced a bill that would see the U.S. government purchase 1 million bitcoins as a "Strategic Bitcoin Reserve" to mirror the size and scope of the gold reserves held by the country. Two of the 2024 presidential candidates, Donald Trump and Robert F. Kennedy, appeared to endorse this plan for a "strategic national bitcoin stockpile."[16] Time will tell how these specific initiatives unfold, but what is more important is the broadening of the Overton window, allowing such ideas that were previously unthinkable to enter public discourse.

CHAPTER 16

Bitcoin and the Environment

Bitcoin mining is on track to consume all of the world's energy by 2020.

—*Newsweek*, 2017

A s of 2024, bitcoin accounts for approximately 0.6 percent of global energy consumption per year (127 terawatt-hours per year), according to the Cambridge Bitcoin Energy Consumption Index. This is comparable to the amount of energy required to run clothes dryers.[1] Air-conditioning consumes approximately 2,000 terawatt-hours per year (about seventeen times that of bitcoin). The traditional banking and payments industry is estimated to consume over twenty-eight times more energy than bitcoin (and when Bitcoin Lightning is compared to instant payment services in the banking system, bitcoin is said to be millions of times more energy efficient per transaction than the traditional system).[2] In recently disclosed email communications with Martti Malmi from 2010,[3] Satoshi Nakamoto's prescience on this point is remarkable:

> Ironic if we end up having to choose between economic liberty and conservation . . .
> If [bitcoin] did grow to consume significant energy, I think it would still be less wasteful than the labour and resource intensive conventional banking activity it would replace. The cost would be an order of magnitude less than the billions in banking fees that pay for all those brick and mortar buildings, skyscrapers and junk mail credit card offers.[4]

—Satoshi Nakamoto, May 3, 2009

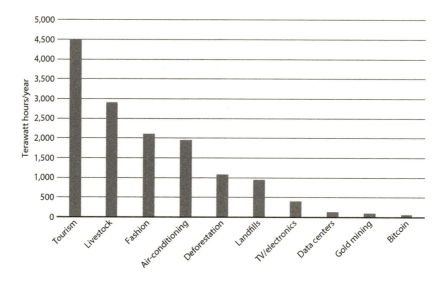

16.1 Comparison of bitcoin's emissions to other sources of emissions. *Source:* KPMG.

Although bitcoin accounts for about 0.6 percent of annual global energy consumption, the figure that is actually relevant for this discussion is bitcoin's share of emissions contributing to environmental harm. This is a much lower figure, approximately 0.13 percent.[5] The reason for this significantly lower share of emissions compared to actual energy consumption is the outsized proportion of renewable energy used in bitcoin mining.

RENEWABLE ENERGY

It is estimated that approximately 60 percent of global bitcoin mining relies on sustainable energy sources, primarily hydro, solar, and wind power.[6] Some miners are even certified to be running on 100 percent renewable energy.[7] Prominent environmental expert and venture capitalist Daniel Batten projects that the bitcoin mining industry is on track to be 80 percent sustainably powered by the end of 2030.[8] For context, the International Energy Agency (IEA) World Energy Outlook 2022 estimates that only 28 percent of the world's electricity comes from renewables. Bitcoin's use of renewable energy is, by a very large margin, the highest of any industry globally, and it is growing at a rapid pace. The chart in figure 16.1 provides a detailed breakdown.[9] While these statistics are impressive, what is often missed in the debate is bitcoin mining's role in subsidizing or bootstrapping renewable energy production around the world. This is an aspect that warrants deeper evaluation and understanding.

Renewable energy sources like solar and wind are becoming cheaper globally, but their integration into the energy market faces challenges. This is particularly the case in remote locations with less developed infrastructure. These renewable projects typically produce excess energy with no immediate buyers. This is where bitcoin mining presents a unique and revolutionary opportunity. Bitcoin mining operations possess a distinctive advantage because of their flexibility and portability, which makes them adept, like no other known energy consumer, at being able to consume stranded energy. Mining machines can be transported across thousands of miles at low cost in the back of a truck. They can be switched on and off at any time, at will. Mining operations can be established in any region where electricity costs are minimal. This trait aligns perfectly with renewable energy projects, which usually offer lower electricity rates than traditional fossil fuels.

This price advantage is especially pronounced in areas that have surplus renewable energy capacity. For example, during the rainy season, hydroelectric plants might generate more power than the grid can absorb, leading to potential waste of this renewable resource. Bitcoin miners can capitalize on this excess by situating their operations close to such renewable energy sources. By purchasing the surplus electricity, bitcoin mining provides a consistent revenue stream to these projects, thereby enhancing their financial sustainability and encouraging the expansion of renewable energy infrastructure.[10]

This is a symbiotic relationship. Renewable energy projects gain a dependable customer in bitcoin miners, who in return access a cheaper and greener supply of electricity. This makes renewable projects more economically feasible and stimulates further investment and development in renewable energy technologies. Through this mechanism, bitcoin mining can play a pivotal role in supporting the global transition toward more sustainable energy solutions.

> Bitcoin mining is the only profitable use of energy in human history that does not need to be located near human settlement to operate. The long-term implications of this are world changing and hiding in plain sight . . .
>
> Historically, our energy challenge has been to move the power to the people. With Bitcoin, we can move the people to the power.[11]
>
> —Ross Stevens

Ross Stevens, founder and CEO of Stone Ridge Asset Management, notes that bitcoin's unique ability to use energy, independent of location, can revolutionize energy economics. He envisions a future where bitcoin mining takes place in remote locations and leads to the development of infrastructure such as roads, housing, and schools, potentially fostering new human settlements around these operations. This could reverse the historical trend of bringing energy to where people live. Instead, bitcoin might draw people to where energy is most abundant and inexpensive. Just as cities like New York and Tokyo arose around natural trade routes before the era of fossil fuels, bitcoin could spur the growth of communities around new energy hubs.[12] As bitcoin potentially drives the creation of low-cost, clean energy on a large scale, we could see a future where an increasing portion of the global population lives near abundant, cost-effective energy sources.

Alex Gladstein, author and chief strategy officer of the Human Rights Foundation, has described bitcoin's transformative potential in different parts of Africa.[13] For example, Mount Mulanje in Malawi, a landscape of dramatic beauty and historical scars from the slave trade and resource exploitation, is on the cusp of a bitcoin-driven transformation. Only a fraction of Malawians have access to electricity, but the introduction of bitcoin mining by companies like Gridless, a Kenyan company backed by Twitter founder Jack Dorsey, is turning what was once wasted energy into a valuable commodity. Excess electricity from local renewable sources is now powering bitcoin mining operations, providing a new revenue stream that funds community electrification without dependence on aid or subsidies. Gladstein notes that this model is a blueprint for change not just in Malawi but across Africa. It demonstrates that the surplus energy of remote areas can drive economic development, turning dormant natural resources into power for progress. By utilizing the excess heat from bitcoin mining, local industries can also benefit. For example, tea plantations may use ASIC miners for drying tea leaves, an essential process in tea production.[14]

This model, where bitcoin mining provides a financial incentive to harness and utilize surplus renewable energy, represents a shift in energy economics. It offers a path forward where rural communities can thrive by monetizing their natural resources, sparking local development, and enhancing quality of life. It exemplifies a future where the intrinsic value of natural resources can be unlocked, turning isolated areas into hubs of economic activity.

Bitcoin is often framed by critics as a waste of energy. But in [Malawi], like in so many other places around the world, it becomes blazingly clear that *if you aren't mining Bitcoin, you are wasting energy*. What was once a pitfall is now an opportunity. Bitcoin miners can be thought of as dung beetles, scraping up the waste energy that no one else wants and transforming it into something valuable.[15]

—Alex Gladstein

There is a rapidly growing list of similar examples from other parts of Africa and from around the world:

Kenya: Gridless uses solar-powered containerized data centers for bitcoin mining.[16] This model promotes off-grid renewable energy solutions and provides reliable power to nearby communities.

Ethiopia: With ample hydro and geothermal resources, Ethiopia has emerged as a hotspot for bitcoin mining. CleanSpark uses renewable energy from geothermal plants to power their mining operations and contribute to the national grid.[17] This helps Ethiopia diversify its energy mix and generate additional revenue for renewable projects.

Zimbabwe: Zimbabwe recently legalized bitcoin, and early ventures like BitMari aim to utilize locally produced solar energy for mining.[18] This could encourage further solar development in a country facing ongoing energy shortages.

Iran: Facing economic sanctions and energy limitations, Iran encourages bitcoin mining to utilize its natural gas reserves for both domestic use and energy-intensive mining operations. This approach incentivizes renewable energy exploration.

Argentina: Argentina boasts abundant wind and solar potential, but grid limitations hinder full utilization. Bitcoin mining companies like Luxor Technologies collaborate with local renewable projects to create demand and promote infrastructure development.[19]

El Salvador: After adopting bitcoin as legal tender, El Salvador is leveraging geothermal energy from volcanoes to power bitcoin mining. This aligns with its goal of achieving carbon neutrality by 2030.

Texas, United States: Texas has abundant wind and solar energy resources, but grid limitations and low demand often hinder their full utilization. Several bitcoin mining companies have set up operations in Texas, purchasing excess renewable energy and contributing to grid stability. One such example is Riot Blockchain, which is partnering with wind farm developers to power its mining operations.[20]

Kazakhstan: Despite having vast renewable resources, Kazakhstan relies heavily on coal for energy. Bitcoin mining companies, attracted by cheaper electricity rates, have started setting up shop. This creates demand for renewable energy and incentivizes local authorities to invest in infrastructure development.

Quebec, Canada: Quebec has an established hydroelectric grid with excess capacity during off-peak hours. Bitcoin miners leverage this by operating during these times, utilizing clean energy and providing an additional revenue stream for the province.

Iceland: Utilizing its abundant geothermal and hydroelectric energy resources, Iceland has attracted bitcoin mining operations keen to leverage the country's renewable energy. This demand from miners helps to support and justify Iceland's investment in renewable energy, contributing to the country's status as a leader in sustainable energy use.

Methane Flaring

The mobility, portability, and flexibility of bitcoin mining presents another major benefit that is often lost on environmental critics or deliberately ignored. This relates to flaring of methane emissions. According to the World Bank, methane (CH_4) has a global warming potential up to eighty times greater than carbon dioxide.[21] It is said to account for approximately 30 percent of global warming.[22] Methane arises from various human activities, including oil and gas production, animal agriculture, and waste decomposition in landfills. When this gas cannot be captured or utilized, it is often flared, converting it to carbon dioxide (CO_2), which has lower, but still significant, warming potential according to climate experts.

Bitcoin mining comes into play as an innovative solution for the use of this otherwise wasted energy. By setting up mining operations near flaring sites, miners can convert methane directly into electricity to power their operations, effectively reducing methane emissions while creating an additional revenue stream. The long-term implications of this could be significant. By providing a profitable use for flared methane, this practice can incentivize the capture and use of methane that would otherwise be released into the atmosphere or inefficiently burned.

The ability of bitcoin mining to use methane flaring raises the prospect of bitcoin not just reducing its carbon footprint but actually becoming carbon negative in the long term. Jamie Coutts of CMT Research estimates that bitcoin miners currently use methane flaring to capture three megatons of CO_2 emissions.[23] This represents over 7 percent of all emissions produced by bitcoin mining. As this number increases in the coming years, it is not hard to envisage bitcoin having a net carbon negative footprint, which Daniel Batten projects could be achieved by 2028.[24]

World's Best ESG Asset

Across six critical metrics, bitcoin is arguably the world's best environmentally friendly industry.[25]

ESG Metric	Bitcoin Rank
Mitigate methane profitably with existing technology	1
High current level of methane mitigation	1
Sustainable fuel use (%)	1
Industry growth and emissions decoupled	1
Low, declining emission intensity	1
Major energy source is renewable	1

From a social perspective (the S of ESG), we have discussed throughout this book the life-changing impact that bitcoin is having around the world in promoting human rights and financial inclusion among millions of people living under authoritarian regimes and in unstable economies. And from a governance perspective (the G of ESG), we have discussed throughout part IV how bitcoin can play a role as an apolitical and incorruptible form of money with the potential to change geopolitics forever.[26]

SUBJECTIVE VALUE AND MORAL POLICING

The value of an activity is highly subjective. For some, the aesthetic and cultural importance of Christmas lights, symbolizing joy and tradition during the holiday season, may justify their enormous energy consumption. For many others, Christmas lights are a waste of energy and contribute to climate change. For some, clothes dryers represent a justifiable use of energy. For others, it is an egregious waste when a clothesline through your living room will suffice. Some may see bitcoin's energy consumption as necessary for maintaining a decentralized, secure financial system that offers financial inclusion and autonomy beyond the reach of traditional banking systems and authoritarian governments to over 1 billion unbanked people around the world. Others may see it differently. The underlying principle is that value is subjective. And value policing is dangerous.

French philosopher and historian Paul-Michel Foucault offered a lens through which to view the debate on energy consumption and the dangers of value policing. His concept of power/knowledge suggests that what is considered "valuable" or "wasteful" is often determined by power structures.[27] Foucault suggests that power is not simply a matter of direct coercion or physical force but is exercised through the production and control of knowledge. In the context of energy consumption, what is deemed a "valuable" use of energy versus a "wasteful" one is often a result of narratives shaped by those in positions of power (i.e., those in government, environmental organizations, or multinational corporations) and with control over the media. These entities help construct the narratives that define responsible or irresponsible energy use, often embedding their own interests and values within the narratives.

Value policing limits individual freedom and stifles diversity by imposing a homogenized view of what constitutes acceptable energy use. It would help to examine the power dynamics at play in these debates, and question whose interests are served by particular energy consumption norms and values. Understanding these interests may help untangle the complex web of motivations behind the positions held in the debate:

1. Environmental groups focused on carbon emissions often express sensationalist sound bites about bitcoin's energy consumption in order to capture attention. There is a tendency to simplify the narrative to make a more compelling case for immediate action. This can sometimes lead to scapegoating. Bitcoin is seen as a high-value target that attracts the attention of broader audiences in discussions about carbon footprints and sustainability. Environmentalists often lack the time or incentive to undertake the complex analysis needed to understand the nuanced topic of bitcoin's energy consumption that we have discussed in this chapter.[28] For environmentalists, bitcoin is a dream poster child for capturing the public's attention. Could there be anything more

attention-grabbing than "a speculative, valueless, online casino chip that consumes more energy than nations, and boils oceans"?

2. Banks and traditional financial service providers have long held a monopoly on financial transactions and wealth management. Bitcoin poses a direct challenge to this monopoly by offering a decentralized alternative. These institutions might oppose bitcoin on energy consumption grounds as a way to discredit it and protect their own industries from the threat that bitcoin poses.

3. Governments and regulatory authorities have a vested interest in maintaining control over their national currencies and financial systems. Bitcoin operates outside the traditional financial regulatory frameworks and thus represents a challenge to this control. Highlighting the energy consumption of bitcoin can serve as a justification for imposing regulations or outright bans on bitcoin mining, as seen in some countries.

4. Energy companies are acutely aware of the growing public environmental concern over climate change sustainability. Engaging in or supporting debates on energy consumption, whether criticizing the energy use of technologies like bitcoin or advocating for energy-efficient practices, can be part of their strategy to enhance their public image. Deflecting attention from their own culpability may be the primary motivation.

5. There are many competing platforms and currencies within the cryptocurrency community. Some use far less energy than bitcoin because of different consensus mechanisms (e.g., Proof-of-Stake as opposed to Proof-of-Work, as discussed in chapter 4). Proponents of these alternative cryptocurrencies might emphasize bitcoin's energy usage to promote their own, "more energy-efficient platforms" as better alternatives.[29]

What this list illustrates is that the only way that meaningful progress can be made is through ethical engagement and awareness of the complexities and contradictions inherent in this subject. "Rightness" of energy use often depends on broader sociopolitical contexts and the competing needs and values of diverse populations.

Value policing is dangerous. It oversimplifies the diverse nature of human values, and it risks imposing a binary standard of good or bad, where a nuanced one is warranted instead. What we need is more dialogue and education rather than judgment and division.

PART V

The Philosophy

CHAPTER 17

Sovereign Prerogative

"What time is it?" asked Louis XIV. "It is whatever time your Majesty pleases," came the reply.

"Sovereign prerogative" refers to the rights, powers, and privileges that are exclusively reserved for the sovereign state or monarchy.[1] It implies the sovereign's status as the ultimate source of power and authority ("God-given," traditionally) inside the realm. It bestows on the sovereign a wide spectrum of authorities that are agreed to be beyond the scope of the laws that apply to ordinary citizens. These authorities have varied across dominions through the ages but typically have included legislation; governance; foreign policy; defense; security; administration of justice; and, important for the purposes of this discussion, monetary control.

The philosophical justifications for this prerogative over monetary policy have been debated for thousands of years and span, among other disciplines, political theory, ethics, and economics. Debates on the topic typically revolve around the inherent conflict between centralized political power and individual liberty. It would be helpful to consider the perspectives of certain key thought leaders on this topic.

Renowned seventeenth-century English philosopher Thomas Hobbes proposed certain ideas that are seen as foundational for the sovereign's authority over money. In *Leviathan* (1651), he introduced the concept of the social contract."[2] Underlying this idea was the notion that people willingly give up part of their liberties to the sovereign in exchange for protection and order, thereby escaping the "solitary, poor, nasty, brutish, and short" life outside civilized society.

This formed the basis for Hobbes's conception of a strong, centralized authority for the proper and useful functioning of a political system for the benefit of its subjects. From this perspective, sovereign control over money was a logical extension of the state's responsibility for preserving order and hence avoiding the chaos of competing or conflicting currencies.

John Locke, another eminent English philosopher from the same period, also offered some influential perspectives in his work, *Two Treatises of Government* (1689), which laid the foundation for subsequent debate on the subject.[3] From his point of view, sovereign control over money is justified as a way of safeguarding property rights by providing the masses with a stable medium of exchange, which is critical for economic activities and the protection of wealth.[4] Some of the earliest policy debates regarding the government's power to set and change interest rates credit Locke.[5] His arguments were highly influential in the evolution of monetary policy—in particular, his belief that social and economic stability depend on the government's role in maintaining a stable currency.[6]

Italian diplomat and sixteenth-century philosopher Niccolò Machiavelli may have also played a part in the debate. Known for his view that "it is better for a ruler to be feared than loved," his thinking may have influenced the techniques by which governments achieved and kept their sovereign prerogative over monetary policy. He emphasized the importance of the creation of a centralized and omnipotent political class. Mobilizing monetary resources for the state's military objectives was a key rationale for the state's control over the realm's economic affairs. Otherwise, it would mean that the state would have to depend on willing contributions from private citizens before going to war.[7]

On the other side of the debate, Austrian economist and political philosopher Friedrich von Hayek fiercely attacked the government's monopoly over money. In his book *The Denationalization of Money*, he advocated for competition in the creation of money and for letting private entities print their currencies.[8] He criticized sovereign power as being prone to mismanagement and abuse that would lead to economic cycles of boom and bust. In his view, competition in the monetary domain was vital in order to avoid inflation, improve monetary stability, and promote economic freedom.[9]

American economist Milton Friedman argued against centralized control of monetary policy. Proposing a rule-based approach, he said that the central bank's responsibility should be restricted to guaranteeing a consistent and predictable increase in the money supply.[10] He blamed discretionary monetary policy for causing economic unrest and argued that misaligned political incentives typically result in poor economic outcomes.

Murray Rothbard, American libertarian and anarcho-capitalist, expanded the critique by challenging the validity of the state itself and therefore its power over money. Like any service, he said, money should be subject to market forces; its manufacture and control should be entrusted to the private sector.[11] He viewed sovereign control over money as being intrinsically coercive and violative of personal liberty, resulting in inefficiencies and unfair allocation of resources.[12]

> In sum, freedom can run a monetary system as superbly as it runs the rest of the economy. Contrary to many writers, there is nothing special about money that requires extensive governmental dictation. Here, too, free men will best and most smoothly supply all their economic wants. For money as for all other activities of man, liberty is the mother, not the daughter, of order.[13]
>
> —Murray Rothbard

The philosophical debate between the justification and criticism of sovereign monetary control reflects a broader tension between the quest for stability, order, and efficiency on one side, and freedom, competition, and individual rights on the other. It engages with deep questions about the nature of authority, the purpose of the state, and the rights of individuals.

THE SEPARATION OF CHURCH AND STATE

It is human nature to prefer the status quo. Most people would find the notion of separating money and state to be conceptually radical and unsettling. A treasonous notion! Many likely felt the same way in medieval Europe with respect to the separation of church and state. While it may seem an alien concept now, at that time, people were deeply accustomed to the church's intertwinement with political authority. Intolerance and persecution of religious minorities were the norm, with rulers using religion to legitimize their power. This led to violent conflicts, including the Crusades and other religious wars in Europe. Spiritual authority went hand in hand with political coercion.

The origins of the entanglement of religion and the state goes back thousands of years. In ancient Mesopotamia, Hammurabi claimed his right to rule was granted by the gods. In ancient Egypt, pharaohs were considered divine beings, directly representing the gods on Earth. This link between political power and religious legitimacy ensured that rulers could maintain control by presenting themselves as divinely sanctioned. In ancient Greece, Socrates was sentenced to death on grounds of impiety: failing to acknowledge the gods designated by the state.

In 1534, when Henry VIII contrived to divorce Catherine of Aragon and remarry to produce a male heir, the pope of the Roman Catholic Church refused to oblige. The separation that hitherto existed between the Roman Catholic Church and the English monarchy presented an inconvenience to Henry. He therefore decided to break from the church and establish the Church of England, with himself as the ruler—effectively unifying church and state. The king's Lord Chancellor, Thomas More, resigned in protest, refusing to acknowledge Henry as the supreme head of the church, believing that only the pope held that authority. He was arrested and executed for treason. He declared poignantly before his death, "I die the King's good servant, but God's first." His defiance exposed the dangers of intertwining political power with religious authority. And his martyrdom symbolized the cost of resisting state control over religion during that period.

In the seventeenth century, Locke, Voltaire, and other Enlightenment thinkers began advocating for the separation of church and state. The French and American revolutions in the eighteenth century were pivotal moments. In France, the French Revolution in 1789, led to the confiscation of church property and the secularization of the state. The U.S. Constitution, ratified in the very same year, enshrined religious freedom and prohibited the establishment of a state church. The phrase "separation of church and state" is derived from a statement by Thomas Jefferson mentioning a "wall of separation between Church & State." The "wall" he was referring to was the First Amendment of the U.S. Constitution, which declared that the state shall pass "no law respecting an establishment of religion, or prohibiting the free exercise thereof."

The separation of church and state was a transformative moment in human history. It took strong men with great vision to accomplish. Governance was reshaped forever by removing religious authority from politics. In the context of monetary policy, it is arguable that a separation of money and state could be an even more significant event in history. Until now, humanity lacked the tools to decouple the two. Bitcoin, with spatial salability that exceeds that of fiat and temporal salability that exceeds that of gold (see chapter 10), combined with unprecedented powers of censorship resistance and unconfiscatability, offers a groundbreaking opportunity that has never existed before. It represents humanity's best chance yet to achieve this civilizational milestone.

SELF-SOVEREIGNTY

"Self-sovereignty" refers to the right of individuals to control their own lives and make decisions without coercion. As a necessary means to achieving this objective, the libertarian philosophy advocates for the minimal role of government in the lives of individuals.[14]

The philosophy of self-sovereignty is evident in every aspect of bitcoin's design, from its peer-to-peer network to its consensus mechanism, and the emphasis on users taking personal custody of their funds. Author Erik Cason notes that bitcoin offers humanity an unprecedented tool in the battle for self-sovereignty: "Any single human—no matter their station of birth, class of wealth, or creed of faith—may choose to put their economic, social, and political rights into a new digital commonwealth that is beyond the power of any and all governments to violate."[15]

In bitcoin, code is law. The security, integrity, and transactability of the asset are enforced through code and decentralized consensus rather than by a legislature, executive, and judiciary. By engaging in a different strategy of law that abandons the need for authority and violence, bitcoin creates a new form of social contract that is unprecedented in history. As Cason argues,[16] bitcoin inverts the dictum of sovereign power as surmised in Hobbes's work, *Leviathan*,[17] from "authority, not truth makes legitimacy" into "truth, not authority makes legitimacy."

In a world where the state is increasingly omnipotent and omnipresent, the most powerful tool to resist government overreach is our economic power. The ability to allocate our wealth to the digital realm, thereby curtailing the growth of unchecked and overbearing state authority, is an incredibly profound notion. Bitcoin offers the most potent, nonviolent, and ingenious tool conceivable in this regard.

Bitcoin provides a path for society to value liberty and also to embrace the responsibilities it entails. For example, if you lose your private keys, you lose your funds. There is no customer support you can call or bank you can sue in court. Liberty comes with the responsibility of managing one's own assets and making decisions free from the paternalistic oversight of the state and financial institutions.

Liberty means responsibility. That is why most men dread it.[18]

—George Bernard Shaw

A Permissioned Existence

The question isn't who is going to let me; it's who is going to stop me.[19]

—Ayn Rand

As Benjamin Franklin was leaving Independence Hall on the last day of debate at the Constitutional Convention in 1787, a woman asked him, "Well, Doctor, what have we got—a Republic or a Monarchy?" Franklin replied: "A Republic, *if you can keep it*."[20] Franklin's comment is of immense significance to American political philosophy. Through those famous words, he emphasized the critical responsibility of the people to stay vigilant and guard against government excesses. It is quite clear that the risk of government overreach was at the forefront of his mind. He thought it vitally important that citizens keep the state in check in order to ensure the protection of their fundamental rights.

In a world where survival is linked directly to economic activities, the management of money is part of the very fabric of human life. Yet, society has allowed the subtle but ubiquitous notion of permission to permeate almost every facet of our daily financial transactions.[21] Layer upon layer of invisible permissions from banks and other financial intermediaries dominate our lives without even our full awareness. We can comfortably ignore their existence as long as the permissions are easily granted. The moment they are denied or withdrawn, however, one becomes acutely conscious of their inescapability. This reality depicts a troubling relinquishment of power to the state and other institutional authorities—precisely the risk that Franklin warned against over two centuries ago.

As crypto entrepreneur Erik Voorhees has commented, financial freedom is no longer a right but a privilege dependent on compliance and good behavior. He observes that needing permission to transact is just a step away from needing permission to exist.[22] The historical journey from a world less encumbered by financial regulation to the present state of affairs reveals a gradual, yet seemingly unstoppable, erosion of economic freedoms.

> Consider the average man of a hundred years ago, and the average man of today. Who was more economically free? 120 years ago, there wasn't even an income tax. Things were so radical that you were permitted to keep what you earned![23]
>
> —Erik Voorhees

There is a sharp contrast between the degree of liberty and freedom enjoyed by our ancestors and our permissioned life today. This decline is often presented as a natural progression—a necessary evil in order to enjoy the benefits of order and security that the state affords society in return. But does it really have to be this way? Or might it be a deliberate encroachment into one's supposedly inalienable rights under the guise of public interest and collective good—an easier pill to swallow?

Our daily lives operate under a veil of manufactured consent.[24] Every day we negotiate a maze of preapproved choices, each one with embedded permissions. In the financial world, we have entirely lost the ability to opt in or to opt out of the great variety of permissioned systems used in our financial transactions. The permissioned state has woven itself into the fabric of life.

State power manifests in many ways, many that we may not even be consciously aware of. French philosopher Michel Foucault introduced the concept of panopticism, which is the principle that power can be exercised merely through visibility.[25] In other words, the very possibility of being watched ensures that individuals police themselves without the need for physical restraints or even legal restrictions. Self-censorship is a manifestation of this phenomenon. It leads to a form of self-discipline, where individuals adjust their behavior to conform to norms and expectations. This happens even in the absence of an actual observer.

As Quentin Skinner argues in his essay, "The Sovereign State," the proper method of assessing the legitimacy of a state's actions must be to ask whether they are fair or just.[26] When we ask that question, the inescapable part of the answer is that individual rights must take priority over any notion of common good. The reason is that the arbiter of this common good is not nature or God. Rather it is a group of human individuals, sometimes elected but most often not. And where there are humans, decision-making is always subject to all manner of bias, vested interests, coercion, and corruption. In a truly free and just society, it may be argued that individual rights should override any attempt by a centralized body that deems the violation of your rights to be necessary to promote public interest.

> Each person possesses an inviolability founded on justice that even the welfare of society as a whole cannot override.[27]
>
> —John Rawls

Thomas Jefferson famously stated: "The price of freedom is eternal vigilance." He emphasized the responsibility of individual citizens to remain cautious about government authority and its excesses. His statement was an acknowledgment of the constant struggle involved in preserving one's liberty and ensuring that devices of the state put in place in the name of defending the public are not turned into apparatuses of control. He called for a vigilant citizenry that demands transparency and accountability from the state. He advocated for the questioning of authority rather than submissive acquiescence and conformity.

Bitcoin is a revolutionary countermovement to our prevailing world of permissioned existence. It represents a nonviolent rebellion. With its foundational principles of decentralization, transparency, and autonomy, bitcoin offers a means to exert individual liberty. It offers billions of people the prospect of reclaiming the freedom to transact and, by extension, the freedom to exist. It is a technological response to the omnipresent threat of panopticism. It is a deep philosophical manifesto advocating for a society governed by objective rules rather than mandates by decree. And it invites a reevaluation of our relationship with money, authority, and each other as humans. Jefferson may have approved.

DECENTRALIZED POWER

Does power typically tend toward centralization or decentralization in the natural world? Ant colonies and beehives, for instance, illustrate the operation of decentralized power and decision-making. Each ant in an ant colony follows certain basic rules and responds to local cues. However, a system of incentives creates a collective intelligence of the colony, enabling each ant to achieve remarkable feats such as foraging, building nests, and defending against threats, all without a central authority. One might mistake the queen ant as some sort of central figure or ruler, but that is not the case. Despite her title, the queen ant's role could not be more different from that of an all-powerful human monarch. The queen is vital for reproduction and sometimes influences colony organization through pheromones. Much of the colony's activities are actually carried out by workers following decentralized rules. The queen's role does not involve direct management of these tasks.

Honeybee hives exhibit decentralized decision-making through their swarm intelligence. Worker bees communicate and collaborate to manage hive functions such as food collection, brood care, and hive maintenance. The hexagonal structure of honeycombs, a result of individual bees' actions rather than a predetermined design, illustrates the effectiveness of decentralized processes. The coordinated functioning of a bee swarm is testament to how decentralized networks can achieve sophisticated, coordinated behavior through distributed efforts. And again, the queen bee is not the ruthless insect ruler one might imagine: she is no Bloody Mary. She sticks to her job of laying eggs and issuing pheromone-based guidance to ensure cohesion of the colony, rather than orchestrating a reign of terror and surveillance over her swarm.

Schools of sardines follow similar processes of decentralized power and consensus. Without a single leader, they move together in coordinated patterns. This symphony of movement is achieved by virtue of each fish following a few simple rules: maintain a certain distance from one's neighbor and align with nearby fish. The result is that the school of thousands of small and individually vulnerable sardines are collectively able to evade predators and efficiently find food. Flocks of starlings exhibit decentralized consensus-based decision-making. Individual birds follow local rules to maintain formation and navigate collectively to a desired destination. They avoid predators and travel efficiently as a result.

Author Brandon Quittem has written about the decentralized operation of fungal networks in this context.[28] Lacking any sort of centralized brain, they function as a distributed intelligence network capable of sending information bidirectionally over long distances. The fungal network contains millions of end points, each searching for food and defending its territory. The networks form a decentralized consensus on the use of resources, reproduction, and defense. This decentralized structure has made them one of the most adaptive and robust organisms on Earth, having survived millions of years through several mass extinction events.

So why did human civilizations take such a different approach to power and governance? Vast volumes of research and analysis have no doubt been devoted to this question in the fields of political theory and sociology. But the discussion in this chapter invites you to consider what influence money itself might have had—particularly the capture, corruption, and manipulation thereof by a privileged few. One wonders what society might have looked like through history if it had the gift of a nonmanipulatable, unconfiscatable, uninflatable, and uncensorable money. Would that have enabled us to instead organize around more egalitarian governance structures inspired by the natural order of other forms of life? The discussion later in this chapter regarding bitcoin and violence offers food for thought in this regard.

Throughout human history, power has formed a natural alignment with centralized systems. As discussed earlier in this chapter, rulers and kings claimed divine right—powers bestowed upon them directly by God. They preserved this centralized chain of custody of divine power, never considering the need for its dispersion into society. Democracy emerged as a revolutionary system in ancient Greece and has been humanity's best effort at achieving such dispersion of power. Yet it still retains a concentration of authority at the top rather than achieving a full dispersion throughout society. As Winston Churchill remarked, "Democracy is the worst form of government except for all the others."

What does a true dispersion of power look like in human society? One might imagine an open network of people or organizations—a network that is permissionless to join or leave. It would be devoid of hierarchical structures and powerful authorities. It would achieve, by some magical means, the dilution of all forms of concentrated decision-making power. It would be a form of participatory governance, preserving and prioritizing individual rights. These ideals might sound familiar when considering bitcoin's governance system. But the concepts are by no means new in the field of philosophy.

> Power is everywhere; not because it embraces everything, but because it comes from everywhere . . . Power is not an institution, and not a structure; neither is it a certain strength we are endowed with; it is the name that one attributes to a complex strategic situation in a particular society.[29]
>
> —Michel Foucault

Foucault challenged the notion that power is inherently centralized. Instead, he suggested that it permeates all levels of social interaction.[30] In his view, power is not merely exerted from the top down by the governors over the governed. He argued that power, in its natural form, is exercised within a network of relationships that spans the entire social body. It arises from knowledge and discourse, and it is present in each individual social relationship rather than being the exclusive domain of select individuals or institutions that are assigned the ability to govern society at large.[31]

Spanish sociologist Manuel Castells, who has done extensive work on the concept of a network society, has certain observations on this point. Castells's network society is the result of networks (built on information and communication technologies) emerging as the dominant form of social organization.[32] These networks are flexible and adaptive and, most importantly, they are in stark contrast with the hierarchical organizations of the industrial age. They represent the birth of a new digital era of egalitarian societal structures, marking a shift in traditional centralized power structures. One of Castells's key concepts is the "space of flows," which refers to human interaction in the digital age that is dynamic and continuous, transcending geographical boundaries.[33]

Bitcoin is not exactly a tool of societal governance. But its monetary properties resonate with most of the above concepts. It operates within the "space of flows" wherein it enables instant global transactions that are not bound by physical constraints of traditional currencies. It aligns with the concept of the network society, operating on a global and open peer-to-peer network. It helps to circumvent traditional hierarchical structures and has been embraced by various groups to challenge the established centralized financial order. Millions around the world continue to adopt bitcoin's censorship-resistant and immutable properties as a counterpoint to the repressiveness of traditional banking systems. Given the fundamental role that money plays in society, it is possible that bitcoin could also influence social change from centralized to decentralized power.

Bitcoin Is Anarchy

As bitcoin expert Shinobi has observed, bitcoin is inherently anarchic.[34] The notion of anarchy might conjure up images of chaos, disorder, and dysfunction, but in reality, what it represents is a system based on voluntary cooperation, free from rulers. This idea is inextricably linked to the functionality of bitcoin as a decentralized network. With no central figure in charge, bitcoin operates on the voluntary participation of its users. This is an inherently anarchic system.

Much like the concept of anarchy, bitcoin challenges traditional notions of governance and control. Both structures rely on a shared belief in a certain value system rather than any sort of mandate regarding what is true or false or what is right or wrong. This contrasts with conventional governance structures and financial systems that are based on subjective principles and the coercive powers of authorities.

In an anarchic system, there is no governing body imposing rules. You simply opt into rules that you agree with, as opposed to having them forced upon you. This is how bitcoin operates. For instance, any changes to bitcoin's protocol through hard or soft forks follow this voluntary principle. There is no overarching governance structure dictating the evolution of its consensus rules. If you do not agree with a proposed code upgrade, simply do not update your node. If you have a different view on how bitcoin should operate, feel free to change your node software and convince others to join you.

Bitcoin has rules without rulers. As a participant in the consensus system, the most you can do is signal—that is, put up some kind of flag or flare saying that you intend to go a certain way and that if others want to follow, they can, but no one is forcing anyone.[35] While there are different forms of "voting" involved in the bitcoin consensus mechanism, all this represents really is a form of signaling. The power of some or all the system participants to ignore your signal is ultimately what gives power to this governance mechanism. Jameson Lopp notes that, in this governance model, the power of the veto is as strong as, or even stronger than, the power of the majority to impose their will.[36]

The lack of centralized control, the voluntary nature of participation, and the decentralized consensus on its rules encapsulate the anarchic spirit of bitcoin. It is a system that relies on free association driven by self-interest. And it strips away any need for order maintained through coercion. By embracing an anarchic form of governance, bitcoin challenges people to reconsider preconceived notions of order and governance in the context of financial systems.

A society that will trade a little liberty for a little order will lose both and deserve neither.

—Thomas Jefferson

BITCOIN AND VIOLENCE

The relationship between bitcoin and violence is a highly underappreciated topic that is of profound significance. The historical roots of violence trace back to the acquisition or defense of personal property. The vast majority of violent acts through history, be it at the interpersonal level or the transnational level, originate from the need to acquire or defend, and this has almost always related to physical property. The desire to acquire or defend such property stems from the inherent value or worth that people have attached to such physical property, be it land, resources, or other objects and possessions. These acts of violence have shaped the maps of nations and paths of civilizations for thousands of years. They have influenced the lives of countless humans through time. The quest for wealth and the power derived therefrom have been the primary causes of virtually all human strife.

Studies have explored the relationship between war and resource richness. The resource curse theory suggests that countries rich in natural resources are more prone to experiencing civil wars, coups, and other forms of internal conflict.[37] This is clear in the case of colonialism, which was almost entirely driven by the desire to annex territories around the world that had abundant resources. The desire for gold, diamonds, and rubber drove Europeans in the late nineteenth century to Africa and to divide the continent among themselves.[38] Similar motivations propelled the annexation of India a century prior.

The key aspect to appreciate here is that all these properties that were the subject of conquest, invasion, and plunder were physical. There never existed anything of value that was not physical and that resided entirely in the intangible and ethereal realm. Enter bitcoin. Once you appreciate the paradigm shift that has occurred here, it is not difficult to see its incredible significance for humanity.

The emergence of digital property marks a fundamental change in the historical dynamics of the acquisition and defense of property. Unlike physical assets, which have always been the focus of personal and international conflict, digital property exists in a realm where conventional methods of aggression and coercion become far less effective. The dematerialization of property into digital form changes everything.

Digital assets are not limited to any one physical place; thus, they are not vulnerable to conventional techniques of physical assault and capture. The deployment of armies to annex another party's bitcoin is futile. Bitcoin's security comes from cryptography. Its custody involves keeping one's private keys—a string of words—safe. You could simply memorize these private keys and move around the world with nothing but the clothes on your back. Forcing someone to divulge their private keys through physical coercion is perhaps the only way to extort their bitcoin. But the way to guard against this risk is far simpler than building armies, weaponries, and other defense capabilities to protect physical property. Rather, it would involve good privacy practices and robust systems for storing and safeguarding private key information. It is much easier to keep your ownership of bitcoin secret than it is to do the same with your gold bars, real estate, stock portfolio, or bank balances. The words comprising one's bitcoin private keys may be split up and secretly stored in different locations around the world. Multisignature solutions exist whereby it is impossible to extort another's bitcoin without the involvement of multiple cosigners, who may be individuals or institutions located in several countries. Protecting digital wealth relies on cryptographic security, operational secrecy, and the responsible management of private keys. On this basis, we are potentially entering an era where physical barriers that have guarded wealth throughout history could become less relevant.

> Now that the cost of protection has rapidly plummeted, a return on investment from attempting to extort is just not possible. Information-age assets are increasingly fleeing into these areas where they can secure protection behind cryptography. That's a big deal because now, holders of capital (whether it's the ultra-rich or people in the developing world) can secure protection of their money for free using open-source software . . . At the end of the day, it changes the economics of violence and it makes violence not so profitable anymore.[39]
>
> —Trace Mayer

This paradigm shift has several global and societal ramifications. It can potentially alter the very nature of human interaction, both domestically and internationally. If the need to defend against physical attacks on personal property and national territories were to wane, it would naturally shrink the size and relevance of the state. Nations might reallocate resources formerly reserved for military and defense into other sectors like education, health care, and infrastructure. It could usher in an era where countries and societies are less distrustful and fearful of one another and more willing to increase cooperation to solve problems like public health, poverty, and environmental destruction.

In a world where value is dematerialized and nearly immune to physical violence and seizure, the primary means by which people may acquire property would be by engaging in trade and offering goods and services of value to each other in exchange for bitcoin. Incentive structures might change dramatically into being driven by positivity and optimism as opposed to insecurity and protectionism. We may see a greater shift toward meritocracy, creativity, and collaboration at the domestic and international level.

While the complete demonetization of physical property is not imminent, the advantages of a digital commodity—such as its ease of transfer, privacy, and immunity to physical seizure—are impossible to ignore. This recognition may drive a gradual, but unstoppable, migration of value from the physical realm to the digital realm. And with that migration, we may gradually see a shift in the way we conceptualize wealth and security. This in turn may alter the way we treat one another across borders and cultures. It may lay the foundation for a future where cooperation and respect are more valued than conquest and domination.

CHAPTER 18

The Cypherpunks

We cannot expect governments, corporations, or other large, faceless organizations to grant us privacy out of their beneficence.

—Eric Hughes

The cypherpunks are a group of digital activists who advocate for strong privacy-enhancing technologies in the age of the internet and growing government surveillance. They have been engaged in an active social and political movement on this front since the late 1980s. The name "cypherpunk" is a humorous fusion of the words "cipher," a method for encrypting and decrypting data, and "cyberpunk," a genre of science fiction that emerged in the 1980s and is set in a lawless dystopian world dominated by computer technology.[1] The term "punk" signifies a rebellious, antiestablishment attitude with a focus on countercultural themes.

"A Cypherpunk Manifesto," written by Eric Hughes in 1993, is a seminal document that is considered the founding text of the movement. It begins with the following statement: "Privacy is necessary for an open society in the electronic age. Privacy is not secrecy. A private matter is something one doesn't want the whole world to know, but a secret matter is something one doesn't want anybody to know. Privacy is the power to selectively reveal oneself to the world."[2]

The central philosophy of the manifesto is that privacy is a fundamental right. It proposes cryptography as a way to protect individual freedoms against surveillance and control by governments and corporations. The cypherpunks and their manifesto were a major inspiration behind the creation of bitcoin. The principles laid out in the manifesto have direct relevance to bitcoin, particularly in regard to privacy.

The cypherpunks pioneered the idea that the internet (and the government and large corporations that control it) would not automatically guarantee privacy rights. They therefore believe that it is vital for individuals to protect their privacy proactively. Their solution was to develop innovative, privacy-enhancing tools to help this cause: "cypherpunks write code" is a defining motto that captures this spirit of taking practical action to develop software, rather than wasting time debating theory and engaging in political controversy. Actions speak louder than words.

The manifesto and broader culture inspired a generation of activists, programmers, and technologists to develop and disseminate cryptographic tools, leading to the creation of technologies like secure email; the Tor network; and, of course, bitcoin. Julian Assange, Adam Back, Bram Cohen, Hal Finney, and Satoshi Nakamoto himself were active participants in the cypherpunk movement.

Most of the concerns expressed in the manifesto are unfolding today in an eerie sense of coincidence, particularly with regard to mass surveillance, data collection by corporations, and the erosion of civil liberties online. The countermovement to this trend espoused by the cypherpunks is deeply ingrained in the spirit of bitcoin. Satoshi was influenced by these ideas, and bitcoin itself can be seen as a realization of the manifesto's vision.

WHY PRIVACY?

> Arguing that you don't care about the right to privacy because you have nothing to hide is no different than saying you don't care about free speech because you have nothing to say.
>
> —Edward Snowden

Privacy is important to ensure human dignity, safety, and self-determination. It empowers people to think and act independently, free from scrutiny, influence, and pressure. Bitcoin technical expert Giacomo Zucco has emphasized the need for a separation between personal identity and monetary transactions to ensure a currency's sustainable operation.[3] He outlines two aspects essential for this separation: deniability and fungibility:

- Deniability refers to the ability of individuals to credibly deny any connection to their past monetary transactions. As we know, those in possession of money are perpetual targets of criminal activity. Privacy with respect to one's wealth and financial dealings is crucial to minimize the risk of robbery, blackmail, kidnapping, and so on. Therefore, being able to separate one's identity from monetary transactions is vitally important for one's personal safety and freedom. Privacy is also critical for ensuring that parties can engage in political and social activities without fear of reprisal.

- Fungibility is about the indistinguishability of monetary units from one another. We often think of this feature of money as primarily necessary to improve transactability. However, there is a key privacy element that is often missed. Fungibility allows recipients to disregard any past associations of the currency, which lowers verification costs for money receivers. They no longer need to worry about the chain of custody of that specific note or coin that they received in a commercial exchange. Ironically, know-your-customer (KYC) regulations contradict the historical use of money to enable merchants to transact without detailed knowledge of their customers. Nonfungible goods are deemed unsuitable for use as money because of the need to verify past ownership.

Bitcoin allows users to engage in financial transactions with a degree of anonymity—pseudonymity. While all your transactions are visible on the public ledger, they are not directly linked to your personal identity. Bitcoin addresses do not list the owner's name, address, and other contact information. However, they are potentially traceable. For example, your Internet Protocol (IP) address can be associated with your transaction. Also, if you move your bitcoin to a cryptocurrency exchange, you instantly become identifiable because of the KYC information you provided to the exchange during the account-opening process. There is an entire industry dedicated to surveilling the bitcoin ledger, connecting dots and making ownership assumptions, a process known as chain analysis. The information generated is ostensibly for use by law enforcement but, as is invariably the case, it is also subject to misuse.

The better one's privacy practices, the greater the level of anonymity one may enjoy. Refraining from reusing bitcoin addresses is one such privacy-enhancing practice because it reduces (although it does not eliminate) the ability to trace the address back to you. By way of illustration, assume that you sent bitcoin to your self-custody address in ten different transactions. The first nine were from addresses that did not have any personally identifiable information (PII) associated with them. However, the tenth transaction was from a cryptocurrency exchange that has all your PII. You have now effectively disclosed to the world (or at least to the cryptocurrency exchange) that your receiving address plus all other hitherto anonymous addresses likely belong to you too.

CoinJoin

CoinJoin is a method for increasing privacy in bitcoin transactions—it is essentially an anonymization tool. It works by combining multiple bitcoin payments from multiple users into one single collaborative transaction. The transaction will have several outputs of the same amount, which makes it virtually impossible to track each output back to the original input. By doing this, users may obfuscate the trail of ownership of their individual bitcoin amounts. The result is that your bitcoin is fungible again with no provable means of associating it with past transactions. There is no alteration to the bitcoin ledger as such. It is simply a mixing of your bitcoin with other users' bitcoin to obscure your transaction history.

The use of CoinJoin and similar privacy-enhancing technologies has been a topic of a great deal of philosophical debate regarding the question of whether an individual's right to privacy should be subjugated to the state's responsibility to fight crime. Governments argue that financial transparency is necessary to combat illegal activities like money laundering, tax evasion, and financing of terrorism. They contend that technologies like CoinJoin make it more challenging to track the flow of money, potentially shielding illegal activities from detection. Based on this stance, there have been several prosecutions of CoinJoin developers in the United States.[4] For example, in June 2024, the cryptocurrency "mixer" (offering CoinJoin and similar services) Samourai Wallet was shut down by the government, and its founders were charged with money laundering and operating an unlicensed money transmitter business. In 2022, Tornado Cash, another cryptocurrency mixer, was sanctioned by the Office of Foreign Assets Control (OFAC).

There are several arguments that such actions by the government are illegal and unconstitutional. For one, CoinJoin is merely open-source code that may be protected as free speech under the First Amendment of the U.S. Constitution. The charged and sanctioned individuals did no more than write code that was made available to the public.

From a policy standpoint, as discussed earlier, individuals may have various legitimate reasons to seek privacy, ranging from protecting personal safety by hiding wealth from potential thieves to preventing corporations from tracking and monetizing their commercial activities. CoinJoin can be seen as merely a tool that empowers users to maintain their autonomy and privacy in the digital age. Privacy in financial transactions is not a concept unique to bitcoin. Traditional financial systems offer various forms of anonymizing services: cash being foremost among them. Cash transactions do not leave a physical or digital trail, and using cash is perfectly legitimate. Tools like CoinJoin can be viewed as the digital equivalent of using cash in a private and anonymous way.

As we discussed in part III, financial surveillance can be a tool of political repression in countries with authoritarian governments. Surveillance tools are increasingly used by the state to track funding for opposition groups or to punish anyone seen as a threat. CoinJoin and similar technologies can protect people subject to such oppression.

The reality is that criminal organizations often find ways to circumvent regulatory frameworks, restrictions, and government surveillance. It is unfortunately only the ordinary, law-abiding citizens who are left to suffer the consequences of reduced privacy. Privacy technologies can level the playing field by providing all users with tools that protect against unwarranted surveillance. The development of technologies like CoinJoin drives innovation in security and privacy, which are crucial in the digital age. Discouraging or criminalizing such innovations could stifle the development of new technologies. Again, the debate between privacy and regulatory oversight in bitcoin transactions exemplifies a broader tension between individual liberties and state intervention on security grounds.

PERSONAL RESPONSIBILITY

Personal responsibility is a theme that cuts through the Cypherpunk Manifesto: "We must defend our own privacy if we expect to have any." A key principle of the cypherpunk movement is that people should be in charge of their own data, and they should fight for it if necessary because it is unlikely to be handed to them by the state and large corporates. This is every individual's personal responsibility.[5] The manifesto emphasizes steps that people may take to ensure their digital privacy, including the use of cryptography and secure communication technologies. The personal responsibility extends to people needing to educate themselves on the tools and practices necessary to safeguard their digital information.

These principles apply directly to bitcoin. As a peer-to-peer platform, bitcoin is no more than code that you download on your computer or smartphone and use to transact directly with other users. You have the individual responsibility to secure your private keys and take necessary measures to protect your privacy. If you misplace your private keys or disclose them through poor privacy practices, or if you type in the wrong destination address for a bitcoin transaction because you were not paying attention, you will lose your money, and you will have only yourself to blame. There is no helpdesk to call that can reverse transactions.

Personal responsibility extends to one's obligation to the broader community, too. This includes promoting ethical behavior, contributing to security and privacy best practices, and helping to educate others on these fronts. The decentralized nature of bitcoin relies on the collective action and responsibility of its users to maintain the network's integrity and trust.

OPEN-SOURCE COLLABORATION

The responsibility to engage in open and collaborative behavior is another theme that cuts through the Cypherpunk Manifesto: "*We must come together* and create systems which allow anonymous transactions to take place." Cypherpunks realize this ideal through open-source development of software and community collaboration in the advocacy for cryptography and privacy-enhancing technologies.[6] Transparency, peer review, and collaborative development are core values that are seen as necessary to achieve online security and privacy for society at large.

The implicit idea throughout the manifesto is that a collective effort is necessary to achieve its objectives. The cypherpunks were clearly not focused only on personal privacy. The goal was to start a broader community movement to help spread awareness and disseminate cryptographic tools. This spirit of collaboration is central to the open-source movement, where developers from around the world contribute to a project, share knowledge, and collectively improve the software. Contributions are traditionally voluntary from individuals who share a common goal.

Open-source software is made freely available for anyone to use, modify, and distribute. Many of the technologies advocated by cypherpunks, including those used in bitcoin, are open source, which allows for continuous peer review, thus ensuring that vulnerabilities can be identified and addressed by the community on an ongoing basis.

Satoshi released bitcoin as open-source software, inviting developers worldwide to examine the code, identify potential flaws, and contribute to its development. Since it was released in 2009, over 99 percent of Satoshi's code has been rewritten by strangers from around the world whose identity is unknown to most bitcoin users. That is the nature of open-source software development. Bitcoin's success is largely the result of its open-source nature because it facilitates widespread scrutiny and testing of its protocol to an extent that may not have been achievable in a centralized enterprise. Thousands of developers continuously scrutinize bitcoin's code and contribute to its maintenance. They feel a collective ownership of it and a sense of responsibility toward it. Decisions about changes to the protocol are made through community consensus, with various stakeholders (developers, miners, node operators, and users) participating in the process.

The cypherpunks have had an unmistakable impact on bitcoin and continue to influence it philosophically to this day. Among many influences, the most obvious one may be bitcoin's decentralized approach to governance, which reflects the cypherpunk belief in community input and consensus to achieve the cypherpunk ideological ends.

CHAPTER 19

Time Preference

"Time preference" or "time discounting" in economics refers to the relative valuation placed on receiving a good or cash earlier compared with receiving it later. Decisions relating to time preference affect one's health, wealth, and happiness, and also, as Adam Smith first recognized, determine the economic prosperity of nations.[1] A high time preference indicates an inclination to prefer short-term returns or instant gratification, and a low time preference indicates the opposite.

Modern behavioral economics is a field that has done extensive research on time preference. The famous marshmallow test is an experimental design that measures a child's ability to delay gratification. The child is given the option of waiting for a period to get their favorite treat, or if they do not wait for the required period, receiving a less-desired treat. The minutes (or seconds) a child waits measures their ability to delay gratification—in other words, their time preference.

HIGH TIME PREFERENCE

People with high time preference tend to be (relatively) more present oriented. They place extra value on consuming sooner. They prefer instant gratification and are less inclined to save and invest. One's orientation depends on perceptions of the future. Some people, like small children, may find it difficult to grasp the concept of the future. While others, like the severely ill or elderly, think less of future consumption because they know there may not be any. By contrast, those with a low time preference are more future oriented. They delay gratification and have a clear vision of the benefits they wish to enjoy at a future date. Such people are more inclined to save and invest. Savings and investment, as opposed to immediate consumption, are what cause long-term economic growth, not just for the individual in question but for society at large.[2]

Inflation encourages high time preference because of the belief that prices will rise in the future ("buy today because prices will be higher tomorrow"), making goods more expensive and savings less valuable. Low interest rates further exacerbate high time preference because consumers are encouraged to take advantage of low borrowing costs to buy things today on credit. Individuals and businesses take on debt for immediate consumption rather than saving or investing in long-term, more sustainable projects. This dynamic is seen as a driving force behind consumerism, which is the theory that consumption of goods and services is economically desirable and contributes to societal value, personal success, and happiness.

Bitcoin heralds a return to the philosophy of a noninflationary "hard money" where the value of savings is expected to remain stable or increase over time, encouraging thoughtful consumption. It presents an economic incentive to delay gratification, invest wisely, and consider the long-term value and utility of purchases. In this way, bitcoin could be seen as an antidote to the impulsiveness and wastefulness encouraged by consumerism. As a noninflationary asset, it could promote a culture of sustainability and mindful consumption. The choice between the two paths is not just an economic decision but also a moral and philosophical one.

Although the period after World War II is often seen as the beginning of the consumerist era across the industrialized world, historian William Leach locates its roots in the United States around the turn of the century. Through the 1890s, shops were rapidly expanded, mail-order shopping surged, and the new century saw massive multistorey department stores covering millions of acres of selling space.[3] Today, it is said that 16 percent of the global population consumes 80 percent of its resources, the United States accounting for the lion's share of that consumption.

> The cardinal features of this culture were acquisition and consumption as a means of achieving happiness; the cult of the new; the democratization of desire; and money value as the predominant measure of all value in society.[4]
>
> —William Leach

The philosophical underpinnings of consumerism are complex. One might say that it has its roots in hedonism, which refers to the prioritization of pleasure in one's life. Hedonism theorizes that pleasure is the sole form of intrinsic value. In the hedonistic philosophy, pleasure or happiness is the highest ideal.[5] This philosophical mindset often results in a materialistic culture, where pleasure translates into the acquisition of material goods. Consumerism can be seen as an extension of these philosophies, where societal and personal well-being is measured by the ability to consume and display wealth.

We buy things we don't need with money we don't have to impress people we don't like.[6]

—Dave Ramsey

Research suggests, however, that while material goods can provide temporary pleasure, they do not necessarily lead to long-term happiness. This highlights the paradox at the center of consumerist hedonism.[7] Several studies have shown that materialistic people experience more negative emotion and less meaning in their lives. The quest for this elusive meaning in life is often channeled into further consumption of goods and services that symbolize certain identities or social statuses.[8]

Besides these internal emotional and psychological problems that consumerism causes, the (arguably) bigger issue relates to its negative externalities. Consumerism is a leading cause of environmental degradation. It also perpetuates social inequalities. The preference for quick, cheap consumption can lead to a proliferation of poor-quality products in sectors like food and architecture, as discussed below. Economic policies driving consumerism often result in increased public and private debt because they rely on borrowing to finance the endless binge of consumeristic spending. "Move fast and break things" is a Silicon Valley venture capital mantra that is a derivative of this underlying philosophical malignancy—headline eye-catching metrics are pursued by burning vast amounts of capital (in a game of valuation-driven musical chairs), often turning a blind eye to the absence of sustainable underlying profitability of businesses.

Proponents of consumerism on the other hand (likely from the Keynesian "free money" school of thought), may claim that it drives economic growth, innovation, and improved standards of living. They might argue that it offers individuals freedom of choice and the ability to "express oneself" through consumption.

The Environment

Consumerism and environmentalism are philosophically at loggerheads. Household consumption and mass production of products place incredible stress on the environment. These stresses include pollution, waste generation and overconsumption of natural resources, to name just a few.

Insatiable demand for new products drives the unsustainable extraction of raw materials. This extraction and production often involve harmful processes that can damage the environment. For example, the mining of minerals and metals can cause air and water pollution, and deforestation can lead to loss of biodiversity. The use of fossil fuels may contribute to climate change through the emission of greenhouse gases. Global supply chains often exploit workers and resources in developing countries where the lack of regulations and oversight lead to unchecked environmental harm.

Overconsumption refers to the act of consuming resources that cannot be replenished or that cannot sustain themselves at the rate we are consuming them. Take the logging industry as an example. Timber is used for shelter, heat, cooking, and paper products. According to the United Nations, overconsumption of timber has resulted in the loss of over 1 million acres of forest land since 1990. Natural resources need time to replenish. Overfishing is another example—fish populations need time to restore after extensive commercial fishing. According to the World Bank, almost 90 percent of global marine fish stocks are fully exploited or overfished. Earth.Org estimates that overfishing has wiped out more than 70 percent of specific shark populations in recent decades.

Disposal of waste and unwanted goods is a major problem for the environment. Landfill sites are responsible for the contamination of soil and groundwater. Contaminating materials like lead and mercury spread into the soil and groundwater. According to the International Union for the Conservation of Nature, an estimated 20 million metric tons of plastic litter ends up in the environment each year. The Center for Biological Diversity estimates that, at current rates, plastic waste in our oceans will outweigh all the fish in the sea by 2050.

As pointed out by economist and author Juliet Schor, the demand for consumer goods is linked directly to resource extraction rates that far exceed the Earth's capacity for regeneration.[9] The psychological drive of consumerism, such as the constant pursuit of material possessions, often results in a cycle of consumption and waste. "Treadmill of consumption" is the phenomenon where the incessant and insatiable need to consume leads to increased resource depletion and waste production without a corresponding increase in life satisfaction.[10]

Food Industry

Consumer food choice is influenced by a complex mix of biology, economics, geography, and social interactions. However, people choose food most often based on what they can afford. The current hierarchy of global food prices is such that empty calories are cheap, whereas nutrient-rich foods are expensive.[11] Thus, more and more people inevitably turn to foods that are high in calories, sugars, fats, and salt but that lack essential nutrients like fiber, vitamins, and minerals.

Fast-food options have led to the rise of processed foods at the expense of nutritional value. The long-term consumption of such diets contributes to health problems, including obesity, diabetes, heart disease, and other chronic conditions. Most of the world's population will soon be living in cities far removed from farms, fields, and fisheries. As a result, short, local food supply chains will have to transition to urban or national systems of food processing, storage, distribution, and retail. Fresh local foods will give way to more processed foods.

The unsustainable demand for food is fueling the production and use of pesticides and fertilizers at an equally unsustainable pace. According to the United Nations, about 385 million cases of unintentional acute pesticide poisonings are estimated to occur every year, with approximately eleven thousand deaths.[12] Pesticides are now ubiquitous in the environment, including in soils, sediments, and surface and groundwater, at levels exceeding environmental standards or guidelines. This is leading to serious environmental and health impacts.

As economies grow, many traditional foods give way to low-cost imported grains and added sugars. The dual burden of cheap, ample calories and more scarce and more expensive nutrients is now a common feature of the food supply around the world. As urbanization takes hold around the world, poverty and obesity are paradoxically becoming linked.[13] As fast foods proliferate to meet skyrocketing consumption, local food cultures and traditions are lost forever. Homogenization of diets takes hold around the world, and cultural richness associated with food becomes a thing of the past.

The implications of unhealthy diets place a significant burden on healthcare systems. The rise in diet-related diseases necessitates increased health-care services, medical interventions, and public health campaigns, imposing economic and social costs on societies.

Architecture

Throughout history, architecture has depicted the heart and soul of a locality, a nation, and its citizens, with architects being the storytellers. The Taj Mahal captured the eternal love of the Indian emperor for his spouse. The Pantheon depicted ideals of democracy and philosophy. The columns of the Colosseum show gladiatorial combat, public spectacle, and the majesty of the Roman empire. Machu Picchu's stone masonry demonstrated the Incas' connection to the natural environment. And the Forbidden City of China portrays imperial power and harmony. The dominant driver of these architectural marvels has always been clear: aesthetics to inspire generations.

The architectural style of the consumerist era has taken a different turn. To maximize available space to meet consumer demands, we see boxy high-rise buildings, devoid of any sort of character or artistic appeal. The demands are for high-density living or retail space rather than aesthetics and culture. Buildings embrace minimalism and simple forms rather than the ornamentation of the past. The use of prefabricated, mass-produced materials leads to standardized homogenous designs. Maximizing floor space and branding opportunities take precedence over all else. And the quest for cost-effectiveness leads to generic and repetitive forms over unique architectural marvels built as timeless sources of inspiration. The dominant drivers of this new era are very clear: functionality and cost-effectiveness.

Time preference lies at the core of these shifts. Rapid construction and short utility override durability and aesthetics. Planned obsolescence means that buildings and products are created with artificially limited useful life or a purposely frail design so that they become obsolete after a certain period of time, when they are deemed unfashionable and replaced.

Mental Health

Consumerism-driven high time preference has been shown to affect mental health. It contributes to a culture of comparison and competition, emphasizing individualism over collectivism. People are judged as being superior based on how much they consume, with high prestige equating to high consumption. This focus on what you own and on what people think of you takes priority over building meaningful relationships. Studies show how this has led to increasing anxiety, depression, low self-esteem, and a sense of isolation, particularly among younger and more impressionable individuals.

Those who cannot conform to high levels of consumption are deemed failures for not achieving a good life, and the failure is viewed as the fault of the individual.[14] Consumerism thus exacerbates social inequalities because it is designed to reinforce social and wealth disparities. People who cannot meet consumption expectations are deliberately marginalized in society. The endless cycle of desire and dissatisfaction, along with social comparison (facilitated by advertising and social media) have extremely negative long-term psychological implications for society at large.

LOW TIME PREFERENCE

Stoicism is an ancient Graeco-Roman philosophy from around 300 BCE that is based on the principle that the practice of virtue should be the ultimate pursuit in life. Virtues in everyday life include wisdom, courage, self-control, justice, and life lived in harmony with nature. Aristotelian ethics emphasizes similar principles. The philosophy of a life based on low time preference may find its roots in these teachings. It is the antithesis of consumerism and materialism.

Investing Practices

Seneca the Younger was a Stoic philosopher of Ancient Rome. His essays and letters constitute some of the most important foundations of ancient Stoicism.[15] He served as tutor and adviser to Nero before the emperor (in keeping with his reputation) ordered him to be killed. Images of Seneca's stoic and calm suicide are iconic and have been the subject of many great works of art. Despite advocating for simplicity, self-control, and the virtues of Stoicism, Seneca's life presented a paradox—he was one of the wealthiest men in Rome, owning vast estates and financial investments. Well aware of this contradiction, he addressed it in his writings, arguing that wealth itself is not inherently bad; rather, it is the attachment to wealth and the inability to live without it that are problematic.

High time preference typically signifies a hedonistic attachment to materialistic consumption. Low time preference, on the other hand, is the inclination to value future rewards more than present rewards. One's orientation on the time preference continuum has major implications with regard to money and investing. A low time preference would typically result in a greater willingness to forgo immediate consumption or gains in favor of more significant future returns. An investor with such a mindset may be more likely to invest in assets that do not provide immediate yield but are expected to appreciate over time; such an approach demonstrates patience and foresight.

A mindset of sacrificing present consumption and prioritizing the future emphasizes saving money. Long-term planning, risk aversion, and wealth accumulation are considered virtues. These values sit in stark contrast with concepts from Keynesian economics such as the paradox of thrift—the economic theory that personal savings are a net drag on the economy, especially during a recession. To address the paradox of thrift and remediate the problem of excess savings in an economy, Keynesian economists would typically respond by lowering interest rates, thereby encouraging borrowing and spending. The theory is that people must continue spending (consuming) so that the wheels of the economy continue turning at all times, at all costs.

The modern economy can be challenging for people who do not own physical assets like property, commodities, or other scarce assets and investments. As discussed in part III, monetary expansion is projected to continue unabated. As this ever-growing money supply flows into hard assets, those who own such assets benefit; those who do not are left further and further behind, exacerbating wealth disparities.[16] Inflation continues to hit younger generations who rely on daily wages and lack any form of buffer or hedge against inflation. Such individuals find it increasingly difficult to afford a basic standard of living.

These challenges often lead people, particularly younger people, to seek risky investments in a desperate bid to make ends meet. In an environment with low interest rates, conventional savings accounts will never come close to compensating for inflation rates over people's lifetimes. Thus, they invariably resort to more speculative investments in order to earn potentially greater profits. (Ironically, many see bitcoin as one such speculative investment, demonstrating a lack of appreciation of its true uniqueness and long-term investment thesis.)

An environment with low interest rates and rising living costs is the perfect setup to drag people further and further into debt. People are trapped in cycles of debt repayment to cover immediate needs, consuming a significant portion of their incomes. Credit card debt, student loans, and payday loans compound the problem, making escape from debt increasingly unrealistic.

Bitcoin, as a scarce commodity, enables individuals to store the fruits of their labor in a form that may be resistant to inflationary degradation over time. Unlike fiat currencies, which can lose purchasing power because of indiscriminate expansion of the money supply, bitcoin's purchasing power may appreciate over time (as it has done since its inception if you block out short-term volatility)[17] because of its scarcity and increasing demand for it. The prospect of being part of a rising tide of global adoption of an absolutely scarce commodity—an asset monetizing for the first time in history right before our eyes—might encourage individuals to save rather than spend. The appreciation potential of bitcoin incentivizes users to think long term about their financial well-being. Individuals may choose to forgo immediate consumption in favor of investing with the expectation of future financial security.

Note that the contention of this chapter is *not* that bitcoin is some sort of panacea that will herald a reversal of environmental destruction, improve dietary practices and mental health, and usher in a renaissance of aesthetically pleasing architecture. Rather, this is a discussion of the critical role that money plays in shaping incentives and inspiring human action. "Fix the money, fix the world" is a popular bitcoin meme on social media. This chapter is an exposition of the societal implications of the manipulation of money by central banks, specifically through inflationary policies that foster a consumption-driven culture. The contention of this chapter is that environmental destruction, erosion of food quality, decline in architectural value, and the burgeoning mental health crisis are largely symptomatic of a deeper malaise rooted in monetary policy.

Bitcoin emerges as a tool of resistance against many nihilistic societal trends. The gold standard represented a historical attempt to anchor currency to a tangible standard and curb the excesses of fiat currency manipulation. Despite its sound monetary principles (scarcity being foremost among them), the gold standard was ultimately abandoned because it was beleaguered by its practical limitations and inefficiencies, as discussed in chapter 2. Bitcoin, however, is presented as transcending these limitations and offers a digital hard money in the fight against the consumerist affliction that plagues society. Bitcoin offers humanity a chance to redirect the self-destructive trajectory of unchecked consumerism toward a future where sustainability and well-being are paramount.

CHAPTER 20

Narratives and Memes

I n Moscow's prisons in the 1990s, packs of Marlboro cigarettes attained the status of money. People would accept payment in Marlboro packs and individual cigarettes even if they did not smoke. This system is still prevalent today in prisons around the world, including in the United States (where it competes with instant ramen packs as the in-prison legal tender). The practice of using cigarettes as money may date back to German World War II prisoner-of-war camps. It is said that when large backlogs of delayed Red Cross packages finally arrived, sometimes injecting thousands of cigarette packs into the money supply at a camp, it caused inflation in prices.[1]

How do such systems of consensus emerge among humans? Philosopher John Searle draws a distinction between facts that exist in the world only by virtue of human agreement and facts that exist independent of any human opinions. The fact that Mount Everest has snow at its summit or that water boils at 100°C or that you cease to be alive when your heart stops beating fall into the latter camp, which he refers to as "brute facts." They exist regardless of our interpretation and beliefs. The agreement among inmates of prisons that tobacco wrapped in paper has value (even when an inmate might not be a smoker themself), falls into the former camp, which he refers to as "institutional facts." Money is an institutional fact.

How are these institutional facts born and perpetuated? According to author Yuval Harrari, societal constructs play a primary role in shaping the value systems that underlie institutional facts like money. Core to these societal constructs are narratives or, as he puts it, stories:

> The most successful story ever invented isn't a religious story about some god, but rather the story of money. The British pound is only valuable because everybody

believes it's valuable. And everybody believes it is valuable because they believe the stories told by the government, the Bank of England, and the major corporations. As long as everybody believes in this story, I can go to the supermarket, hand a colourful piece of paper to a stranger, and get bread in return. That doesn't work with chimpanzees: they don't believe in money and would never agree to give you a banana in exchange for some colourful pieces of paper. That's why we control the world, and the chimps don't.[2]

—Yuval Noah Harari

In other words, chimps prefer brute facts, and have trouble with institutional facts because of comparatively lower capacity to comprehend and deal with stories.

The power of social constructs, narratives and stories applies to investments, too. The essence of any enduring investment thesis is not merely found in numbers, charts, or economic indicators. It is also rooted in philosophical narratives that underpin the investment thesis.

The human brain has always been highly tuned toward narratives, whether factual or not, to justify ongoing actions, even such basic actions as spending and investing. Stories motivate and connect activities to deeply felt values and needs. Narratives "go viral" and spread far, even worldwide, with economic impact.[3]

—Robert Shiller

Robert Shiller, a Nobel laureate in 2013, introduced the concept of "Narrative Economics." In his book on the subject, he discusses popular narratives that often influence investment decisions and spread via a contagion similar to diseases in their transmission.[4] He argues that, while traditional economic models assume that decision-making is entirely driven by self-interested actions, narratives in society are also a powerful force. Narratives have an impact on people's understanding of how the world works, and the dangers that may affect them.

The power of narratives to influence investment decisions by affecting the human psyche and triggering herd mentality was clear to Satoshi too. He knew what thread to pull when he tried to encourage people to buy some bitcoin in 2009:

It might make sense just to get some in case it catches on. If enough people think the same way, that becomes a self-fulfilling prophecy.[5]

—Satoshi Nakamoto

Narratives provide a broader context and a deeper understanding of an investment's purpose and place within the economic and social landscape. They help investors align with long-term values rather than short-term trends. They offer a philosophical framework for evaluating paradigm shifts that are beyond immediate market dynamics and volatility. A philosophical grounding in one's value system is crucial for developing resilient investment theses that withstand near-term market volatility. Investment strategies based on core values are more likely to maintain their course in the face of adverse events.

Philosophical narratives attract like-minded investors, thus creating a community of stakeholders invested in the success of the mission for reasons that go beyond financial returns. They imbue investment theses with depth, purpose, and endurance, and enable them to navigate the ebbs and flows of markets while remaining anchored to a larger vision.

Narratives spark cultural revolutions. As Shiller noted, the power of narratives to influence cultural trends by going viral is further affected by information technology. Shiller argues, for instance, that the invention of the printing press and newspapers contributed to the Dutch tulip mania in the seventeenth century. In the age of the internet and social media, the viral element involved in narratives taking hold has never been stronger.

The importance of philosophical and cultural narratives cannot be overstated when it comes to bitcoin. This is especially true given bitcoin's unique position as an asset without a revenue stream, corporate governance, leadership team, or even a physical form. Like gold, bitcoin's value is heavily derived from the collective belief in its worth and utility. This belief system is anchored and propagated through compelling narratives that capture the imagination and conviction of its users and proponents.

Central to sustaining bitcoin's narratives are memes and the vibrant culture surrounding them. Bitcoin memes do more than entertain—they are a powerful tool for distilling complex ideas about economics, sovereignty, and privacy into accessible and relatable content. They leverage the power of the internet and social media to the fullest extent possible. They help foster a sense of community and shared purpose, which are essential for a decentralized network where consensus and collective action are key. They encapsulate the culture of bitcoin and emphasize its antiestablishment roots. And they are instrumental in building and sustaining the belief in bitcoin's mission. The following sections offer brief descriptions of a small selection of bitcoin's most iconic memes.

Be Your Own Bank

The phrase "be your own bank" encapsulates bitcoin's core philosophy. It refers to the ability of individuals to have full control over their own money and to bypass the traditional financial services industry. In the banking system, banks act as intermediaries that hold and manage people's money and facilitate transactions. Bitcoin offers an alternative. It enables individuals to store, manage, and transact their wealth independently, 24 hours a day, 365 days a year, in a self-reliant and self-sovereign way. By holding the private keys to your bitcoin, you have sole ownership and responsibility for your money, free from the limitations and influence of third parties. By eliminating the banking system as an intermediary, you gain censorship resistance and insulation from bank failures. The meme highlights bitcoin's potential to disrupt and disintermediate the banking industry.

Vires in Numeris

The Latin phrase "vires in numeris" translates to "strength in numbers." It is symbolic of the inherent superiority of numbers over fallible humans. Unlike fiat currencies, which are subject to the whims of governments, central banks, and the people who run them, bitcoin operates on the principles of mathematics and cryptography. By placing trust in mathematical principles rather than human institutions, bitcoin represents a philosophical shift toward decentralized, trustless systems and away from centralized systems prone to corruption. It symbolizes a departure from blind faith in human and institutional authority toward a transparent and egalitarian approach rooted in numerical certainty.

Not Your Keys, Not Your Coins

The meme "not your keys, not your coins" originated as a warning regarding the ownership and security of bitcoin. It captures an important principle of bitcoin ownership: if you do not control the private keys to your wallet, you do not truly own the coins stored in that wallet. The phrase gained prominence as a way to emphasize the importance of self-custody and the risks associated with storing bitcoin on exchanges or in wallets controlled by third parties where you are subject to risks like exchange bankruptcy, fraud, and hacks. Gary Gensler, chair of the U.S. Securities and Exchange Commission (SEC) and notorious crypto-skeptic, released a YouTube video in February 2023 where he too vocalized the meme "Not your keys, not your crypto."

Bitcoin Sign Guy

On July 12, 2017, during Federal Reserve chair Janet Yellen's testimony before the House Financial Services Committee, an unnamed individual strategically positioned himself to be visible in the camera shot behind her and held up a notepad with "Buy Bitcoin" written on it. The act was seen live on television and quickly became an iconic moment in the bitcoin community. The timing and setting of the act underscored the contrast between the traditional centralized and inflationary financial policies represented by Yellen and bitcoin as a means to opt out. In particular, the meme captured the antiestablishment sentiment that is at the heart of bitcoin. In April 2024, the said notepad was sold for a price of $1 million, signifying its cultural significance.

HODL

A common misconception is that HODL is an abbreviation for "hold on for dear life." Fortunately, this is not true as it would have made for a rather underwhelming meme. HODL, in fact, originates from a misspelling of the word "hold" in a humorous, yet insightful, blog post in 2013, wherein the author argues about the futility of attempting to time the market. In essence, HODL encourages investors to adopt a long-term view and resist the temptation of short-term gains. HODL-ing reflects a pragmatic response to bitcoin's notorious price volatility. Rather than succumbing to the whims of short-term market fluctuations, HODLers choose to weather the storm and remain confident in the eventual appreciation of bitcoin's value. This resilience against volatility contrasts with the high-risk, high-reward nature of attempting to time the market, which often leads to losses.

Beyond its practical implications, the HODL meme has fostered a sense of community among bitcoiners. By promoting a shared commitment to holding onto bitcoin despite short-term volatility, the meme has helped forge bitcoin's collective identity and spirit. It encapsulates a philosophy of long-term investment, resilience against market volatility, and skepticism toward market timing.

Honey Badger

The meme comparing bitcoin to a honey badger originates from the honey badger's reputation for being fearless and tough. The meme suggests that bitcoin, like the honey badger, is resilient and unstoppable in the face of adversity. Despite regulatory challenges, exchange bankruptcies, crypto industry scams, market volatility, ideological rifts within the community, and unrelenting criticisms from financial experts and the news media, bitcoin has continued to grow and scale new heights in market capitalization and global adoption. This meme emphasizes bitcoin's ability to withstand various challenges with unshakable resilience.

Laser Eyes

The laser-eyes meme originated in 2021 when individuals began editing their social media profile pictures to include laser beams shooting from their eyes. The meme symbolized a collective commitment to maintain a laser-like focus on bitcoin's journey until it reached the milestone of $100,000 per bitcoin. Many critics of the meme argue that those sporting laser eyes often come across as dogmatic and toxic. The meme is seen by some as emblematic of a fundamentalist, almost religious zeal within the bitcoin community. It is intertwined with another meme—"bitcoin maximalism"—the philosophy that any and all blockchain-related development should happen on bitcoin alone because it is the only truly decentralized blockchain.

Those who criticize the meme often ignore the value of unyielding dogma in all cultural revolutions. The bitcoin culture evolved organically. No amount of investment from Silicon Valley, Wall Street, or other global institutions or governments can re-create a unifying grassroots culture as powerful as this. It is immutable, irreplicable, and path dependent, just like bitcoin itself. It did not emerge from hefty investments or glossy marketing campaigns. It was forged in the fires of antiestablishment ideals, honed through relentless commitment to cypherpunk principles, and solidified in the hands of those who subscribe to a simple and humble philosophy: run a bitcoin node, self-custody your savings, and convert your hard-earned wages into satoshis. The clichéd symbols of crypto success—the Lamborghinis and penthouses—are antithetical to this culture, which calls for a stoic, low time preference; a simple life; and prioritizing what is real and true.

Bitcoin, like gold, derives its value from a collective belief in its worth. This belief system mirrors the evolution of philosophical doctrines through the ages. They demand unwavering adherence to foundational ideologies. Consider the monastic principles by which monks in the Middle Ages meticulously and dogmatically transcribed sacred texts to ensure their endurance, and their resistance to adulteration over hundreds of years. Bitcoin's resilience also hinges on resisting dilution. Its strength lies in simplicity and adherence to its original vision and avoiding complexities that could undermine its true essence. Single-minded focus is critical to ensuring that bitcoin remains relevant through decades, centuries, or millennia, like gold has. The laser-eyed bitcoin maximalists represent the stoic battle-hardened guardians of this philosophy.

CHAPTER 21

Bitcoin Is a Mirror

Two roads diverged in a wood, and I—
I took the one less traveled by,
And that has made all the difference.

—Robert Frost

The study of bitcoin is a revealing philosophical journey. On the one hand, it involves an analysis of the nature and intricacies of the innovation itself. On the other, it holds a mirror to one's own cognitive predispositions, ideologies, and biases. It reveals personal convictions. For example, it compels one to pinpoint their position on the continuum between individual liberty and governmental control. It demands intellectual humility, especially for those distinguished by advanced degrees and professional achievements, to embrace the Socratic admission: "I know that I know nothing."[1] And it encourages fallibilism, the practice of critically examining and questioning established beliefs and widely accepted truths.

The Dunning-Kruger effect—a cognitive bias wherein individuals with limited knowledge overestimate their competence—can be particularly relevant here.[2] The more you learn about bitcoin, the more you realize the vastness of what you have yet to understand. One is reminded of the words of ancient Tamil poet Avaiyar from around 100 BCE: "What you have learned is a mere handful; what you have not learned amounts to an entire world."

Throughout history, individual responses to significant innovative advancements have varied widely. Each landmark innovation, from the wheel to the internet, has encountered its share of contemporary skeptics. Here are some notable examples:

> The Americans have need of the telephone, but we do not. We have plenty of messenger boys.
>
> —Sir William Preece, chief engineer of the British Post Office, 1876

> Heavier-than-air flying machines are impossible.
>
> —Lord Kelvin, president of the Royal Society, 1895

> The horse is here to stay but the automobile is only a novelty—a fad.
>
> —President of the Michigan Savings Bank, 1903

> Who the hell wants to hear actors talk?
>
> —H. M. Warner, Warner Brothers, 1927, on the prospects of sound in film

> I think there is a world market for maybe five computers.
>
> —Thomas Watson, president, IBM, 1943

> Television won't last because people will soon get tired of staring at a plywood box every night.
>
> —Darryl Zanuck, 20th Century Fox, 1946

> Remote shopping, while entirely feasible, will flop.
>
> —Time Magazine on the prospects for online shopping, 1966.

> The truth is no online database will replace your daily newspaper.
>
> —Clifford Stoll, *Newsweek* article entitled, "Internet? Bah!," 1995

> The growth of the Internet will slow drastically ... most people have nothing to say to each other! By 2005 or so, it will become clear that the Internet's impact on the economy has been no greater than the fax machine's.
>
> —Paul Krugman, Nobel Prize–winning economist, 1998

When the electric bulb was introduced in 1880, critics raised safety concerns around electrical fires, accidents, and potential health hazards. Gas companies threatened by the advent of electric lighting argued that it was harsher and less reliable compared to the established gaslight. Cultural critics mourned the loss of the warm glow of gaslight and the natural rhythm of day and night, fearing that electric light would disrupt urban aesthetics and societal norms.

When bicycles were first introduced around the same period in the late nineteenth century, they were met with various scare-mongering claims. Skeptics warned that cycling could damage reproductive organs and lead to infertility. Some believed that cycling could lead to psychological issues such as hysteria and psychosis, and physical deformities like bent spines and legs due to the posture and repetitive motion involved. The freedom and mobility provided by bicycles were seen as threats to traditional gender roles, prompting fears of increased promiscuity and moral decay among women. Doctors also warned that women using the newfangled contraption could lead to a terrifying medical condition called bicycle face.[3] The *Literary Digest* in 1895 proclaimed: "Over-exertion, the upright position on the wheel, and the unconscious effort to maintain one's balance tend to produce a wearied and exhausted 'bicycle face.'" Symptoms included "a hard, clenched jaw and bulging eyes."[4]

Daniel Batten suggests that society's negative responses to new technologies stem from an inherent human survival instinct. On the savannah, if an early human saw a large indistinct shape on the horizon and was unsure if it was a predator or prey, assuming it was dangerous and being wrong meant losing a potential meal. But assuming it was harmless and being wrong could have meant becoming a meal. This instinct to err on the side of caution in the face of uncertainty is ingrained in evolutionary psychology. When confronted with novel technologies whose impacts are not yet understood, people tend to default to negative assumptions.[5]

Bitcoin has faced its share of harsh and vehement criticism along with numerous declarations of its demise right from its inception. There is a website that tracks bitcoin obituaries—that is, each time someone in a major media publication has declared bitcoin to be dead. The count currently stands at 415. As this book goes to press, bitcoin's fundamentals (e.g., its mining hash rate, node distribution, and price) have never looked better. In the history of obituaries, bitcoin may be unsurpassed in the number of times it has emerged from the dead, bigger and stronger than ever before. If you bought $100 worth of bitcoin each of those 415 times the media declared it dead, you would have over $100 million today.[6]

Skepticism is certainly not a bad thing. It undoubtedly plays a crucial role in both the advancement of knowledge and the safeguarding of society from untested or fallacious claims. It drives rigorous inquiry, forming the backbone of the scientific method. In everyday life, a healthy dose of skepticism can protect individuals from scams, propaganda, and misinformation. Thus, while skepticism can sometimes slow acceptance of a new innovation, it ultimately serves to build a more robust framework for its understanding, validation, and adoption. The pattern of skepticism that bitcoin has been subjected to is not unique or unusual—it is a universal rite of passage.[7]

The manner in which humans instinctively react to new technologies may also reflect deep philosophical orientations toward the future and the human capacity to shape it positively or negatively.[8] Technological optimism can be traced back to the Enlightenment and its emphasis on the belief in progress.[9] The optimism of the Enlightenment was grounded in a confidence that knowledge and rationality could lead to continuous improvement in human conditions.

The Industrial Revolution is a prime historical analogy for optimism versus pessimism in technology. Optimists saw the massive technological changes as ways to elevate living standards, improve health, and democratize access to goods. In contrast, pessimists focused on the dark side: worker exploitation, environmental degradation, and the loss of artisanal skills and community values. The Luddites, for example, famously resisted technological advancements in weaving, fearing job loss and a breakdown of their social fabric.

After World War II, the development of nuclear technology epitomized the stark dichotomy of technological optimism and pessimism. On one hand, optimists heralded the atomic age as a promise for unlimited clean energy and a force for world peace through deterrence. On the other, pessimists saw the atomic bomb as a potential harbinger of global annihilation and harbored fears about the ability to control it.

Bitcoin's potential to serve as a better form of money for humanity perhaps appeals to those with a natural proclivity to choose optimism over pessimism or, in some cases, nihilism. On another front, bitcoin may also appeal to those who are predisposed to distrust institutions and, in particular, the state.[10] Many of bitcoin's ardent backers from its earliest days subscribe to philosophies ranging from classical liberalism to libertarianism and anarchism. To them, bitcoin is a means to challenge the status quo and assert individual autonomy.

Those on the other end of the philosophical spectrum view the state as a legitimate authority entrusted with maintaining social order and providing essential services. Drawing from thinkers such as Thomas Hobbes and John Locke, proponents of placing trust in the state prioritize the role of government in safeguarding citizens' rights and promoting the common good.[11] They often perceive bitcoin as a threat to this vision and its decentralized nature as undermining the state's ability to regulate and stabilize the economy. One's socioeconomic background may perhaps have the greatest impact on one's instinctive reaction to bitcoin:

> Anyone born into a reserve currency like the euro, yen, or pound has financial privilege over the 89 percent of the world population born into weaker systems.[12]
>
> —Alex Gladstein

In the comfort of our well-appointed living rooms, seated in a cozy armchair by the gentle warmth of a fireplace, it is easy to cast a skeptical eye on bitcoin. From this vantage point of privilege, bitcoin's perceived lack of intrinsic value, short-term volatility, and notoriety for facilitating money laundering are fodder for dismissal or even scorn.

But there are millions who do not enjoy this luxury perspective. For instance, in March 2024, it was reported that Iran was introducing a new law under which funds may be automatically deducted from the bank accounts of women who fail to comply with the compulsory hijab requirement.[13] Enforcement would be through artificial intelligence and facial recognition technology that would scrutinize online content and identify violators. Ordinarily, being fined through traditional means allows for a range of responses—ignoring the fine, lodging an appeal, or bracing for repercussions. Imagine the shock of waking up one morning, however, to find half your bank account drained without forewarning or explanation. This stark reality unveils a chilling truth: the funds in your bank account were never yours in the first place.

What recourse might bitcoin sceptics offer an Iranian woman faced with such tyranny? If only there existed a technological tool that allowed invisible and private self-custody of one's life savings beyond the reach of any authority![14]

> Most people don't realize this, but Satoshi opened a portal from the physical realm into the digital realm . . . Bringing conservation of energy and matter, objectivity, truth, time, and consequence into the digital realm, delivering property rights, freedom, and sovereignty that is separate from the physical and the political realm, to humanity.[15]
>
> —Michael Saylor

As we discussed in chapter 12, the digital era has provided oppressive regimes far greater means than ever to quash dissent through financial surveillance. While the methods employed vary among regimes, their objective remains consistent: to silence voices of opposition and subdue freedom of expression through economic coercion. This creates pressing challenges to human rights in an era dominated by digital technologies.

Maslow's hierarchy of needs is a psychological theory proposing that human needs can be arranged in a hierarchical order, with basic safety needs forming the foundation, followed by needs for love, esteem, and self-actualization at the top. Individuals progress through these levels as lower-level needs are satisfied, with higher-order needs fulfilled only after lower-level ones are. The hierarchy of needs suggests that individuals are motivated to fulfill their most basic needs first before progressing to higher-order needs.

Most readers of this book would likely find themselves on the upper echelons of Maslow's psychological hierarchy, far removed from the immediate concerns of safety and basic survival. For people in privileged positions, it is crucial to recognize how socioeconomic disparities mold philosophical judgment.[16] This is particularly important when grappling with questions surrounding the pressing need for financial empowerment and individual freedoms that are not immediately relevant to us or necessarily relatable given our backgrounds and upbringing.

To those with less socioeconomic privilege, bitcoin represents much more than just a speculative investment or a conduit for underground transactions. It symbolizes a lifeline when autonomy over one's finances and livelihood are systematically stifled.

"Bitcoin is bigger than any government," declared Larry Fink, chair and CEO of the $10 trillion asset management firm BlackRock, in a 2024 Fox Business interview,[17] sending many ardent bitcoin critics into disarray. There is clearly a growing recognition of bitcoin as a tool of unprecedented power for the reclamation of financial self-sovereignty from oppressive government and institutional authorities. In the words of Victor Hugo, "No army can withstand the strength of an idea whose time has come."

The thing about bitcoin is that such perspectives are not immediately apparent. Only a comprehensive and deep study can yield such a holistic understanding. Regrettably, to this day, far too many continue to rely on "tulip mania" and "beanie babies" as analogies to criticize bitcoin's perceived lack of value.[18]

In a 2020 shareholder letter, Ross Stevens, founder and CEO of Stone Ridge Asset Management, quotes David Foster Wallace: "There are these two young fish swimming along and they happen to meet an older fish swimming the other way, who nods at them and says 'Morning, boys. How's the water?' And the two young fish swim on for a bit, and then eventually one of them looks over to the other and says, 'What's water?'"[19] Sometimes the most obvious, most important realities are the ones that are hardest to see. Stevens argues that today one of our "What's water?" questions is "What's money?" In the conceptual framing of this book, this is where first principles thinking and a holistic approach might hold the key. Such an analysis might trigger a revaluation of bitcoin's primary technological, economic, political, and philosophical proposition: the separation of money and state.

> Money is a very old convenience but the notion that it is a reliable artefact to be accepted without scrutiny or question is, in all respects, a very occasional thing—mostly a circumstance of the last century.[20]
>
> —John Kenneth Galbraith

Is bitcoin humanity's money of the future? Nobody knows. What can be said with certainty, however, is that bitcoin does not fit traditional molds, and the most common cognitive error people make in passing judgment is trying to fit a square peg into a round hole. A good place to start studying the subject is simply to open one's mind to the possibility that maybe, just maybe, after fifteen years of critics being wrong, there might actually be more to the matter than a cursory examination yields.

Notes

PREFACE

1. Stephen Foley and Jane Wild, "The Bitcoin Believers," *Financial Times*, June 14, 2013.
2. The concept of digital gold is, in fact, decades-old. Nick Szabo in 1998 introduced Bit Gold in his paper, "Formalizing and Securing Relationships on Public Networks," which may not have been the first such reference. Nick Szabo, *First Monday* 2, no. 9 (1997), https://doi.org/10.5210/fm.v2i9.548.
3. Nathaniel Popper's book *Digital Gold* had in fact just been published at the time, but it unfortunately eluded me.
4. Interview with Laura Shin on the Unchained Podcast, November 29, 2017.
5. Aristotle, *Nicomachean Ethics*, trans. W. D. Ross (Batoche, 1999), 1–109. In this foundational text on ethics, Aristotle introduces the concept of eudaimonia, meaning "flourishing" or "well-being," which he describes as the highest good for humans.
6. Ernest Hemingway, *A Moveable Feast* (Scribner, 1964), 12.

1. WHY ARE WE TALKING ABOUT THIS?

1. The Buddhist text Tittha Sutta, contains one of the earliest versions of the story, dated around 500 BCE.
2. Posted by Satoshi Nakamoto on the BitcoinTalk forum on July 5, 2010, https://satoshi.nakamotoinstitute.org/quotes. All quotes from Satoshi are sourced from this page.
3. Gigi, "Bitcoin Is Time," January 14, 2021, dergigi.com.
4. The quote is widely attributed to George Bernard Shaw, but the precise origin is unknown.
5. There may be legal assurances (e.g. confidentiality agreements), but they rely on external factors for enforcement that are outside peer-to-peer exchange.
6. Posted by Satoshi Nakamoto on the BitcoinTalk forum on August 27, 2010.
7. John Oliver, *Last Week Tonight with John Oliver*, HBO, March 11, 2018.
8. Aristotle, *Metaphysics*, in *The Complete Works of Aristotle: The Revised Oxford Translation*, vol. 2, ed. J. Barnes (Princeton University Press, 1984).

9.   Aristotle, *Physics*, in J. Barnes (Ed.), *The Complete Works of Aristotle: The Revised Oxford Translation*, vol. 1, ed. J. Barnes (Princeton University Press, 1984).

10.   In his work, *Posterior Analytics*, Aristotle observed that each science consists of a set of first principles that are necessarily true and knowable directly, and a set of truths that are both logically derivable from and causally explained by the first principles. A. P. Martinich and Avrum Stroll, "Epistemology," *Encyclopedia Britannica* (Encyclopedia Britannica, 2024).

11.   John Kenneth Galbraith, *Money: Whence It Came, Where It Went* (Houghton Mifflin Harcourt, 1975).

12.   Attributed to Henry Ford by Charles Binderup (March 19, 1937), Congressional Record–House, vol. 81, 2528.

13.   The Dutch tulip mania occurred in 1637 in the Netherlands when the prices of tulip bulbs skyrocketed before collapsing dramatically, marking one of the first recorded speculative bubbles.

14.   George Selgin, "Synthetic Commodity Money," *Journal of Financial Stability* 17 (2015): 92–99.

15.   Plato, *Plato: Complete Works—Charmides*, ed. J. M. Cooper, trans. R. K. Sprague (Hackett, 1997). Cited in Chiara Thumiger and Hynek Bartoš, *Holism in Ancient Medicine and Its Reception*, chap. 4, Hippocratic Holisms (Brill, 2020).

16.   Shameem Anwar, *Success Needs Your Holistic Approach!*, Medium, October 19, 2020, https://medium.com/@shameemanwar.sa/success-needs-your-holistic-approach-e1a0954ea5b6.

2. BITCOIN AND MONEY

1.   This example is from Gigi's paper—"Bitcoin Is Time," January 14, 2021, dergigi.com.

2.   Gigi, "Bitcoin Is Time."

3.   Felix Martin, *Money: The Unauthorized Biography* (Knopf, 2014). Statistics from the Federal Reserve Bank of St. Louis and the Bank of England, respectively, for November 2011.

4.   Gigi, "Bitcoin Is Time."

5.   Gigi's paper, "Bitcoin Is Time," was the first to introduce this idea. The paper is one of the most important pieces of literature on bitcoin.

6.   Nick Szabo, "Shelling Out: The Origins of Money," 2002, https://nakamotoinstitute.org/shelling-out/.

7.   Gigi, "Memes vs. the World," 2021, dergigi.com.

8.   Carl Menger, "On the Origin of Money," *Economic Journal* 2, no. 6 (1892): 239–55.

9.   It is also theoretically possible to mine gold on asteroids, which are believed to contain gold in concentrations much higher than those found on Earth. Technological advancements and space missions by NASA and private companies are exploring the feasibility.

10.   Horatio Sam-Aggrey, "Assessment of the Impacts of New Mining Technologies: Recommendations and the Way Forward," *WIT Transactions on Ecology and the Environment* 245 (2020), https://www.witpress.com/elibrary/.

11.   Ross L. Stevens, "Stone Ridge Shareholder Letter," December 15, 2020, https://www.casebitcoin.com/stone-ridge-2020-shareholder-letter.

12.   Operation Fish was the relocation of British money and gold ingots from the United Kingdom to Canada for safekeeping during World War II. It was the largest known

movement of physical wealth in history. See Robert Low, "Operation Fish," Bank of Canada Museum, May 8, 2018, https://www.bankofcanadamuseum.ca/2018/05/operation-fish/.

13. Layer 2 protocols refer to protocols built on top of Bitcoin (layer 1 protocol) that enable instantaneous transactions without having to wait for Bitcoin's ten-minute settlement cycle. Examples include the Lightning Network and Liquid Network. While they provide the convenience of day-to-day instantaneous and low-fee transactions, they lack the finality and security of layer 1 final settlements on the Bitcoin protocol. See chap. 3 of this book.

14. A key aspect of bitcoin transactions is that the "cost" involved in sending bitcoin is independent of the amount of bitcoin being sent. This contrasts with physical commodities or fiat where costs increase commensurately with the value transacted.

15. United States Treasury Department, "The Use and Counterfeiting of United States Currency Abroad" (September 2006), https://www.federalreserve.gov/boarddocs/rptcongress/counterfeit/counterfeit2006.pdf.

16. Fire assay is considered the most reliable method for accurately determining the content of gold, silver, and platinum-group metals (except osmium and ruthenium) in ores or concentrates. See "Fire Assay Analysis" (Geneva: SGS), https://www.sgs.com/en/services/fire-assay-analysis.

17. X-ray fluorescence (XRF) analyzers are devices that use X-rays to measure the purity of precious metals without destroying them. Drawell, "How Does an XRF Gold Analyzer Work," 2023, https://www.drawellanalytical.com/how-does-an-xrf-gold-analyzer-work/.

18. GIA, "Use the Touchstone Method for Testing Purity in Karat Gold," 2024, https://www.gia.edu/gia-news-research-bench-tips.

19. Clint Siegner, "How to Test Gold & Silver at Home: 5 Proven Bullion Testing Methods, Money Metals Exchange," 2022, https://www.moneymetals.com/guides/how-to-test-gold-and-silver-at-home.; "How Can I Tell if My Gold Is Real or Gold-Plated?," AMPEX Knowledge Center, 2023, https://learn.apmex.com/learning-guide/bullion/how-can-i-tell-if-my-gold-is-real-or-gold-plated/.

20. Britannica Money, *Origins of Coins*, https://www.britannica.com/money/coin/Origins-of-coins.

21. GoldBroker, "Counterfeit Gold: How to Spot Fake Gold," 2024, goldbroker.com, https://goldbroker.com/investing-guide/counterfeit-gold-how-to-spot-fake-gold; Global Bullion Suppliers, "Are There Gold Bars Filled with Tungsten at Major Banks?," January 30, 2019, https://globalbullionsuppliers.com/en-us/blogs/blog/are-there-gold-bars-filled-with-tungsten-at-major-banks?.

22. Britannica Money, *Parting, Casting, Separation & Refining*, https://www.britannica.com/science/metallurgy/Ferrous-metals.

23. David Bowers, "Gold Coins: Their History, Professional Coin Grading Services," 2002, pcgs.com/news/gold-coins-their-history.

24. Britannica Money, *Gold—Element, Precious Metal, Jewelry*, https://www.britannica.com/science/gold-chemical-element/Properties-occurrences-and-uses.

25. In practical terms, the physical nature of gold can introduce slight variations in purity and form, which might necessitate assay or verification, especially in large transactions.

26.   By way of example, on November 8, 2016, the Indian government announced the demon-etization of Rs.500 and Rs.1,000 currency notes, rendering 86 percent of the country's cash in circulation invalid overnight to combat black money and counterfeit currency. This sudden move led to severe cash shortages, long queues at banks, and significant disruptions to daily life and economic activities, especially for those reliant on cash transactions.

27.   When a country imports more than it exports, it runs a trade deficit. Importing large amounts of gold can contribute significantly to this deficit because gold is a valuable commodity. To manage or reduce a trade deficit, governments may restrict gold imports to decrease the outflow of money used to purchase gold from abroad.

28.   A. M. Riggsby, *Ownership and Possession Roman Law and the Legal World of the Romans* (Cambridge University Press, 2010); Jeremy Waldron, "Property and Ownership," *The Stanford Encyclopedia of Philosophy* (2023).

29.   The expression, "possession is nine-tenths of the law" originates from an old Scottish proverb: "possession is eleven points in the law, and they say they are but twelve." Its earliest written record dates back to 1616, when Thomas Draxe mentioned "possession is nine points of the Law" in his work, *Bibliotheca Scholastica* (London, 1633).

30.   Anne O'Donnell, *Power and Possession in the Russian Revolution* (Princeton University Press, 2024); G. Mkodzongi, *Land and Agrarian Transformation in Zimbabwe: Rethinking Rural Livelihoods in the Aftermath of the Land Reforms* (Anthem Press, 2020).

31.   Ryan C. Perkins, "The 1947 Partition of India & Pakistan," *Spotlight at Stanford* (2024), https://exhibits.stanford.edu/1947-partition/about/1947-partition-of-india-pakistan.

32.   "The Bitcoin Network Has Been Working For . . . ," https://bitcoinuptime.org/.

33.   Vijay Boyapati's paper, "The Bullish Base for Bitcoin," March 2, 2018, originally proposed a similar scorecard which was the inspiration for this scorecard.

34.   Malcolm Gladwell in his 2000 book, *The Tipping Point: How Little Things Can Make a Big Difference*, uses the term to describe the moment when an idea or trend crosses a thresh-old, tips, and spreads like wildfire. In his book, Gladwell explores how seemingly minor changes can trigger a tipping point, leading to paradigm shifts. Malcolm Gladwell, *The Tipping Point: How Little Things Can Make a Big Difference* (Little, Brown, 2000).

35.   Saifedean Ammous, "Economics of Bitcoin as a Settlement Network," *Satoshi Nakamoto Institute* (May 19, 2017), https://nakamotoinstitute.org/mempool/economics-of-bitcoin-as -a-settlement-network/.

36.   See Saifedean Ammous, *The Bitcoin Standard: The Decentralized Alternative to Central Banking* (Wiley, 2018).

37.   Posted by Satoshi Nakamoto on the BitcoinTalk forum on February 11, 2009.

38.   Posted by Hal Finney on the BitcoinTalk forum on December 30, 2010, https:// bitcointalk.org/index.php?topic=2500.0.

39.   See Jonathan Bier, *The Blocksize War* (Author, 2021).

3. BITCOIN'S ARCHITECTURE

1.   Leslie Lamport, Robert Shostak, and Marshall Pease, "The Byzantine Generals Problem," *ACM Transactions on Programming Languages and Systems* 4, no. 5 (1982): 382–401.

2. Lamport, Shostak, and Pease, "The Byzantine Generals Problem."

3. Satoshi Nakamoto, "Bitcoin: A Peer-to-Peer Electronic Cash System," https://bitcoin.org/bitcoin.pdf, 2008.

4. Andrew Poelstra, "On Stake and Consensus," *Nakamoto Institute*, 2015, https://cdn.nakamotoinstitute.org/docs/on-stake-and-consensus.pdf.

5. David Chaum, "Security Without Identification: Transaction Systems to Make Big Brother Obsolete," *Communications of the ACM* 28, no. 10 (October 1985): 1030–1044; Nick Szabo, "Bit Gold," *Unenumerated* (blog), December 27, 2008, https://unenumerated.blogspot.com/2005/12/bit-gold.html.

6. *Bit Nodes*, https://bitnodes.io, accessed November 2, 2024; *TimechainStats*, https://timechainstats.com, accessed November 2, 2024.

7. Crypto.com Research and Insights Team, "Crypto Market Sizing Report 2022: Global Crypto Owners Reached 425 Million by the End of 2022," January 19, 2023, https://crypto.com/research/2022-crypto-market-sizing-report.

8. While the internet is the most common means of broadcasting, it is possible to use other means, such as ham radio, mesh networks, and even SMS text messaging.

9. See Simon Singh, *The Code Book: The Science of Secrecy from Ancient Egypt to Quantum Cryptography* (Anchor Books, 1999).

10. The private key is a randomly generated 256-bit number. The public key is derived from the private key using a mathematical operation called elliptic curve multiplication. This is a one-way function that takes the private key and multiplies it by a point on an elliptic curve. The result is a point on the elliptic curve (a pair of coordinates x, y) which is the public key.

11. Breaking SHA-256 encryption through brute force would require attempting up to 2^{256} (approximately 1.16×10^{77}) different combinations, an astronomically large number. The computational effort needed for such an exhaustive search would demand an energy consumption so vast that it could theoretically exceed the energy output of the Sun, which is about 3.8×10^{26} watts. See National Institute of Standards and Technology (NIST), *FIPS PUB 180–4, Secure Hash Standard (SHS)*, August 2015, https://csrc.nist.gov/pubs/fips/180-4/upd1/final.

12. President Barack Obama's keynote address at the South by Southwest Festival, March 2016.

13. The puzzle involves finding a value that, when hashed using the SHA-256 hash function, produces an output that begins with a number of zero bits.

14. A fork in the blockchain occurs when two miners solve the cryptographic puzzle simultaneously, leading to two competing versions of the blockchain. Nodes might temporarily follow different chains until consensus is reached on which chain is the valid one. The ten-minute interval reduces the likelihood of such conflicts by providing enough time for information to spread across the network (considering internet speeds and geographical distribution of nodes), thus reducing the chances of miners working on competing chains.

15. The block subsidy last changed from 6.25 bitcoins per block to 3.125 bitcoins per block on April 20, 2024.

16. See chap. 7 of this book.

17. Robert Breedlove may have been the first to describe this analogy.

18. Shinobi, "Why Is Bitcoin Censorship Resistant?" *Bitcoin Magazine*, January 23, 2024, https://bitcoinmagazine.com/markets/why-is-bitcoin-censorship-resistant.

19.   Shinobi, "Why Is Bitcoin Censorship Resistant?"

20.   Adam Smith, *An Inquiry into the Nature and Causes of the Wealth of Nations*, ed. Edwin Cannan (Methuen, 1904).

21.   Smith, *An Inquiry into the Nature and Causes of the Wealth of Nations*.

22.   Gigi, "Bitcoin Is Time," January 14, 2021, dergigi.com.

23.   Poelstra, "On Stake and Consensus."

24.   Gigi, "Bitcoin Is Time."

25.   Nakamoto, "Bitcoin."

26.   Gigi, "Bitcoin Is Time."

27.   Besides the Lightning Network, see the Liquid Network for an example of a side chain that attempts to solve the same issue.

28.   See Jack Mallers, "Bitcoin as a Payment Rail to Disrupt the World" (episode number 672), *The Pomp Podcast* (podcast audio), September 27, 2021, https://podcasts.apple.com /us/podcast/672-bitcoin-as-a-payment-rail-to-disrupt-the-world/id1434060078?i =1000536730110.

4. PROOF-OF-WORK VERSUS PROOF-OF-STAKE

The epigraph to this chapter is from an email from Satoshi Nakamoto to Martti Malmi on May 3, 2009.

1.   For example, in 2022, Greenpeace launched a campaign called "Change the Code, Not the Climate," urging Bitcoin to change its code to a Proof-of-Stake consensus system. Their campaign emphasized the significant reduction in energy consumption that Proof-of-Stake could bring over Proof-of-Work.

2.   See chap. 2 of the book regarding the hard fork that created Bitcoin Cash.

3.   Ethereum.org, "Proof-of-Stake (POS)," January 31, 2024, updated September 3, 2024, https://ethereum.org/en/developers/docs/consensus-mechanisms/pos/.

4.   Quotes are used around "randomly" here because the process is still deterministic; that is, everyone must agree on the same validator set. By contrast, in Proof-of-Work, anyone who solves for the nonce is entitled to add their block to the blockchain. See Scott Sullivan, "A Bitcoiner's Guide to Proof-of-Stake," *Substack*, August 30, 2022, https://scottmsul .substack.com/p/a-bitcoiners-guide-to-proof-of-stake.

5.   Ethereum.org, "Proof-of-Stake (POS)."

6.   Theoretically, the only way to consolidate mining power among a few would be to prevent acquisition of mining machines by somehow disrupting supply chains. Imagine the costs involved to achieve something like that, even if it were theoretically possible, compared to the costless exercise it would be for Proof-of-Stake validators to achieve the same censorship result.

7.   Posted by Satoshi Nakamoto on the BitcoinTalk forum on August 7, 2010.

8.   Lyn Alden, *Broken Money: Why Our Financial System Is Failing Us and How We Can Make It Better* (Timestamp Press, 2023), 360.

9.   Hugo Nguyen, "Work Is Timeless, Stake Is Not," *Medium*, October 12, 2018, https:// hugonguyen.medium.com/work-is-timeless-stake-is-not-554c4450ce18.

10.   Nick Szabo, "Shelling Out: The Origins of Money," 2002, https://nakamotoinstitute.org /shelling-out/.

11. Alden, *Broken Money*, 361.
12. Andrew Poelstra, "On Stake and Consensus," *Nakamoto Institute*, 2015, https://cdn.nakamoto institute.org/docs/on-stake-and-consensus.pdf.
13. Poelstra, "On Stake and Consensus."
14. Satoshi Nakamoto, "Bitcoin: A Peer-to-Peer Electronic Cash System," https://bitcoin.org /bitcoin.pdf
15. Gigi, "PoW Is Essential: A Failure to Understand Proof-of-Work Is a Failure to Understand Bitcoin," 2021, https://dergigi.com/threads/pow-is-essential.
16. Alden, *Broken Money*.
17. This specific topic about bitcoin's long-term security budget is discussed in chap. 5.
18. See chap. 3 of this book. The discussion in this hypothetical scenario is similar to the discussion in chapter 3, but it warrants a review because of its critical importance.
19. See chap. 3.
20. Sullivan, "A Bitcoiner's Guide to Proof-of-Stake."
21. Sullivan, "A Bitcoiner's Guide to Proof-of-Stake."

5. LONG-TERM SECURITY BUDGET

1. Jonathan Bier, *The Blocksize War* (Author, 2021).
2. Bier, *The Blocksize War*.
3. Bitcoin blockspace refers to the finite 4-megabyte capacity within a bitcoin block used to record and confirm transactions on the blockchain.
4. In the case of Lightning transactions, the initial setup transaction (channel opening) as well as the final closeout transaction (channel closing) must be settled on-chain at the Bitcoin base layer.
5. Dillon Healy, "Even Without Mining Subsidy, These Two Factors Will Protect Bitcoin into the Future," *Bitcoin Magazine*, December 29, 2022, https://bitcoinmagazine.com /technical/bitcoin-security-without-mining-subsidy.
6. Alex Gladstein, "Stranded: How Bitcoin Is Saving Wasted Energy and Expanding Financial Freedom in Africa," *Bitcoin Magazine*, January 24, 2024, https://bitcoinmagazine.com /check-your-financial-privilege/stranded-bitcoin-saving-wasted-energy-in-africa. See chap. 16 in this book for a detailed discussion on this point.

6. HOW DO YOU KILL BITCOIN?

1. This idea is from a discussion with Jameson Lopp.
2. *Bit Nodes*, https://bitnodes.io, accessed November 2, 2024;
3. Jamie Dimon, CEO of JPMorgan, stated at a U.S. Senate hearing in December 2023: "I've always been deeply opposed to bitcoin, crypto, etc. . . . If I was the government, I'd close it down."
4. Michael Saylor, CEO of MicroStrategy, has described seven layers of security that arise from Bitcoin's Proof-of-Work system. See Robert Breedlove, *The "What Is Money?" Show*, October 13, 2021.
5. Cambridge Bitcoin Electricity Consumption Index, "Bitcoin Network Power Demand," University of Cambridge, Cambridge Center for Alternative Finance, updated every twenty-four hours, https://ccaf.io/cbeci/.

6. Despite being technically debunked, there were several ardent adherents to the "China 51 percent attack" thesis (e.g., financial commentator, Mike Green). The thesis has now all but vanished since the events of May 2021.

7. Conversation with Jeff Booth, Vancouver, June 2023

8. Jimmy Song, "Op Ed: Bitcoin Mining Attacks Are Overblown," *Bitcoin Magazine* January 21, 2019, https://bitcoinmagazine.com/business/op-ed-bitcoin-mining-attacks-are-overblown.

9. See Alex De Vries, "Bitcoin's Growing Energy Problem," *Joule* 2, no. 5 (2018): 801–805.

10. Song, "Op Ed: Bitcoin Mining Attacks."

11. Song, "Op Ed: Bitcoin Mining Attacks."

12. Song, "Op Ed: Bitcoin Mining Attacks."

13. Posted by Satoshi Nakamoto on the BitcoinTalk forum on June 17, 2010.

14. Post on X.com, March 29, 2024.

15. Shinobi, "Adversarial Thinking for Attacks on Bitcoin," *Bitcoin Magazine*, April 26, 2022, https://bitcoinmagazine.com/technical/adversarial-thinking-for-attacks-on-bitcoin.

16. Jonathan Bier, *The Blocksize War* (Author, 2021).

17. Chris Bernhardt, *Quantum Computing for Everyone* (MIT Press, 2019).

18. Shor's algorithm, developed by Peter Shor, is a quantum computing algorithm created in 1994 that can factor large numbers into their prime components efficiently, posing a potential threat to classical encryption methods based on the difficulty of factorization.

19. Roger Huang, "Here's Why Quantum Computing Will Not Break Cryptocurrencies," *Forbes*, December 21, 2020, https://www.forbes.com/sites/rogerhuang/2020/12/21/heres-why-quantum-computing-will-not-break-cryptocurrencies.

20. I. Stewart et al., "Committing to Quantum Resistance: A Slow Defence for Bitcoin Against a Fast Quantum Computing Attack," *Royal Society Open Science* 5, no. 6 (2018).

21. Stewart et al., "Committing to Quantum Resistance."

22. QuantumExplainer.com, "Quantum Computing's Impact on Bitcoin," March 4, 2024, https://quantumexplainer.com/quantum-computings-impact-on-bitcoin/.

23. Deloitte, "Quantum Computing and the Bitcoin Blockchain," 2024, https://www2.deloitte.com/nl/nl/pages/innovatie/artikelen/quantum-computers-and-the-bitcoin-blockchain.html.

7. ONCE-IN-HISTORY INVENTION

1. Adam Back is a renowned cryptographer and computer scientist. He is cited in the Bitcoin whitepaper, and his prior inventions formed some of the primary building blocks for bitcoin. The epigraph to this chapter comes from a tweet he posted on X.com on May 23, 2021.

2. Jack Dorsey, posted on X.com, May 15, 2021.

3. This expression is attributed to Robert Breedlove.

4. Robert Breedlove, "An Open Letter to Ray Dalio re: Bitcoin," *Medium*, November 9, 2019, https://breedlove22.medium.com/an-open-letter-to-ray-dalio-re-bitcoin-4b07c52a1a98.

5. The creator(s) of Bitcoin assigned themselves a masculine gender; therefore, it seems appropriate to respect that choice.

6. See the discussion relating to Bitcoin's "difficulty adjustment" in chap. 3 of this book.

7.   Christine Kim, "A Breakdown of Ethereum Supply Distribution Since Genesis," *Galaxy*, 2022, https://www.galaxy.com/insights/research/breakdown-of-ethereum-supply-distribution-since-genesis/.

8.   Vitalik Buterin was rumored to have sold some of his ETH in 2023, which he denied. However, he admits to having sold some of his pre-mined coins in 2018 for personal gain. See Terence Simwara, "Vitalik Buterin: 'I Haven't Sold ETH for Personal Gain Since 2018,'" Bitcoin.com News, October 18, 2023, https://news.bitcoin.com/vitalik-buterin-i-havent-sold-eth-for-personal-gain-since-2018/.

9.   Several public companies, including MicroStrategy, Tesla, and Marathon Digital Holdings, hold significant amounts of bitcoin on their balance sheets as this book goes to press.

10.   Given the pseudonymous nature of bitcoin transactions, it is impossible to derive conclusive ownership statistics. These figures are rough approximations—guesstimates—based on clustering algorithms that collate and group bitcoin addresses. The numbers are also constantly fluctuating. See Glassnode, "The Shrimp Supply Sink: Revisiting the Distribution of Bitcoin Supply," (2023).

11.   GlassnodeInsights, "The Shrimp Supply Sink: Revisiting the Distribution of Bitcoin Supply," *Glassnode*, March 15, 2023, https://insights.glassnode.com/bitcoin-supply-distribution-revisited/.

12.   See the discussion about environmental concerns relating to Proof-of-Work in chap. 16 of this book.

13.   See the discussion on Proof-of-Stake versus Proof-of-Work in chap. 4 of this book.

14.   Michael E. Porter, "Strategy and the Internet," *Harvard Business Review* 79, no. 3 (2001), https://hbr.org/2001/03/strategy-and-the-internet; David S. Evans and Richard Schmalensee, "The Industrial Organization of Markets with Two-Sided Platforms," *Competition Policy International* 3, no. 1 (2007): 151–179.

15.   One notable figure among the early adopters was Hal Finney, a renowned cryptographer who received the first bitcoin transaction from Satoshi in January 2009. Finney was an early supporter of the concept of digital currency and contributed to its development through coding and problem solving.

16.   There are numerous apps that integrate Lightning, for example, through the Bakkt app, Starbucks customers can make bitcoin Lightning payments. Strike is another service that is widely adopted around the world, including in El Salvador, where it allows for virtually free cross-border remittances as well as day-to-day point-of-sale payment services.

17.   The chart excludes stablecoins, which are not relevant to this discussion because they are pegged directly to fiat currencies and, therefore, track their value one for one (on a good day!).

18.   Quote from Ben Mezrich, *Bitcoin Billionaires: A True Story of Genius, Betrayal and Redemption* (Little, Brown, 2019).

19.   Posted by Hal Finney on the BitcoinTalk forum on June 4, 2011, https://bitcointalk.org/index.php?topic=11765.msg169026#msg169026.

20.   Nassim Nicholas Taleb, *Antifragile: Things That Gain from Disorder* (New York: Random House, 2012).

21. Peter Thiel and Blake Masters, *Zero to One: Notes on Startups, or How to Build the Future* (Crown Business, 2014).

22. Thiel and Masters, *Zero to One*.

23. Thomas Schelling, *The Strategy of Conflict* (Harvard University Press, 1960).

24. Anil Patel, *The Bitcoin Handbook: Key Concepts in Economics, Technology and Psychology* (Konsensus Network, 2023).

25. Patel, *The Bitcoin Handbook*.

8. MONEY AND THE STATE

1. While this is the consensus view among economists, it does remain controversial. See Felix Martin, *Money: The Unauthorized Biography—from Coinage to Cryptocurrency* (Vintage, 2014), 27–29.

2. Carl Menger, "On the Origins of Money," *Economic Journal* 2 (1892): 239–55.

3. Niall Ferguson, *The Ascent of Money: A Financial History of the World* (Penguin, 2009), 26.

4. Margaret Bunson, *The Encyclopedia of Ancient Egypt* (Gramercy, 1991). 268.

5. Nik Bhatia, *Layered Money: From Gold and Dollars to Bitcoin and Central Bank Digital Currencies* (Independent Publishing, 2021). 8.

6. Herodotus, *Clio*, translated by Rev. William Beloe (Philadelphia: M'Carty and Davis, 1844), 31, quoted in John Kenneth Galbraith, *Money: Whence It Came, Where It Went.* (Houghton Mifflin, 1975).

7. Galbraith, *Money*.

8. Guinness World Records, "First Paper Money," https://www.guinnessworldrecords.com /world-records/first-paper-money.

9. Guinness World Records, "First Paper Money."

10. Hanhui Guan, Nuno Palma, and Meng Wu, "The Rise and Fall of Paper Money in Yuan China, 1260–1368," *Economic History Review* 77, no. 4 (2024): 1222–1250.

11. John Lanchester, "The Invention of Money: In Three Centuries, the Heresies of Two Bankers Became the Basis of Our Modern Economy," *The New Yorker* (July 29, 2019), https://www.newyorker.com/magazine/2019/08/05/the-invention-of-money.

12. Marco Polo, *The Travels of Marco Polo*, trans. Henry Yule (John Murray, 1871).

13. Stephen Quinn and William Roberds, "The Evolution of the Check as a Means of Payment: A Historical Survey," *Federal Reserve Bank of Atlanta Economic Review* 93 (2008): 1–28.

14. Gunnar Wetterberg, *Money and Power: From Stockholms Banco 1656 to Sveriges Riksbank Today* (Sveriges Riksbank, 2009), 38, https://www.riksbank.se/en-gb/about-the-riksbank /history/historical-timeline/1600-1699/first-banknotes-in-europe/.

15. Bhatia, *Layered Money*, 9.

16. John Maynard Keynes, *A Treatise on Money* (Macmillan, 1930).

17. Johannes Wiegand, "Destabilizing the Global Monetary System: Germany's Adoption of the Gold Standard in the Early 1870s," International Monetary Fund (IMF) Working Paper 2019/032, International Monetary Fund.

18. Vaulted, "History of the Gold Standard in America," *Vaulted*, https://vaulted.com /nuggets/history-of-the-gold-standard-in-america/.

19.   Liaquat Ahamed, *Lords of Finance: The Bankers Who Broke the World* (Penguin, 2009).

20.   H. Montgomery Hyde, *John Law* (Allen, 1969).

21.   Ahamed, *Lords of Finance*.

22.   Ahamed, *Lords of Finance*.

23.   Roger Lowenstein, "The Nixon Shock," *Bloomberg Businessweek*, August 4, 2011, https://www.bloomberg.com/news/articles/2011-08-04/the-nixon-shock.

24.   Lowenstein, "The Nixon Shock."

25.   Avik Roy, "Bitcoin and the U.S. Fiscal Reckoning," *National Affairs* 61 (2021), https://nationalaffairs.com/publications/detail/bitcoin-and-the-us-fiscal-reckoning.

26.   Michael J. Graetz and Olivia Briffault, "A 'Barbarous Relic': The French, Gold, and the Demise of Bretton Woods," Yale University Press, Yale Law and Economics Research Paper No. 558, 2019.

27.   Alex Gladstein, "Uncovering the Hidden Costs of the Petrodollar," *Bitcoin Magazine*, September 21, 2021, https://bitcoinmagazine.com/culture/the-hidden-costs-of-the-petrodollar.

28.   The earliest uses of fiat money can be traced back to as early as eleventh-century China. However, 1971 is significant because it marked a shift in the global monetary system to a fiat standard.

29.   Lyn Alden, *Broken Money: Why Our Financial System Is Failing Us and How We Can Make It Better* (Timestamp Press, 2023), 29.

30.   Hammurabi, *The Code of Hammurabi, King of Babylon*, trans. Robert Francis Harper (University of Chicago Press, 1904). 37–39.

31.   See Murray N. Rothbard, *A History of Money and Banking in the United States—The Colonial Era to World War II* (Ludwig von Mises Institute, 2002).

32.   Nick Szabo, "An Unending Variety of Topics," March 23, 2018, *Unenumerated* (blog), https://unenumerated.blogspot.com/.

33.   Wikipedia, "United States Notes," https://en.wikipedia.org/wiki/United_States_Note#cite_note-7.

34.   Elbridge G. Spaulding, *History of the Legal Tender Paper Money Issued During the Great Rebellion* (Express Printing, 1869).

35.   After the Civil War, the United States did return to the gold standard. It was finally abandoned in 1971 under President Richard Nixon.

36.   Posted by Satoshi Nakamoto on the BitcoinTalk forum on February 11, 2009.

37.   Jonathan Ashworth, *Quantitative Easing: The Great Central Bank Experiment* (Agenda Publishing, 2020).

38.   Charley Grant, "Stocks Post Broad Losses After Strong Economic Data," Wall Street Journal, July 6, 2023, https://www.wsj.com/articles/global-stocks-markets-dow-news-06-29-2023-254badaa.

39.   See Milton Friedman, *An Economist's Protest* (Harcourt Brace Jovanovich, 1972).

40.   Nomi Prins, *Permanent Distortion: How the Financial Markets Abandoned the Real Economy Forever* (Hachette, 2022).

41.   See Christopher Leonard and Jacques Roy, *The Lords of Easy Money* (Simon & Schuster, 2022).

42.   Leonard and Roy, *The Lords of Easy Money*.

43. For a discussion on the internal dynamics in the Federal Reserve and insights into the decision-making processes and ideological conflicts, see Leonard and Roy, *The Lords of Easy Money*.

44. Milton Friedman, *Capitalism and Freedom* (University of Chicago Press, 1962).

9. INFLATION: THE HIDDEN TAX

The epigraph to this chapter is from Friedrich A. Hayek, *The Denationalisation of Money* (Institute of Economic Affairs, 1976).

1. Joseph T. Salerno, "The Gold Standard: An Analysis of Some Recent Proposals," *Cato Institute Policy Analysis* 16 (September 9, 1982).

2. Milton Friedman, "Inflation and Unemployment," Nobel Memorial Lecture, delivered December 13, 1976.

3. Howard Schneider, "Powell's Econ 101: Jobs Not Inflation. And Forget About the Money Supply," *Reuters*, February 24, 2021, https://www.reuters.com/article/business/powells-econ-101-jobs-not-inflation-and-forget-about-the-money-supply-idUSKBN2AN2EJ/.

4. Federal Reserve Bank of St. Louis, "Federal Reserve Economic Data," https://fred.stlouisfed.org/.

5. Federal Reserve Bank of St. Louis, "Federal Reserve Economic Data."

6. Board of Governors of the Federal Reserve System, "Credit and Liquidity Programs and the Balance Sheet—Recent Balance Sheet Trends," *Federal Reserve*, accessed July 2024, https://www.federalreserve.gov/monetarypolicy/bst_recenttrends.htm.

7. Steve H. Hanke and Alex K. F. Kwok, "On the Measurement of Zimbabwe's Hyperinflation," *Cato Journal* 29, no. 2 (2009): 353-64.

8. See Domingo Cavallo, "Lessons from the Stabilization Process in Argentina, 1990–1996," Symposium Proceedings: Achieving Price Stability (Kansas City Fed, 1996).

9. Lyn Alden, *Broken Money: Why Our Financial System Is Failing Us and How We Can Make It Better* (Timestamp Press, 2023), viii

10. Steve Forbes, Nathan Lewis, and Elizabeth Ames, *Inflation: What It Is, Why It's Bad, and How to Fix It* (Encounter, 2022).

11. Liaquat Ahamed, *Lords of Finance: The Bankers Who Broke the World* (Penguin, 2009).

12. Saifedean Ammous, *The Bitcoin Standard: The Decentralized Alternative to Central Banking* (Wiley, 2018), 127-28.

13. Ammous, *The Bitcoin Standard*.

14. Ahamed, *Lords of Finance*.

15. Alden, *Broken Money*.

16. Alden, *Broken Money*, 114.

17. *Bank Underground* is the staff blog of the Bank of England, founded to publish the views and insights of the people working for one of the world's oldest central banks. You can visit the blog at https://bankunderground.co.uk/.

18. Alden, *Broken Money*.

19. Alden, *Broken Money*.

20. Patrick McClean, "A Correction 103 Years Late: How the BoE Covered Up Failed War Bond Sale," *Financial Times*, August 8, 2017, cited in Alden, *Broken Money*.

21. Jeff Stein, "U.S. Debt Eclipses $34 Trillion for First Time," *Washington Post*, January 2, 2024, https://www.washingtonpost.com/business/2024/01/02/us-debt-34-trillion-congress/.

22. Committee for a Responsible Federal Budget, "Interest Costs Just Surpassed Defense and Medicare," May 10, 2024, https://www.crfb.org/blogs/interest-costs-just-surpassed-defense-and-medicare.

23. Bank of America Global Investment Strategy—Bloomberg, The Kobeissi Letter, April 9, 2024.

24. Sonali Basak, "Druckenmiller Warns US Debt Crisis Worse Than He Imagined," *Bloomberg*, May 3, 2023, https://www.bloomberg.com/news/articles/2023-05-02/druckenmiller-warns-us-debt-crisis-worse-than-he-imagined.

25. Alden, *Broken Money*.

26. See Nomi Prins, *Permanent Distortion: How the Financial Markets Abandoned the Real Economy Forever* (Hachette, 2022).

27. Luke Gromen, *Peak Cheap Energy and Monetary System Change*, Forest for the Trees, January 2024.

28. Gromen, *Peak Cheap Energy and Monetary System Change*.

29. Luke Gromen has expressed this view in multiple forums. See Lyn Alden, "January 2024 Newsletter: Fiscal and Monetary Divergence," January 4, 2024, https://www.lynalden.com/january-2024-newsletter/.

30. Over the years, the calculation of the consumer price index (CPI) has undergone changes that arguably understate inflation. These adjustments include the introduction of hedonic quality adjustments, which attempt to account for changes in the quality of products, and the substitution effect, where the calculation assumes that consumers will switch to cheaper alternatives as prices rise. Another change is the use of geometric weighting, which gives less weight to goods and services that are rising in price the fastest.

31. John Maynard Keynes, *The General Theory of Employment, Interest, and Money* (Macmillan, 1936).

32. Friedrich A. Hayek, *The Road to Serfdom* (University of Chicago Press, 1944); Hayek, *The Denationalisation of Money*; Ludwig von Mises, *Human Action: A Treatise on Economics* (Yale University Press, 1949).

33. Friedrich A. Hayek, *The Constitution of Liberty* (University of Chicago Press, 2011), 157.

34. Friedrich A. Hayek, "The Pretence of Knowledge," Prize Lecture, December 11, 1974, https://www.nobelprize.org/prizes/economic-sciences/1974/hayek/lecture/.

35. Hayek, "The Pretence of Knowledge;" Friedrich A. Hayek, *Individualism and Economic Order* (University of Chicago Press, 1996).

36. Hayek, *The Constitution of Liberty*.

37. Milton Friedman, *Capitalism and Freedom* (University of Chicago Press, 1962).

38. Friedman, *Capitalism and Freedom*.

39. Friedman, *Capitalism and Freedom*.

40. Lyn Alden, in the context of the debate over commodity money versus fiat. See Alden, *Broken Money*, 45.

41. Jeff Booth, *The Price of Tomorrow: Why Deflation Is the Key to an Abundant Future* (Stanley Press, 2020).

42.   Booth, *The Price of Tomorrow.*

43.   Booth, *The Price of Tomorrow.*

44.   Jeff Booth, foreword to Knut Svanholm's Bitcoin: *Everything Divided by 21 Million* (Konsensus Network, 2022).

10. A STORE OF VALUE

1.   Paul Jones and Lorenzo Giorgianni, "The Great Monetary Inflation," *DocDroid*, May 2020, https://www.docdroid.net/H1fuimX/the-great-monetary-inflation-pdf.

2.   Vijay Boyapati, posted on X.com, February 5, 2024.

3.   Saifedean Ammous, *The Bitcoin Standard: The Decentralized Alternative to Central Banking* (Wiley, 2018), 4-5; Carl Menger, "On the Origins of Money," *Economic Journal* 2 (1892): 239-55.

4.   Ammous, *The Bitcoin Standard.*

5.   Lyn Alden, *Broken Money: Why Our Financial System Is Failing Us and How We Can Make It Better* (Timestamp Press, 2023).

6.   Martti Malmi and Satoshi Nakamoto, Correspondence: "Satoshi - Sirius Emails 2009-2011," 2011, https://mmalmi.github.io/satoshi/.

7.   Jones and Giorgianni, "The Great Monetary Inflation."

8.   See chap. 3 for an explanation of bitcoin's technological breakthrough in achieving absolute scarcity.

9.   BGeometrics, "Bitcoin and M2Growth Global of YoY," *BGeometrics*, https://charts .bgeometrics.com/m2_global.html.

10.   Allen Farrington, "Bitcoin Is Venice," *Medium*, February 13, 2021, https://allenfarrington .medium.com/bitcoin-is-venice-8414dda42070.

11.   Fidelity Digital Assets, "Bitcoin Aspirational Store of Value Revisited," 2023, *Fidelity Digital Assets*, https://www.fidelitydigitalassets.com/research-and-insights/bitcoin -aspirational-store-value-revisited.

12.   See chap. 11 in this book for a discussion about bitcoin's global adoption process.

13.   See chap. 21 in this book.

14.   See chap. 21.

15.   See https://glassnode.com/.

16.   This is already the case with a very large number of individuals around the world who have adopted bitcoin as their unit of account, for example, residents of El Zonte, El Salvador, but it is difficult to come up with a global estimation.

17.   World Bank, "The Global Findex Database," 2021, https://www.worldbank.org/en /publication/globalfindex.

18.   KPMG, "Nigeria's Financial Inclusion: The Way Forward," 2020, https://assets.kpmg.com /content/dam/kpmg/ng/pdf/nigerias-financial-inclusion-the-way-forward.pdf.

19.   Naeha Rashid, "Pakistan's Unbanked," *Tabadlab*, 2022, https://tabadlab.com/pakistans -unbanked/.

11. GLOBAL ADOPTION

1.   All details here about Martti Malmi are from a series of his posts on Twitter (X.com now) on December 18, 2020, https://x.com/marttimalmi?lang=en.

2. Crypto.com, "Crypto Market Sizing Report 2022—Global Crypto Owners Reached 425 Million by the End of 2022," https://crypto.com/research/2022-crypto-market-sizing-report.

3. Tuur Demeester, "The Bitcoin Reformation," *Adamant Research*, 2019, https://adamantresearch.com/files/archive/BitcoinReformation2019.pdf.

4. Fidelity Digital Assets, *Bitcoin Aspirational Store of Value Revisited*, Fidelity Digital Assets, 2024, https://www.fidelitydigitalassets.com/research-and-insights/bitcoin-aspirational-store-value-revisited.

5. Fidelity Digital Assets, *Bitcoin Aspirational Store of Value Revisited*.

6. Fidelity Digital Assets, *Bitcoin Aspirational Store of Value Revisited*.

7. Fidelity Digital Assets, *Bitcoin Aspirational Store of Value Revisited*.

8. Fidelity Digital Assets, *Bitcoin Aspirational Store of Value Revisited*.

9. CFA Institute, FINRA Investor Education Foundation, and Zeldis Research, "Gen Z and Investing: Social Media, Crypto, FOMO, and Family," *CFA Institute*, May 23, 2023, https://rpc.cfainstitute.org/en/research/reports/2023/gen-z-investing.

10. The late Charlie Munger and Warren Buffett have been famously critical of bitcoin, calling it "rat-poison squared," https://www.cnbc.com/2018/05/05/warren-buffett-says-bitcoin-is-probably-rat-poison-squared.html

11. John Kenneth Galbraith, *Money: Whence It Came, Where It Went.* (Houghton Mifflin, 1975).

12. Glassnode Studio, https://glassnode.com/.

13. Glassnode Studio, https://glassnode.com/.

14. See chap. 3 of this book.

15. Vijay Boyapati, "The Bullish Case for Bitcoin," 2018, https://vijayboyapati.medium.com/the-bullish-case-for-bitcoin-6ecc8bdecc1.

16. This adoption path has been discussed by Vijay Boyapati and Anil Patel.

12. THE SURVEILLANCE STATE

1. S. D. Church, *The Exchequer Cloth, c. 1176–1832: The Calculator, the Game of Chess, and the Process of Photozincography, In: The English and Their Legacy, 900–1200* (Boydell & Brewer, 2012).

2. D. Carpenter, *The Struggle for Mastery: Britain 1066–1284* (Oxford University Press, 2004).

3. Sylvia Tomasch, "Surveillance/History," *SPELL*, 2019, https://www.e-periodica.ch.

4. See Michael Wood, *The Domesday Quest, In Search of the Roots of England* (Random House, 2005).

5. David Carpenter, *Magna Carta* (Penguin, 2015).

6. Central Intelligence Agency (CIA) Archives, *USSR: Role of the State Planning Committee (Gosplan), Information Requested by Alan Greenspan*, 1975, https://www.cia.gov/readingroom/docs/CIA-RDP86T00608R000600020031-1.pdf.

7. See International Monetary Fund, "A Study of the Soviet Economy," in *Chapter III.2 The Changing Roles of Monetary and Exchange Rate Policies* (International Monetary Fund, 1991).

8. See Michael Rieger, "A World Without Prices: Economic Calculation in the Soviet Union," 2017, https://www.libertarianism.org/columns/world-without-prices-economic-calculation-soviet-union.

9. International Monetary Fund, "A Study of the Soviet Economy."

10. For a detailed discussion of the Soviet gulag, see Paul R. Gregory and V. V. Lazarev, eds., *The Economics of Forced Labor: The Soviet Gulag* (Hoover Institution Press, 2003). https://openlibrary.org/books/OL9650930M/The_Economics_of_Forced_Labor.

11. For an analysis of the Soviet second economy, see Vladimir G. Treml and Michael V. Alexeev, "The Second Economy and the Destabilizing Effect of Its Growth on the State Economy in the Soviet Union: 1965–1989," Duke Economics Working Paper, 1993, https://papers.ssrn.com/sol3/papers.cfm?abstract_id=15546.

12. Rieger, "A World Without Prices."

13. See Martin Dean, *Robbing the Jews: The Confiscation of Jewish Property in the Holocaust, 1933–1945* (Cambridge University Press, 2008).

14. Frank Bajohr, *'Aryanisation in Hamburg': The Economic Exclusions of Jews and the Confiscation of Their Property in Nazi Germany* (Berghahn, 2002).

15. See Albrecht Ritschl, "Financial Destruction: Confiscatory Taxation of Jewish Property and Income in Nazi Germany," Economic History Working Papers, London School of Economics and Political Science (April 2019).

16. The National Holocaust Centre and Museum, "The November Pogrom (Kristallnacht)." https://www.holocaust.org.uk/the-november-pogrom-kristallnacht.

17. The National Holocaust Centre and Museum, "The November Pogrom (Kristallnacht)."

18. World Jewish Congress, "A Third of Nazis' War Effort Funded with Money Stolen from Jews, Study Finds," 2010, https://www.worldjewishcongress.org/en/news/a-third-of-nazis-war-effort-funded-with-money-stolen-from-jews-study-finds.

19. See Bernard Gordon, *Hollywood Exile, or How I Learned to Love the Blacklist* (University of Texas Press, 2001).

20. For notable examples see Wikipedia, "Hollywood Blacklist," https://en.wikipedia.org/wiki/Hollywood_blacklist#cite_note-1.

21. See Sara Savat, "Free Speech? Nearly Half of Americans Self-Censor, Study Finds," *The Source*, August 6, 2020, https://source.washu.edu/2020/08/free-speech-nearly-half-of-americans-self-censor-study-finds/.

22. Wikipedia, "McCarthyism," https://en.wikipedia.org/wiki/McCarthyism.

23. International Monetary Fund, "Exchange Measures in Venezuela," IMF Staff Papers no. 003, January 1, 1964.

24. Angus Berwick, "How ZTE Helps Venezuela Create China-Style Social Control," *Reuters*, November 14, 2018, https://www.reuters.com/investigates/special-report/venezuela-zte/.

25. Berwick, "How ZTE Helps Venezuela Create China-Style Social Control."

26. Shannon K. O'Neil, "Venezuelan Remittances Don't Just Save Lives," *Council on Foreign Relations*, 2019, https://www.cfr.org/blog/venezuelan-remittances-dont-just-save-lives.

27. Elias Ferrer, "Venezuela's Crypto Rebirth: Interview with Enrique De Los Reyes," *Forbes*, March 6, 2024, https://www.forbes.com/sites/eliasferrerbreda/2024/03/06/venezuelas-crypto-rebirth-interview-with-enrique-de-los-reyes/?sh=6359c5495d78.

28. Moises Rendon, "Can Cryptocurrency Help Venezuela?," *Center for Strategic & International Studies*, September 7, 2018, https://www.csis.org/analysis/can-cryptocurrency-help-venezuela.

29. World Bank Group, "Iran Economic Monitor, The Economy at a Crossroads," https://documents1.worldbank.org/curated/en/178111623662609713/pdf/Iran-Economic-Monitor-The-Economy-at-a-Crossroads.pdf.

30.   Iran International, "Iran to Deduct Fines from Bank Accounts of Women Defying Hijab," *Iran International*, March 11, 2024, https://www.iranintl.com/en/202403111235

31.   Mohammed Rasool, "Iran Is Pivoting to Bitcoin," *Vice News*, November 30, 2020, https://www.vice.com/en/article/qjppx3/iran-bitcoin-us-sanctions.

32.   Rasool, "Iran Is Pivoting to Bitcoin."

33.   Yuras Karmanau and Dasha Litvinova, "A Timeline of Restrictive Laws That Authorities Have Used to Crack Down on Dissent in Putin's Russia," *AP News*, March 6, 2024, https://apnews.com/article/russia-election-repressive-laws-dissent-5927d8932736636a9339fdcbaebd2331.

34.   Karmanau and Litvinova, "A Timeline of Restrictive Laws."

35.   Karmanau and Litvinova, "A Timeline of Restrictive Laws."

36.   Anna Baydakova, "Crypto Becomes Lifeline for Russian Emigrés Opposing Putin's War in Ukraine," *CoinDesk*, April 25, 2022, https://www.coindesk.com/layer2/2022/04/25/crypto-becomes-lifeline-for-russian-emigres-opposing-putins-war-in-ukraine/.

37.   Freedom House, "Expanding Freedom and Democracy," 2024, https://freedomhouse.org/.

38.   For more information, see Committee to Protect Journalists (CPJ), https://cpj.org/.

39.   Freedom House, "Freedom in the World 2024: Russia," 2024, https://freedomhouse.org/country/russia/freedom-world/2024.

40.   Catharine Tunney, "Ottawa's Use of Emergencies Act Against Convoy Protests Was Unreasonable, Violated Charter, Court Rules," *CBC/Radio-Canada*, January 23, 2024, https://www.cbc.ca/news/politics/emergencies-act-federal-court-1.7091891.

41.   Alex Tapscott, "Bitcoin Offers Freedom from Political Repression—and That's a Key to Its Future," *Fortune* (2021), https://fortune.com/2021/02/18/bitcoin-censorship-political-repression-deplatforming-china-belarus-russia-nigeria-crypto/.

42.   Economist Intelligence Unit, "Where Democracy is Most at Risk," *The Economist*, February 14, 2024, https://www.economist.com/graphic-detail/2024/02/14/four-lessons-from-the-2023-democracy-index.

43.   Andrew M. Bailey, Bradley Rettler, and Craig Warmke, *Resistance Money: A Philosophical Case for Bitcoin* (Routledge Taylor & Francis Group, 2024).

44.   U.S. Federal Reserve, "Money and Payments: The U.S. Dollar in the Age of Digital Transformation," June 10, 2022, https://www.federalreserve.gov/publications/money-and-payments-discussion-paper.htm

45.   Ludwig von Mises, *The Theory of Money and Credit*, trans. H.E. Batson (Liberty Fund, 1981).

13. GOVERNMENTS WILL BAN BITCOIN

1.   Email sent by Satoshi Nakamoto to the Cypherpunk Mailing List on November 7, 2008.

2.   Chainalysis Team, "The 2023 Global Crypto Adoption Index: Central & Southern Asia Are Leading the Way in Grassroots Crypto Adoption," *Chain Analysis*, September 12, 2023, https://www.chainalysis.com/blog/2023-global-crypto-adoption-index/.

3.   KuCoin, "KuCoin's into the Cryptoverse Report Reveals 35 Percent of Nigerian Adults Are Crypto Investors," April 12, 2022, https://www.kucoin.com/blog/kucoin-is-into-the-cryptoverse-report-reveals-35-percent-of-nigerian-adults-are-crypto-investors.

4.   Central Bank of Nigeria, "Inflation Rates (Percent), accessed July 14, 2024, https://www.cbn.gov.ng/rates/inflrates.asp.

5. Donald Trump, speech at the 2024 Bitcoin Conference, Nashville, Tennessee, July 27, 2024.
6. See chap. 8 of this book.
7. Tom Blackstone, "Cryptocurrency Adoption and Sentiment Report—Security.org," 2024, https://www.security.org/digital-security/cryptocurrency-annual-consumer-report/; Morning Consult, "Cryptocurrency Perception Study," 2023, https://pro.morningconsult.com/trackers/cryptocurrency-adoption-and-perspectives.
8. Statista, "Number of Bitcoin ATMs in Circulation in Selected Countries as of January 29, 2024," accessed May 22, 2024, https://statistics/343147/number-of-bitcoin-atms-countries/-.

14. LAW AND REGULATION

1. Digital Asset Anti-Money Laundering Act of 2023, https://www.congress.gov/bill/118th-congress/senate-bill/2669/text.
2. Chainalysis Team, "2024 Crypto Crime Trends: Illicit Activity Down as Scamming and Stolen Funds Fall, but Ransomware and Darknet Markets See Growth," *Chainanalysis*, January 18, 2024, https://www.chainalysis.com/blog/2024-crypto-crime-report-introduction/.
3. It is only provisional, however; the $24.2 billion total is likely to increase as more addresses are identified as illicit over time.
4. United Nations Office on Drugs and Crime, "Money Laundering," accessed 13 July 2024, https://www.unodc.org/unodc/en/money-laundering/overview.html.
5. Susie Violet Ward, Bitcoin Welcomes All but It's No Haven for the Naïve Criminal, *Forbes*, August 17, 2023, https://www.forbes.com/sites/digital-assets/2023/08/17/bitcoin-welcomes-all-but-its-no-haven-for-the-naive-criminal/.
6. Post by Eric Balchunas on Twitter.com now X.com on December 21, 2013.

15. BITCOIN AND GEOPOLITICS

The epigraph to this chapter comes from Barry Eichengreen, *Exorbitant Privilege: The Rise and Fall of the Dollar and the Future of the International Monetary System* (Oxford University Press, 2010).
1. Atlantic Council, "Dollar Dominance Monitor," 2024, https://www.atlanticcouncil.org/programs/geoeconomics-center/dollar-dominance-monitor/; Bank of Governors of the Federal Reserve System, "The International Role of the U.S. Dollar—Post-COVID Edition," *FED Notes*, 2023, https://www.federalreserve.gov/econres/notes/feds-notes/the-international-role-of-the-us-dollar-post-covid-edition-20230623.html.
2. Keith Rockwell, "An Exorbitant Privilege Now at Risk? The Once (and Future?) Almighty Dollar," *Wilson Center*, May 1, 2023, https://www.wilsoncenter.org/article/exorbitant-privilege-now-risk-once-and-future-almighty-dollar.
3. Joe Leahy and Hudson Lockett, "Brazil's Lula Calls for End to Dollar Trade Dominance," *Financial Times*, April 13, 2023, https://www.ft.com/content/669260a5-82a5-4e7a-9bbf-4f41c54a6143.
4. China Daily, "Asian Monetary Fund Suggested, as Dollar Has Been Weaponized," *China Daily*, April 7, 2023, http://www.chinadaily.com.cn/a/202304/07/WS642f6140a31057c47ebb8c23.html.

5. Barry Eichengreen, "Sanctions, SWIFT, and China's Cross-Border Interbank Payments System," *Center for Strategic & International Studies*, May 30, 2022, https://www.csis.org/analysis/sanctions-swift-and-chinas-cross-border-interbank-payments-system.

6. Eichengreen, "Sanctions, SWIFT, and China's Cross-Border Interbank Payments System."

7. Eichengreen, "Sanctions, SWIFT, and China's Cross-Border Interbank Payments System."

8. Jamil Anderlini, "China Calls for New Reserve Currency," *Financial Times*, March 23, 2009, https://www.ft.com/content/7851925a-17a2-11de-8c9d-0000779fd2ac.

9. Tom Robinson, "How Iran Uses Bitcoin Mining to Evade Sanctions and "Export" Millions of Barrels of Oil," *Elliptic*, May 21, 2021, https://www.elliptic.co/blog/how-iran-uses-bitcoin-mining-to-evade-sanctions.

10. Chelsey Cox, "Treasury Warns Against Russia's Efforts to Evade Sanctions with Cryptocurrencies," *CNBC*, September 20, 2022, https://www.cnbc.com/2022/09/20/treasury-department-russia-avoid-sanctions-using-crypto.html.

11. Treasury Secretary Janet Yellen Testimony Before the House Financial Services Committee, Financial Services Committee, U.S. House of Representatives, July 9, 2024, https://financialservices.house.gov/calendar/eventsingle.aspx?EventID=409309.

12. Conversation with Tyler Meade, July 2024.

13. Satoshi Nakamoto, "Andreas Antonopoulos: Bitcoin Neutrality, Bitcoin 2013 Conference," *YouTube*, June 10, 2013, https://www.youtube.com/watch?v=BT8FXQN-9-A.

14. Posted by Saifedean Ammous on Twitter.com (now X.com) on May 15, 2021.

15. Library of Congress, "*Federalist Papers*: Primary Documents in American History, Full Text of *The Federalist Papers*," https://guides.loc.gov/federalist-papers/full-text.

16. Donald Trump, speech at the 2024 Bitcoin Conference in Nashville, Tennessee; Robert F. Kennedy, speech at the 2024 Bitcoin Conference in Nashville, Tennessee; Cynthia Lummis, speech at the 2024 Bitcoin Conference in Nashville, Tennessee.

16. BITCOIN AND THE ENVIRONMENT

1. KPMG, "Bitcoin's Role in the ESG Imperative," *KPMG*, 2023, https://kpmg.com/kpmg-us/content/dam/kpmg/pdf/2023/bitcoins-role-esg-imperative.pdf.

2. Michel Khazzaka, "Bitcoin: Cryptopayments Energy Efficiency," *SSRN*, April 20, 2022, https://ssrn.com/abstract=4125499.

3. Martti Malmi and Satoshi Nakamoto, Correspondence: "Satoshi - Sirius Emails 2009–2011," 2011, https://mmalmi.github.io/satoshi/

4. Email from Satoshi Nakamoto to Martti Malmi on May 3, 2009.

5. Andrew M. Bailey, Bradley Rettler, and Craig Warmke, *Resistance Money: A Philosophical Case for Bitcoin* (Routledge, 2024).

6. Bitcoin Mining Council, "Bitcoin Mining Council Confirms Year on Year Improvements in Sustainable Power and Technological Efficiency," August 9, 2023, https://bitcoinminingcouncil.com/bitcoin-mining-council-survey-confirms-year-on-year-improvements-in-sustainable-power-and-technological-efficiency-in-h1-2023//.

7. Marvie Basilan, "ESG Expert Talks Evolving Bitcoin Mining Narrative, 'Impunity' in Other Industries' Energy Use," *International Business Times*, July 19, 2024, https://www.ibtimes.com/exclusive-esg-expert-talks-evolving-bitcoin-mining-narrative-impunity-other-industries-energy-3737422.

8. Basilan, "ESG Expert Talks Evolving Bitcoin Mining Narrative."

9. Daniel Batten, "The Bitcoin ESG Forecast: All Time Highs," December 12, 2023, *Bitcoin ESG Forecast*, https://www.batcoinz.com/p/issue-002-all-time-highs.

10. Lyn Alden, "Bitcoin's Energy Usage Isn't a Problem. Here's Why," *Lyn Alden Investment Strategy*, August 2021, updated January 2023, https://www.lynalden.com/bitcoin-energy/.

11. Ross Stevens, "Stone Ridge 2020 Shareholder Letter," *CaseBitcoin*, December 15, 2020, https://www.casebitcoin.com/stone-ridge-2020-shareholder-letter.

12. Stevens, "Stone Ridge 2020 Shareholder Letter."

13. Alex Gladstein, "Stranded: How Bitcoin Is Saving Wasted Energy and Expanding Financial Freedom in Africa," *Bitcoin Magazine*, January 24, 2024, https://bitcoinmagazine.com/check-your-financial-privilege/stranded-bitcoin-saving-wasted-energy-in-africa.

14. Gladstein, "Stranded."

15. Gladstein, "Stranded."

16. https://gridlesscompute.com/.

17. https://www.cleanspark.com/.

18. https://www.bitmari.com/.

19. https://luxor.tech/mining/.

20. https://www.riotplatforms.com/.

21. https://www.worldbank.org/en/programs/gasflaringreduction/about.

22. KPMG, "Bitcoin's Role in the ESG Imperative."

23. Daniel Batten, "10 Images That Forever Changed Our Perceptions About Bitcoin and Energy," 2024, https://batcoinz.com/10-images-that-forever-changed-our-perceptions-about-bitcoin-and-energy/.

24. Daniel Batten estimates that we need only thirty-five more midsize venting landfills that use methane as a power source for mining to mitigate the emissions of the entire bitcoin network. David Batten, "Bit Intelligence—21 Voices, How Bitcoin Goes Carbon Negative by 2028," *YouTube*, June 2024, https://youtu.be/sr-RGdbyRDQ?feature=shared.

25. Daniel Batten, "The Bitcoin Facts That Every Investment Committee Must Know," November 16, 2023, https://batcoinz.com/the-bitcoin-facts-that-every-esg-investment-committee-should-know/.

26. Alex Gladstein, "Bitcoin Global Utility: Commerce and Freedom," Bitcoin Conference, Nashville, Tennessee, 2024.

27. According to Michel Foucault, knowledge and power are not separate entities but are intertwined and mutually reinforcing. Knowledge is both a product of power and a tool for exercising power. In other words, what we know and how we come to know it are deeply influenced by power relations, and this knowledge in turn reinforces those power structures. See Michel Foucault, *Discipline & Punish: The Birth of the Prison* (Vintage, 1995).

28. See, for example, the claim by Greenpeace USA, https://www.greenpeace.org/usa/clean-up-bitcoin/#:~:text=Bitcoin%20is%20fueling%20the%20climate,to%20its%20energy%2Dhungry%20code, and its rebuttal summarized in Teuta Frankovic, "Greenpeace Ripple Donation Allegations Put Environmental Charity Funding Under Scrutiny," ccn.com, March 22, 2024, https://www.ccn.com/news/crypto/greenpeace-ripple-donation-allegations-puts-charity-under-scrutiny/.

29. See the analysis comparing Proof-of-Work and Proof-of-Stake in chap. 4 of this book.

17. SOVEREIGN PREROGATIVE

The epigraph to this chapter come from Philip Coggan, *Paper Promises: Money, Debt and the New World Order* (Hachette, 2011).

1. See Martin Loughlin, *The Prerogatives of Government, Foundations of Public Law* (Oxford: Oxford Academic, 2010).

2. See Thomas Hobbes, *Leviathan*, ed. Christopher Brooke (Penguin Classics, 2017).

3. John Locke, *Two Treatises of Government*, ed. Peter Laslett (Cambridge University Press, 1988).

4. Locke, *Two Treatises of Government*.

5. See John Locke, *Some Considerations of the Consequences of the Lowering of Interest and the Raising of the Value of Money*, ed. Patrick Hyde Kelly (Clarendon Press, 1991).

6. Locke, *Some Considerations of the Consequences*.

7. See Niccolo Machiavelli, *The Prince*, trans. W. K. Marriott (Dover, 1992).

8. Friedrich A. Hayek, *The Denationalisation of Money* (Institute of Economic Affairs, 1976).

9. Friedrich A. Hayek, *Individualism and Economic Order* (University of Chicago Press, 1996).

10. Mario I. Blejer and Paul Wachtel, "A Fresh Look at Central Bank Independence," *Cato Journal* 40, no. 1 (Winter 2020): 105–320.

11. See Murray N. Rothbard, *Anatomy of the State* (Ludwig von Mises Institute, 1974).

12. Rothbard, *Anatomy of the State*, 112.

13. Murray N. Rothbard, *What Has Government Done to Our Money?* (Ludwig von Mises Institute, 1963).

14. See Eric Mack, *Libertarianism* (Polity Press, 2018).

15. Erik Cason, "Cryptosovereignty: The Encrypted Political Philosophy of Bitcoin, *Bitcoin Magazine*, August 23, 2023, 29.

16. Cason, "Cryptosovereignty."

17. Hobbes, *Leviathan*.

18. Bernard Shaw, *Man and Superman: A Comedy and a Philosophy* (Archibald Constable, 1903).

19. This quote is attributed to a character in Ayn Rand's novel, *The Fountainhead*.

20. Catherine Drinker Bowen, *Miracle at Philadelphia: The Story of the Constitutional Convention, May to September 1787* (Little, Brown, 1966).

21. Erik Voorhees, Keynote Speech, Permissionless II, Austin, September 11, 2023.

22. Voorhees, Keynote Speech.

23. Voorhees, Keynote Speech.

24. Voorhees, Keynote Speech.

25. Michel Foucault, *Discipline and Punish: The Birth of the Prison* (Pantheon, 1977), 195.

26. Hent Kalmo and Quentin Skinner, *Sovereignty in Fragments* (Cambridge University Press, 2010), 45.

27. John Rawls, *A Theory of Justice* (Belknap Press of Harvard University Press, 1971).

28. Brandon Quittem, "Bitcoin Is a Decentralized Organism (Mycelium)—Part 1/4," *Medium*, December 11, 2018, https://medium.com/@BrandonQuittem/bitcoin-is-a-decentralized-organism-mycelium-part-1-3-6ec58cdcfaa6.

29. Michel Foucault, *The History of Sexuality* (Pantheon, 1978), https://search.library.wisc.edu/catalog/999500522802121.

30. Jonathan Gaventa, "Power After Lukes: A Review of the Literature, Brighton," *Powercube*, August 2003, https://www.powercube.net/wp-content/uploads/2009/11/power_after_lukes.pdf.

31. Gaventa, "Power After Lukes."

32. See Manuel Castells, *Networks of Outrage and Hope: Social Movements in the Internet Age* (Wiley, 2015).

33. Castells, *Networks of Outrage and Hope.*

34. Shinobi, "Bitcoin Is Pure Anarchy," *Bitcoin Magazine*, January 30, 2024, https://bitcoinmagazine .com.

35. Jameson Lopp, *Presentation: Decentralized 2018* (2018), https://www.youtube.com/watch ?v=_IMzSCSeM68.

36. Lopp, *Presentation: Decentralized 2018.*

37. See Terry O'Brien, *The Bottom Billion: Why the Poorest Countries Are Failing and What Can Be Done About It* (Oxford University Press, 2007).

38. Saul David, "Slavery and the 'Scramble for Africa,'" *BBC History*, February 17, 2011, https://www.bbc.co.uk/history/british/abolition/scramble_for_africa_article_01.shtml.

39. Trace Mayer, "How Bitcoin Destroys The Economics Of Violence," Hidden Secrets of Money Series, Episode 8, with Mike Maloney, May 1, 2018, https://www.youtube.com /watch?v=aNPuGIX1xmY

18. THE CYPHERPUNKS

1. Michael Naftaliev, "The Cypherpunks: The Group That Sparked a Crypto Revolution," *Scytale Digital*, November 23, 2023, https://www.scytale.digital/blog-posts/the-cypherpunks.

2. Eric Hughes, "A Cypherpunk's Manifesto," March 9, 1993, https://www.activism.net /cypherpunk/manifesto.html.

3. Giacomo Zucco, "A Treatise on Bitcoin and Privacy," *Bitcoin Magazine*, March 18, 2020, https://bitcoinmagazine.com/articles/a-treatise-on-bitcoin-and-privacy-part-1-a-match -made-in-the-whitepaper.

4. Mengqi Sun, "Crypto Mixer Samourai Wallet's Co-founders Arrested for Money Laundering," *Wall Street Journal*, April 24, 2024, https://www.wsj.com/articles/crypto -mixer-samourai-wallets-co-founders-arrested-for-money-laundering-df237a4e.

5. John Perry Barlow, "A Declaration of the Independence of Cyberspace," February 8, 1996, https://luongo.pro/cypherpunks/.

6. See Eric S. Raymond, *The Cathedral and the Bazaar: Musings on Linux and Open Source by an Accidental Revolutionary* (O'Reilly Media, 1999).

19. TIME PREFERENCE

1. Shane Frederick, George Lowenstein, and Ted O'Donoghue, "Time Discounting and Time Preference: A Critical Review," *Journal of Economic Literature* 40, no. 2 (2002): 351–401.

2. Andreas Granath, "Time Preference and Success: Is There Any Link?," *Mises Institute*, April 24, 2023, https://mises.org/mises-wire/time-preference-and-success-there-any-link.

3. Kerryn Higgs, "A Brief History of Consumer Culture," *MIT Press Reader*, 2021, https:// thereader.mitpress.mit.edu/a-brief-history-of-consumer-culture/.

4. William Leach, *Land of Desire: Merchants, Power, and the Rise of a New American Culture* (Penguin Random House, 1993).

5. Alexander Dietz, "Explaining the Paradox of Hedonism," *Australasian Journal of Philosophy* 97, no. 3 (2017): 497–510.

6. Dave Ramsey, *The Total Money Makeover: A Proven Plan for Financial Fitness* (Thomas Nelson, 2003).

7. Dietz, "Explaining the Paradox of Hedonism;" Bertrand Russell, *The Conquest of Happiness* (Routledge, 1993).

8. Jean Baudrillard, *The Consumer Society: Myths and Structures* (Sage, 1998), https://doi.org/10.4135/9781526401502.

9. Juliet B. Schor, *The Overspent American: Why We Want What We Don't Need* (Harper Perennial, 1999).

10. Peter Dauvergne, *The Shadows of Consumption: Consequences for the Global Environment* (MIT Press, 2008).

11. Adam Drewnowski, "The Limits to Consumerism," Center for Public Health Nutrition, University of Washington, https://karger.com/books/book/chapter-pdf/3673471/000452376.pdf.

12. United Nations Environment Programme, "Synthesis Report on the Environmental and Health Impacts of Pesticides and Fertilizers and Ways to Minimize Them," United Nations, January 24, 2021, https://www.unep.org/resources/report/environmental-and-health-impacts-pesticides-and-fertilizers-and-ways-minimizing.

13. Drewnowski, "The Limits to Consumerism."

14. See John de Graaf, David Wann, and Thomas H Naylor, *Affluenza* (Berrett-Koehler, 2002); Tim Kasser, *The High Price of Materialism* (MIT Press, 2017).

15. "Letters from a Stoic by Seneca: Book Summary, Key Lessons and Best Quotes," *Daily Stoic*, https://dailystoic.com/letters-from-a-stoic/.

16. Russell, *The Conquest of Happiness*.

17. See chap. 10 of this book.

20. NARRATIVES AND MEMES

1. Daniel Dematos, "Barter and Money in Post-War Germany," *The Tontine Coffee-House*, January 2, 2022, https://tontinecoffeehouse.com/?s=Barter+and+Money+in+Post-War+Germany.

2. Steven Mackenzie, "Yuval Noah Harari: 'We Are Living Inside the Dreams of Dead People,'" *Big Issue*, December 8, 2022, https://www.bigissue.com/culture/books/yuval-noah-harari-we-are-living-inside-the-dreams-of-dead-people/.

3. Robert J. Shiller, "Narrative Economics," *American Economic Review* 107, no. 4 (2017): 967–1004.

4. Fred Schulenburg, "Robert Shiller and the Power of Narratives: How Narratives Can Go Viral and Influence Business and Economies," *Roland Berger*, August 16, 2021, https://www.rolandberger.com/en/Insights/Publications/Robert-Shiller-and-the-power-of-narratives.html.

5. Email sent by Satoshi Nakamoto to the Cypherpunk Mailing List on January 16, 2009.

21. BITCOIN IS A MIRROR

The epigraph to this chapter is from Robert Frost's "The Road Not Taken."

1. Karl Popper has argued for the necessity of falsifiability in scientific theories, advocating for a constant questioning and testing of hypotheses rather than seeking confirmation. This approach necessitates intellectual humility and curiosity because it requires scientists to remain open to the possibility that their theories might be refuted.

2. Brian Duignan, "Dunning-Kruger effect," in *Encyclopedia Britannica* (2024).

3. Joseph Stromberg, "'Bicycle Face': A 19th-Century Health Problem Made Up to Scare Women away from Biking," *Vox*, March 24, 2015, https://www.vox.com/2014/7/8/5880931/the-19th-century-health-scare-that-told-women-to-worry-about-bicycle.

4. Stromberg, "Bicycle Face."

5. 21 Voices, "How Bitcoin Goes Carbon Negative by 2028," Bit Intelligence, June 18, 2024, https://www.youtube.com/watch?v=sr-RGdbyRDQ.

6. Jerry Feng, "Bitcoin is Dead," https://bitcoindeaths.com/, accessed December 12, 2024.

7. 21 Voices, "How Bitcoin Goes Carbon Negative by 2028."

8. In his book *The Singularity Is Near: When Humans Transcend Biology*, Ray Kurzweil explores the outer limits of technological optimism, which is rooted in his belief in the exponential growth of technology, its potential to solve critical problems, enhance human life, and create a future where human and machine intelligence coalesce into a superior form of existence. Ray Kurzweil, *The Singularity Is Near: When Humans Transcend Biology* (Viking, 2005).

9. See Kurzweil, *The Singularity Is Near*; Steven Pinker, *Enlightenment Now* (Penguin, 2019).

10. Jesse Myers, "Why the Yuppie Elite Dismiss Bitcoin," October 30, 2023, *Once-in-a-Species*, https://www.onceinaspecies.com/.

11. See John Dunn, *Locke: A Very Short Introduction* (Oxford University Press, 2003).

12. Alex Gladstein, *Check Your Financial Privilege* (BTC Media LLC, 2022).

13. Iran International, "Iran to Deduct Fines from Bank Accounts of Women Defying Hijab," *Iran International News*, March 11, 2024, https://www.iranintl.news/en/202403111235.

14. See chap. 13 of this book.

15. Michael Saylor, "GALA 2022 Keynote Speech", cited in Lyn Alden, *Broken Money: Why Our Financial System Is Failing Us and How We Can Make It Better* (Timestamp Press, 2023), 379.

16. See Gladstein, *Check Your Financial Privilege*.

17. Jason Nelson, "Bitcoin Is 'Bigger Than Any Government': BlackRock CEO Larry Fink," *Decrypt*, January 12, 2024, https://decrypt.co/212727/bitcoin-bigger-than-any-government-blackrock-ceo-larry-fink.

18. A couple of examples from 2024 alone: in March, Neel Kashkari, president of the Federal Reserve Bank of Minneapolis, described bitcoin as being akin to beanie babies; in January, Shaktikanta Das, governor of the Reserve Bank of India, cautioned that bitcoin could have a tulip mania outcome. These instances are by no means isolated.

19. Ross Stevens, "Stone Ridge 2020 Shareholder Letter," *CaseBitcoin*, December 15, 2020, https://www.casebitcoin.com/stone-ridge-2020-shareholder-letter.

20. John Kenneth Galbraith, *Money: Whence It Came, Where It Went* (Houghton Mifflin, 1975).

Index

GPSR Authorized Representative: Easy Access System Europe, Mustamäe tee
50, 10621 Tallinn, Estonia, gpsr.requests@easproject.com